THE FORMATION OF ECONOMETRICS

THE FORMATION OF ECONOMETRICS

A Historical Perspective

QIN DUO

秦朵

CLARENDON PRESS · OXFORD
1993

Oxford University Press, Walton Street, Oxford OX2 6DP
Oxford New York Toronto
Delhi Bombay Calcutta Madras Karachi
Kuala Lumpur Singapore Hong Kong Tokyo
Nairobi Dar es Salaam Cape Town
Melbourne Auckland Madrid
and associated companies in
Berlin Ibadan

Oxford is a trade mark of Oxford University Press

Published in the United States
by Oxford University Press Inc., New York

British Library Cataloguing in Publication Data
Data available _JP

Library of Congress Cataloging in Publication Data
Qin, Duo.
The formation of econometrics : a historical perspective / Qin Duo.
Includes bibliographical references and indexes.
1. Econometrics—History. I. Title.
HB139.Q3   1993   330'.01'5195—dc20   93–18799
ISBN 0–19–828388–1 (cloth)

1 3 5 7 9 10 8 6 4 2

Typeset by Pure Tech Corporation, Pondicherry, India

Printed in Great Britain
on acid-free paper by
Bookcraft Ltd.
Midsomer Norton, Avon

To the Memory
of My Wai-po

Preface

My interest in the history of how modern economics became formalized in mathematics goes back to my college days in China, when I taught myself the history of economic thought, modern Western economics, and mathematics in preparation for the entrance examination for an M.Phil. programme in economics. I remember how badly I wanted to find books explaining historically the process of formulating economics in mathematical terms whenever I was baffled by theorems in modern Western economics. The desire grew stronger during my M.Phil. studies. The econometrics course in the programme did not appeal to me, because there were few exciting ideas in the textbooks, and the methods presented were not as elegant and rigorous as those in mathematical economics. It was the history of how modern economics became formalized in mathematical terms that I set my heart on then.

My impression of econometrics was completely altered by T. Haavelmo's 1944 monograph and M. Morgan's doctoral thesis on econometric history (later published as a book), the first two books of my reading assignment after I arrived in Oxford. Since then, the more I read of the history of econometrics, the more I am fascinated by the rich ideas in the literature. I have looked into a well of stimulating thought buried beneath a pile of dry formulae.

To link up the two sides is the main purpose of this book. Thus it is written primarily for students of econometrics, like me, who have had, or are having, a dreary and difficult time with textbook econometrics. I expect it also to be helpful to those economists who resort frequently to the econometric tool-kit in their applied studies. I find from my limited reading in the present applied literature that many incorrect uses of econometric methods result from ignorance of the ideas behind them. It seems an ambitious hope to aid professional econometricians with this book. However, some of the issues which they are arguing vehemently about sound so familiar to me that I become worried that they might be going round in circles.

The book originated from my D.Phil. thesis, presented at Oxford University in 1989. I owe a great deal to David Hendry, Christopher Gilbert, and Stephen Nickell for their excellent supervision of the thesis. David Hendry started me on this research project, and I have learnt a lot more from him than the history itself. I feel indebted to Mary Morgan and John Aldrich, my thesis examiners, for their generous help and sincere support for my research. In particular, Mary Morgan patiently went through the early script of this book, and made many very useful comments on it. My thanks also go to Neil de Marchi, Bill Farebrother, Søren Johansen, Zvi Griliches, Dale Jorgenson, Karl Fox, Neil Ericsson, Manuel Arellano, Peter Phillips, Terence Gorman, and many others for their help, advice, and comments.

Special thanks are due to Lawrence Klein not only for introducing me to David Hendry, but also for his readiness to help whenever asked. Paul Samuelson, James Tobin, and Guy Orcutt most willingly gave me interviews and supplied me with much first-hand information on the subject. They have kindly permitted me to quote their words. I am grateful to them all.

This research has been made possible through the generosity of Nuffield College, Oriel College, and Oxford University. I also wish to thank the Rockefeller Archive Centre and the Cowles Foundation for Research in Economics for supporting me in collecting unpublished papers and memoranda, and giving me permission to quote from them in this book.

It is a real challenge to me to write this book in English, not being a native English speaker. I have been quite fortunate in getting help in the language at various stages of my writing. In this respect, I want to extend my thanks to my thesis supervisors and examiners, as well as Christopher Adams, Ian Preston, and Ruben Lee.

It is now time for me to express my distant and sincere thanks to my former teachers, Wu Jia-Pei, Sun Shi-Zheng, Zhang Shou-Yi, to my Chinese colleagues at the Institute of Quantitative and Technical Economics of the Chinese Academy of Social Sciences, and to many of my close Chinese friends. However, my most heartfelt gratitude goes to my family. It would have been impossible for me to have accomplished what I have achieved today without their unceasing affection, support, and tolerance. Their spirit and love has sustained me through this long process of producing this book.

QIN DUO

Oxford
1992

Contents

Introduction

Econometrics is a frontier discipline in the introduction of scientific means and methods into economics. It was born out of the desire to bridge the gap between economic theory and economic data. Mathematical statistics was chosen to supply the building materials for its operational convenience, rigorous logic, and highly abstract character. After nearly a century of attempts to amalgamate economic ideas, mathematical statistics, and data in analysing practical issues of interest, econometricians have not only established the discipline, but have also helped to free economics from its strongly speculative and subjective nature to bring it more into line with scientific principles.

This book examines the history of the formative period of econometric theory from approximately 1930 to 1960. It covers the major events which led to its formation. It focuses upon the process of how tools of mathematical statistics were selected and ideas of mathematical statistics were adapted to combine with economic motivations and enquiries; what insights and advances were achieved in the course of this combination; and what the main problems and issues were that led to its later development up to the present, and that remain worthy of consideration in the light of the situation today. It aims at uncovering the feature, unrecognized in most econometric textbooks, that econometrics is not merely a tool-kit for economics but a subject rich in ideas and theories which have the potential to revolutionize economics.

There has been a remarkable and growing interest in the history of econometrics in recent years. A concise history of econometrics has been produced by R. Epstein (1987); an account of the early period has been provided by M. Morgan (1990); a report of econometric development in Britain is due to C. Gilbert (1988); details of the Cowles programme during 1939–55 has been documented by C. Hildreth (1986); an extensive record of macroeconometric model-building activities from the 1930s up to the 1980s has been prepared by R. Bodkin, L. Klein, and K. Marwah (1991); *Oxford Economic Papers* has published a special issue on the history and methodology of econometrics (1: 1989); and *Econometric Theory* has organized a number of interviews with econometricians whose contributions are recognized to have historic significance.

This book can be considered, in many ways, a complement and sequel to Morgan's (1990) work. However, a crucial issue which, I feel, has so far not been fully investigated, is the process of combination mentioned in the opening paragraph. This forms the basis of the approach adopted here, and this, I believe, should be the key feature of a history of econometric thought. Hence the history requires a treatment in its own right different from the conventional treatment of the history of economic thought.

The general interest in the history of econometrics frequently involves the following questions: How and why have mathematics and statistics swept into economics? What economic problems were mathematical and statistical methods meant to solve, able to solve, and have solved? What methodological impact, if any, has the application of these methods given rise to in econometric as well as in economic thinking? How has econometrics evolved into the system that it has? What are the underlying ideas and purposes of various econometric methods constituting that system? Can developments in econometrics, in the light of its history, eventually achieve its objective of making economic analysis a fully scientific process? It is with these questions in mind that I have chosen to tell the story from the econometric perspective instead of the usual perspective in the history of economic thought, i.e. presenting the story either according to different schools or economic issues. This is clearly reflected in the classification of the chapters.

Chapter 1 records the fundamental event of the probability revolution in econometrics. It focuses upon how probability theory was brought into econometrics in relation to the main econometric modelling issues, such as estimation, identification, and testing. This laid the basis for the formalization of those issues, reported in later chapters. Chapter 2 describes the evolution of the notion of 'model', and the practice and criteria of model construction up to the 1940s. Chapters 3 and 4 narrate the process of how estimation and identification were formalized respectively. Chapter 5 goes on to the issue of testing and reveals some intrinsic problems pertaining to hypothesis-testing, beneath the achievements of formalizing econometrics. The problems are further extended, in Chapter 6, to other issues in association with model construction for the period immediately after the formative phase. This final chapter thus tries to link up the previous chapters and to show particularly what has been left unsolved in the formation of econometrics.

One drawback of arranging the chapters in this way is that there is an unavoidable degree of repetition of events in different chapters. A number of important works have to be dissected for separate discussions under different headings. This is a sacrifice of historical integrity for econometric integrity, and I hope, a worth-while one for the interest of econometricians. At least, the classification has made individual chapters quite independent, and they can be read in this way by those who are concerned with one particular topic. A related point concerns the scope of coverage. By focusing upon the formation of econometric theory, I have devoted relatively little space to the extensive literature of applied econometrics. However, this choice should not be seen as a devaluation of its role. On the contrary, I believe that the development of econometric theory could not have taken place without the impetus from applied studies. Nor is there much description in the book of what may be termed the external story. Again, this does not imply that I underrate the importance of external factors, such as the influence of statisticians and mathematicians, and the general development of science, the limitation of both data availability and computational capacity, the educational background of the individuals concerned, as well as the economic and social environment of the time. I count on various authors for a coverage of these, e.g. Krüger *et al.* (1987) and Gigerenzer *et al.* (1989) for the statistical aspect, Mirowski (1989*a*, 1989*b*) for the scientific aspect, Epstein (1987) and particularly Bodkin *et al.* (1991) for stories about actual model-building activities. Meanwhile, I sketch below a very brief background account of some relevant institutions, individuals, and research projects, by way of introduction.

Most of the pioneering work in applied econometric demand analyses was undertaken at the beginning of this century

4   INTRODUCTION

by American agricultural economists, such as E. J. Working, M. Ezekiel, and F. V. Waugh. Research in this area was largely promoted by the US Bureau of Agricultural Economics, which was established in 1922 (see Fox 1989). Later, among those who worked for the bureau and who made prominent contributions to econometrics were M. A. Girshick and K. A. Fox. A statistical economist, H. L. Moore of Columbia University, also made important contributions to applied demand studies. His interest also extended to statistical analysis of business cycles (see Stigler 1962), and his approach was later developed by his former student H. Schultz, while teaching at the University of Chicago. Contemporarily with Moore's lonely venture into business cycle modelling, a group of Harvard statisticians and economists headed by W. M. Persons launched a research project into business cycle forecasting in the 1920s (see Samuelson 1987). The statistical methods developed by the Harvard group exerted significant influence on the later project of measuring business cycles led by A. F. Burns and W. C. Mitchell of the US National Bureau of Economic Research (NBER) during the 1930s and 1940s. The NBER maintained its opposition to the Cowles formative approach (see below) in the 1940s. The empirically orientated approach of the NBER has given constructive stimulus to the rise of the applied econometric modelling enterprise in the USA since the 1950s.

Early econometric studies in Europe sprouted from several institutions. R. Frisch, one of the founding fathers of econometrics, built up his econometric project at the Oslo Institute of Economic Research. He guided a number of now well-known econometricians at the Institute, such as T. Haavelmo and O. Reiersøl. The Dutch Central Bureau of Statistics and the Netherlands Economic Institute were centres of macroeconometric models. The research was pioneered there by J. Tinbergen, another founding father of econometrics. After he built the first macroeconometric model of the Dutch economy in the mid-1930s, Tinbergen was invited to work on macroeconometric models at the League of Nations in Geneva. T. C. Koopmans was then his collaborator at both the Netherlands Economic Institute and the League of Nations after giving up physics for economics. H. Theil was a student of Tinbergen. Another active institution before the Second World War was the Austrian

Institute for Trade Cycle Research. O. Morgenstern was in charge of the Institute, and A. Wald and G. Tintner were on the staff.

The Econometric Society was established in 1930 by Frisch, I. Fisher of Yale University, and C. F. Roos of Cornell University (see Christ 1952). The Society greatly facilitated academic exchanges between European and American scholars not only in the young econometrics profession but also in mathematical statistics. It thus rapidly promoted the growth of econometrics into a separate discipline. Subsequently, 1932 saw the founding of the Cowles Commission for Research in Economics, a research institution which contributed uniquely to the formalization of econometrics (see Christ 1952; Hildreth 1986). The Commission had a close connection with the Econometric Society from its beginning. Frisch, Roos, H. T. Davis, and Tintner were among its early research staff. After moving from Colorado to Chicago University at the end of the 1930s, the Cowles Commission began to recruit and associate a considerable number of young European researchers who fled to the USA because of the Second World War. Its special contribution to establishing the framework of orthodox econometrics was made mainly under the directorship of J. Marschak, a German-trained economist and formerly the director of the Oxford Institute of Statistics. During the five-year period 1943–8, Marschak gathered together many talented young workers for his research projects, such as Koopmans, Haavelmo, T. W. Anderson, L. R. Klein, L. Hurwicz, and H. Rubin. He also kept the Commission in frequent touch with prominent statisticians who were interested in econometrics and who at the time were mainly at Columbia University, such as H. Hotelling, Wald, and Girshick. The Cowles workers frequently had exchanges and contacts with the American Statistical Association as well. The achievements at the Cowles Commission attracted more ingenious researchers from the late 1940s. Among those associated with econometric studies were O. Reiersøl, C. F. Christ, W. C. Hood, A. Marshall, F. Modigliani, H. S. Houthakker, and H. Simon. Many more visited the Commission for various periods. Econometric researches were soon carried on in other places in the USA as the Cowles Commission shifted its research emphasis on to theoretical and mathematical economics at the beginning of the 1950s.

After the war, econometric activities revived in several places in Europe. In Sweden, H. Wold had been in charge of a continuous econometric research programme at the University of Uppsala throughout the war. He tried to develop a rival model form to the Cowles simultaneous-equations model form. In The Netherlands, H. Theil was mainly responsible for leading econometric research there as the director of the Econometric Institute of The Netherlands School of Economics from the 1950s to the mid-1960s. In Britain, a collective effort to study time-series economic data with an emphasis on applied modelling was organized by R. Stone at Cambridge University in the late 1940s (see Gilbert 1988). His collaborators included Tintner, G. H. Orcutt, D. Cochrane, J. Durbin, and G. S. Watson. Also, J. D. Sargan was a student at Cambridge at that time. He went to teach at Leeds University afterwards and then moved to the London School of Economics, which evolved into a centre for developing dynamic econometric models later in the 1960s. Econometricians in Britain have held an intimate relationship with British statisticians through the Royal Statistical Society.

The following chapters report the contributions made mainly by these figures. The report is written in a manner to allow their contributions to link together in presenting the history. Explanatory notes are added when felt necessary, and commentary is kept to a minimum to maintain as much as possible the objectiveness of the story.

1

The Probability Foundations of Econometrics

Econometrics took shape as a formal subdiscipline of economics towards the end of the 1930s and the beginning of the 1940s. This phase is marked by two key developments: (*a*) a structural modelling procedure, which required econometric models to be built upon a priori theoretical models and sought to confirm the theory by approximately measuring out the associated structure; and (*b*) a stepwise formalization of the general modelling practice. The former determined the exterior position of econometrics as subordinate to theoretical economics, most clearly reflected in the received role of 'measurement'. The latter systematized the interior practice of econometrics, through adapting techniques from mathematical statistics to formalizing econometric modelling steps of estimation, identification, testing, and specification. Both helped to shape econometrics into a discipline separate from those branches of applied economics from which it had sprouted. Furthermore, the view became widely accepted during this stepwise formalization that economic objects should be measured using the general model form of stochastic systems of interdependent variables, and hence that probability theory should be applied as the basis of all the adapted statistical methods in analysing such systems. This helped to differentiate the subject from mathematical economics.

Prior to the 1930s, probability theory was commonly rejected as being unsuitable as a basis for analysing economic data. Only fragmentary statistical methods were used to help to measure economic relationships from data in the early experimental attempts. Changes took place from the 1930s and onwards as more and more statistical methods were tried in the arena of applied economics, and as concern grew stronger to get the applied works using these methods fully justified in standard economics. The changes were also accelerated by the substantial progress made in mathematical statistics with regard to multivariate models since the 1920s, and in the axiomatization of probability theory in the early 1930s. There thus rose a movement to transform economics into a real science.

However, at that time contributions of econometricians to economics were largely reformative rather than revolutionary, as manifested in the gradual dominance of the structural modelling procedure, which orientated econometric tool-makers to conform to economics in systematizing econometric practice with statistical techniques and methods. It was due to these techniques and methods that a probability approach was eventually allowed to creep in. By the time that Trygve Haavelmo argued for a full adoption of the probability approach as the foundation of econometric theory in the early 1940s (Haavelmo 1944)—later referred to as the 'Haavelmo revolution'—it hardly stirred up any fundamental conceptual shifts of a revolutionary significance in econometrics or economics. Nested in the structural procedure, the probability approach was adopted mainly to the extent that no more logical inconsistency should arise in applying statistical techniques to econometrics. A key message of Haavelmo's advocacy—that the probability approach was the right vehicle, not only for bridging the gap between econometrics and theoretical economics, but also for changing economists' viewpoint of a mechanical world into that of a stochastic world—was largely overlooked. The absorption of probability theory into econometrics remained mostly on a technical level, closely associated with the maximum-likelihood method in particular, much more than on an epistemological level. Furthermore, the probability approach appeared immaterial in most subsequent applied econometric studies, where the maximum-likelihood method was scarcely employed (see Chapter 3) and where attention was devoted to measuring the magnitudes of the given a priori theoretical coefficients. Hence, the job of carrying out Haavelmo's probability revolution was virtually incomplete as far as its impact on the whole of econometric thinking and on the basic ideas of economics was concerned. This incompleteness is evident, from the description of later chapters, in the dominance of simultaneous-equations modelling over single-equation modelling, and in the focus on issues of identification and estimation at the expense of hypo-thesis-testing and model specification during the period of econo-metric formalization.

The first section of this chapter sketches the eve of the probability revolution. An introduction to probability methods follows in Section 1.2. Section 1.3 is dedicated to Haavelmo's probabilistic revolution. The following section turns to alternat-ive approaches to the adoption of probability theory. The final section discusses the after-effect and especially the incomplete-ness of the probability revolution.

1.1 The Eve of the Probability Revolution

Econometrics grew rapidly in the 1930s following the founding of the Econometric Society in 1930 and the publication of *Econometrica* in 1933. A particular feature of this growth was the sustained effort among econometricians to bring econometric practice into line with economic theory, through generalizing and formalizing concepts and methods emerging from applied studies. This contributed significantly to the upsurge in the 'scientification' of economics, stimulated by the paradigm of the achievements in modern physics (cf. Mirowski 1989*a*), and the rapid progress in mathematical statistics in the background. Within the developments in economics, four direct factors of growth could be identified: (*a*) the theoretical expansion of general equilibrium economics upon the tradition of the Lausanne school of mathematical economics (cf. Hamouda and Rowley 1988); (*b*) the empirical attempts to measure economic laws mainly by American agricultural economists (cf. Fox 1989); (*c*) the innovative exercises in analysing, explaining, and predicting business cycles; and (*d*) the emergence of a team of professionals working devotedly for 'a unification of the theoretical-quantitative and the empirical-quantitative approach to economic problems' (Frisch 1933*a*). The first factor represented the theoretical-quantitative side, while the third took the side of the empirical-quantitative approach. The second formed the middle-of-the-road.

As pointed out by Morgan (1987, 1990), early econometrics applied mathematical statistics without probability theory.

Probability theory, perceived narrowly in its original context of games of chance, was rejected as inapplicable to econometric problems mainly on the grounds of the non-experimental and highly interdependent nature of economics data (e.g. in the writings of W. M. Persons, O. Morgenstern, and R. Frisch as quoted in Morgan 1987). However, a more fundamental antagonistic force came from theoretical economics, where there prevailed a deep-rooted deterministic viewpoint under the influence of nineteenth-century mechanical physics (see Ménard 1987; Mirowski 1989a, 1989b). Practicality did motivate mathematical economics. But its immediate goal was to make theories into 'operationally meaningful theorems' (Samuelson 1947), where the term 'operational' seemed to denote purely logical deduction by mathematical means without necessarily involving inference from data. As far as mere operationality in this strict sense was concerned, the use of statistics without probability seemed to fit into economic thinking, which was well accustomed to the mode of a priori deductive, nomological formalization.

Problems arose when it came to relating actual economic data to the formulated 'laws', though the two did not appear to be irreconcilable as long as the job was targeted at 'measurement' of those operational theories, as were many of the early statistical demand studies (cf. Morgan 1990, pt. II). An important problem was how one could establish with confidence that the estimated statistical relations corresponded to those desired theoretical relations. Out of this problem grew the concept of 'identification' (cf. Morgan 1990, ch. 6). The early formulation of identification in the sense of uniqueness of coefficient estimates and their interpretation proceeded independently of the probability approach (see Chapter 4). Another related problem was concerned with the interpretation of the error or residual term in an estimated equation (cf. Morgan 1990, ch. 7). The preferred explanation was that the error was due to inaccuracy in data measurement, as reflected in the use of the so-called 'errors-in-variables' form (e.g. Schultz 1930, 1938; Frisch 1934). This interpretation accommodated comfortably early statistical economics and conventional mathematical economics while maintaining a non-probabilistic stand. This was best illustrated in 'confluence analysis' by means of 'bunch maps', the first specifically econometric apparatus invented by Frisch (1934), which was grounded upon a Walrasian type of deterministic system.

However, the non-probabilistic treatment of deterministic variables with observational errors was not without problems. A basic difficulty was the lack of an explicit treatment for 'omitted variables', due to the unrealistic assumption of *ceteris paribus* commonly employed in economics. Early econometricians realized the importance of relaxing this assumption in applied research,[1] but it was quite awkward to specify all the omitted variables by an error term in the errors-in-variables context, where there was already an error term denoting the measurement inaccuracy. At least, the inclusion of another error term would certainly invalidate the heavily used simple estimation methods of least-squares, and require the introduction of more advanced statistical techniques. Yet it was very difficult to pursue the search for better statistical techniques without first specifying clearly the nature and properties of the errors, however they were interpreted.

The strategy of attaching simple statistical techniques to received economic theory represented by deterministic relationships experienced even greater difficulties in business cycle analysis. First of all, there were no well-received economic theories available in this field which could form a reliable basis for measurement. There was especially a lack of partial and dynamic theories capable of describing and explaining the volatile dynamics of the cycles shown in time-series data. Hence, in addition to the usual chores of measurement, econometric researches in this area faced the daunting task of searching for reasonable (with respect to theory) and working (with respect to prediction) models through analysing data, formulating theoretical hypotheses, and testing various competing hypotheses against relevant data (see Chapters 2 and 5). During the early years of econometric history (see Morgan 1990), it was soon proved that the type of representations by Fourier series along the lines of deterministic mathematical analyses was too rigid to work well with data of great mutability. Empirically, it looked more feasible to analyse and factorize economic time-series by the same

---

[1] e.g. Schultz (1938) was aware of the limitations of his results which neglected the effects of other relevant factors and economic relations.

means used in statistics to handle stochastic time-series data. Therefore, when Slutsky argued (1937)[2] that cycles should be viewed as the outcome of a combination of random processes, his view gained rapid acceptance in the profession (see Chapter 2). Around the mid-1930s, models of the 'errors-in-equations' form were adopted widely in applied business cycle studies to account for the greater uncertainty caused by omitted variables. This emphasized the necessity to produce a justification for using more systematic statistics to describe and analyse the randomness of economic data with respect to conventional theoretical formation.

The desire for reliable economic justification in the areas of empirical demand analysis and business cycle study gave rise to a structural modelling procedure during the mid-1930s, later to become the cornerstone of econometric theory. The procedure stemmed from Frisch's invention of a 'structural decomposition' method. The invention was inspired by the desire to systematize the model-searching process in dealing with economic time-series (see Chapter 2). Frisch selected the model form of a *'weight system'* as the appropriate representation of economic dynamics by combining the received concept of 'structure' in economic thought, i.e. a quantifiable economic relation represented in a functional equation, and Slutsky's view that observed economic movements were generated 'through the cumulation of random disturbances' (Frisch 1936). He designed a 'bunch maps' technique for the data-based searching process within the framework of a weight system (cf. Hendry and Morgan 1989). This model form suggested acceptance of a stochastic viewpoint, since the error parts here no longer represented the measurement errors but random shocks. On the other hand, the way that bunch maps were used in modelling implied a formalized process of learning from data by means of statistical inference. Therefore, Frisch's structural method heralded the entrance of probability theory in econometrics, despite his earlier objection to its use.

Hence the introduction of probability theory was in the offing in both demand studies and business cycle analysis.

---

[2] Slutsky's paper was first published in Russian in 1927 with an English summary and was widely known among the leading econometricians at the time before the English version finally came out in *Econometrica* in 1937.

1.2 INTRODUCTION OF PROBABILITY THEORY

As seen in the previous section, Frisch's initiation of the structural decomposition method heralded a programme of formalizing econometrics by means of mathematical statistics. This was stimulated both by growing considerations and discussions in economics from the 1930s, on issues concerning economic decisions in the presence of uncertainty, risk, and expectation, often in probabilistic terms, and by rapid advances in modern mathematical statistics from the early twentieth century.[3]

The taboo against using probability theory in economics began to be removed after F. P. Ramsey put forward the explanation of 'degrees of belief' for probabilities around 1930 (see Hamouda and Rowley 1988). This explanation offered economists a more flexible view of probability theory, giving access to an easy means of handling the complicated and subtle subjective phenomena in economic decision-making. Pioneer analyses of risk and expectation during the 1930s bore a strong revisionist character in that they tended to use individual probabilistic concepts, such as mathematical expectation, with the established mechanistic framework of economics expressed in terms of deterministic mathematics. This was reflected in the labelling of these adapted probabilistic terms as 'certainty equivalents', as did G. L. S. Shackle (1938: 64). The essence of these analyses was to try to simplify the complexity of random behaviour by borrowing certain concepts from probability theory, so as to retain economics in the world of certainty. Thus, this early period of change in economics was called 'the avoidance of uncertainty' by Rowley and Hamouda (1987) (see also Hamouda and Rowley 1988: 52–61). Nevertheless, these rather restricted revisions in conventional economics improved theoretical flexibility in applied studies, as well as opening up the possibility of further shifts of views. The boldest of these occurred mostly in mathematical economics, which, at the time, was very much mixed with econometrics; in fact, mathematical economics was originally part of econometrics (see Frisch 1933a).

---

[3] See Rowley and Hamouda (1987) and Hamouda and Rowley (1988) for more detailed accounts of probability theory in economics in the 1930s; see Kendall (1968) for a more detailed history of mathematical statistics.

A seminal work in the area of introducing probability theory systematically was J. Marschak's 'Utilities and Probabilities in Human Choice' (1937). Marschak tried to utilize the 'degrees of belief' concept of probabilities as a general base to combine estimable probabilities of future events with the existing theoretical discussions of uncertainties in decision-making, mainly by Keynes, Jeffreys, and others. He achieved this by translating their discussion of human choice into that of 'games of chance' so that he was able to merge the utility concept with the probability concept, and then with R. A. Fisher's likelihood function approach to make the theory estimable. Marschak's probability formulation must have exerted significant impact on the thinking of many econometricians through his active participation in the early activities of the Econometric Society, and his prestigious positions, first at the Institute of Statistics of Oxford University, later at the Graduate Faculty of Social and Political Science, New York, and the Cowles Commission for Economic Research.

An even stronger advocacy for randomizing economics appeared in an article in the 1938 *Econometrica* with the title 'Pure Economics as a Stochastical Theory' (Hagstroem 1938). The paper appealed for an extension of the use of probability concepts in the economics literature from describing merely agents' future behaviour, as in the expectation theory, to explaining present day-to-day economic activities. It argued that since probability judgements prevailed in economic life, 'why should not this be reflected in the very basis of the pure theory that tries to interpret the realities of economic action'. The model scheme proposed in the paper was rather an introductory one, but the concluding remarks were quite provocative and far-sighted:

By introducing in the theory of pure economics the stochastical element, it will probably be made more adapted to the needs of practical economics. Indeed, the interpretation of all reality by means of abstract mathematical schemes must pass through the theory of probabilities, and through the practice of statistical observation. This fundamental fact is reflected by stochastical modifications of theories pertaining to different dominions of thought. As regards economic theory, the stochastical point of view seems to us to be clearly inherent in the very object of the research.

However in the applied econometric field, these stimuli from economics paled in comparison with those from the rapid developments of mathematical statistics. The most noticeable of these developments related to topics like regression theory mainly by K. Pearson and G. U. Yule, sampling theory by W. Gosset (Student) and R. A. Fisher, estimation theory by Fisher, E. Pearson, and J. Neyman, hypothesis-testing by Neyman and Pearson, and time-series analysis by Yule, E. Slutsky, and A. Markov, which led to the theory of stochastic processes (see Kendall 1968; Gigerenzer *et al.* 1989).

At the forefront of the statistical influence upon econometrics was the classic sampling and estimation theory. The theory presupposed the clarification of a set of fundamental concepts concerning 'sample' and 'population'. Specifically, estimation was thought to be constructed on individual concrete samples drawn as if at random from some abstract population as a means of making inference from visible phenomena to latent laws. One of the crucial points here was random sampling, which facilitated the use of probability theory in the form of sampling distributions, and especially in formulating the method of maximum-likelihood (ML) point estimation as well as interval estimation. The theory was in fact applied implicitly in setting up formal statistical criteria for evaluating estimated results as characteristics of the probability distribution of samples.

Another important influence came from the development of the theory of statistical testing initiated by Neyman and Pearson who clarified the procedure of statistical inference as centred on hypothesis-testing. They reformulated the testing process rigorously in accordance with the probability scheme. The idea underlying this was that since hypotheses were tentative, they should be viewed as relative statements and therefore be either accepted or rejected with respect to rival statements in any statistical tests. It was also thought that since studies of samples were aimed at studies of populations, estimation of sample characteristics should be taken as a part of and the initial step in testing hypotheses about those populations.

These statistical methods permeated the econometric circle through direct interactions between statisticians and econometricians, which became increasingly frequent in the second half of the 1930s. The year 1936 deserves a special mention. At the summer conference that year of the Cowles Commission for Research in Economics, R. A. Fisher was invited to give three lectures on regression analysis, testing, and inverse probability. He emphasized the importance of viewing regression coefficients from the standpoint of modern statistics, i.e. attention should be paid to information embodied in the variance and covariance of sampling distributions rather than the means. He also advocated the advantages of the ML estimation method (Cowles Commission 1936). Almost concurrently, J. Neyman attended the annual European meeting of the Econometric Society[4] and delivered a 'Survey of Recent Work on Correlation and Covariation' (Neyman 1937a). He explained in detail his method of hypothesis-testing based on the probability scheme. The American winter meeting of the Society that year devoted a whole session to 'Applications of the Theory of Probability to Economic Problems' (Leavens 1937). Fisher's theory in curve-fitting was reiterated and new statistical techniques were introduced at the meeting.

In a flexible atmosphere towards probability concepts in economics, probability theory gained *de facto* acquiescence in econometric practice with the influx and trial of new statistical techniques during the late 1930s. But this was achieved primarily because probability theory underlay the statistical techniques of interest. The theory was brought into econometrics mainly because of the technical requirements for consistent estimation and then verification of the structural relations concerned in the form of weight systems.

The first explicit acceptance of probability theory in the basic econometric scheme came in *Linear Regression Analysis of Economic Time Series*, published in 1937, by Tjalling Koopmans. Being well trained in sciences, Koopmans approached econometrics in a very rigorous and systematic manner.[5] He was aware of 'the urgent need' at the time 'for a basis for appreciation of the reliability of empirical regression equations fitted to eco-

---

[4] Recalling the early activities of the Society in the 1930s, Tinbergen remarked that 'our European meetings were very pleasant because there were only about thirty people participating, so you could actually have profound discussions' (Magnus and Morgan 1987).

[5] 'Koopmans was very well disciplined. He would not let anything go out that wasn't rigorous', as recalled by T. W. Anderson (Phillips 1986).

nomic time-series, which might supply the justification for a procedure based to such an extent on hypothetical foundations' (Koopmans 1937: 7). Koopmans acknowledged that Frisch was correct in emphasizing the particularities of economic data and in provoking far-reaching discussions about the nature of (applied) econometric discoveries. But he pointed out three deficiencies in Frisch's approach to tackling economic data: (a) oversimplification of the premiss of analysis, in so far as Frisch's statistical methods lacked unity and coherence in defining the limitations of estimates from specific sample observations with respect to the abstract and general theoretical suppositions; (b) lack of explicit criteria for evaluating the regression results; and (c) neglect of errors in equations due to sampling errors. All these, Koopmans argued, could be remedied by carefully adapting Fisher's sampling theory based on a probability specification, which had previously been casually shrugged off in econometric circles. Koopmans believed that while Frisch's methods were advantageous in guarding against meaningless regression results with respect to economic theory, Fisher's probability specification provided a better image of the particular–general or concrete–abstract relationship with the concepts and methods of 'sample', 'hypothesis', and 'population'. He felt that it would be very helpful to overcome the deficiencies in Frisch's methods by exploring more fully the information contained in the data through their probability distributions. Furthermore, Koopmans introduced, for the first time, Fisher's classification of the problems in data reduction into 'specification', 'estimation', and 'distribution' to help to clarify the still muddled problems in the reduction of economic data. He also outlined the common statistical criteria for evaluating different estimates, the ML method and the significance t-test method.

Koopmans was cautious about adapting Fisher's statistical methods to an econometric context. For instance, he interpreted the 'repeated sampling' requirement as a hypothetical situation, where 'a repeated sample consists of a set of values which the variables would have assumed if in these years the systematic components had been other independent random drawings from the distribution they are supposed to have' (p. 7). Note that Koopmans still followed Frisch's errors-in-variables approach. He also tried to avoid fitting any of Frisch's defined confluent relations by using Frisch's 'bunch maps' method prior to applying Fisher's statistical methods to economic data (as shown in the example of the world ship-freight market in his 1937 book).

Koopmans's acceptance of probability theory appeared fragmentary and technical, i.e. not related to any of economists' reasoning. Since he was preoccupied with the systematization of the regression procedure in the econometric context, he utilized probability theory only to the extent of identifying the regression residuals in Frisch's framework in terms of probability distributions in order to make a compromise between Fisher's and Frisch's methods. Nevertheless, the methodological implications of his compromise were profound for two reasons. First, he tried to reset Frisch's method on the basis of Fisher's approach when he utilized it subject to the precautions given by Frisch. Secondly, his adoption of Fisher's approach was impartial and free of 'certainty equivalent' considerations in that he proceeded according to the sequence of Fisher's steps of specification, estimation, and distribution, the last of which was to be frequently overlooked by econometricians under the influence of 'certainty equivalents' in economics. However, unaware of much of the significance of Fisher's methodology, Koopmans did not discuss the probability approach. Probability theory was brought in apparently only because it was attached to sampling theory, on which his interest was centred.

Koopmans's book seems to have received considerable attention and favourable comment. Reviews appeared in most of the relevant journals following its publication, all of them strongly recommending it. One regarded it as 'a theoretical treatise on the possibility of using the method of linear regression, together with an appropriate probability theory for making significance tests in the analysis of economic time-series' (Wilks 1938). In particular, Koopmans's results impressed Tinbergen, who presented a considered account of the methods of Fisher, Frisch, and Koopmans successively in his famous work *A Method and Its Application to Investment Activity* (Tinbergen 1939, vol. 1). Adhering to his usual methods of least squares (LS), Tinbergen began to pay more attention to Koopmans's suggestions and to devote some discussion to the regression residuals. Occasionally, he supplemented his analysis with some of Koopmans's methods which were immediately applicable. Probability theory met with no objection (in fact little attention) from Tinbergen. On the whole, many applied economists seemed to be too dazzled by the highly mathematical and technical presentation in Koopmans's book to think about the probabilistic implications underlying them.

1.3 THE HAAVELMO REVOLUTION[6]

The task of thoroughly adopting the probability approach was carried out by Trygve Haavelmo. Haavelmo undertook his econometric studies with Frisch and started his career in elaborating the latter's 'structural decomposition' approach. He soon saw the inconsistency of Frisch's anti-probability position with his approval of Slutsky's random-shock representation in the 'weight system' design. He set out to combine the idea of weight systems with the stochastic essence of Slutsky's approach. Haavelmo argued that 'the structural equations must be taken as laws in the stochastical sense, i.e. as average laws' and that econometric models should take the definite form of 'stochastic structural equations' comprising 'stochastic structural coefficients'[7] (1938). The argument rang similar to 'certainty equivalence' in economics. However, what Haavelmo was trying to do was not to avoid uncertainty by taking probabilistic concepts into economics, but rather to accept uncertainty by converting the outlook of economics from a deterministic to stochastic one. He reiterated that common econometric practice was inferior in superimposing 'additive errors' on the 'exact' and 'ideal' 'theoretical time movement of the variables' (1938, 1940a). To justify this viewpoint, he argued that such a jigsaw of a deterministic system of structural equations and additive error terms might actually give rise to systematic bias in estimating coefficients by classical regression methods, because it prevented modellers from noticing the influence of the error term in each equation on the other equations in the system (1938, 1939, 1943b). This view went beyond the merely conceptual accusation against

---

[6] See also Morgan (1987, 1990); Malinvaud (1988); Spanos (1989); and Nerlove (1990).
[7] This paper was actually given at the same meeting in 1936 where the Neyman–Pearson approach was introduced, as mentioned in Sect. 1.2.

deterministic theories as 'unrealistic' in the face of actual observations. It induced Haavelmo to focus his attention on formalizing several technical aspects of estimating the coefficients of a simultaneous-equation model (SEM) based upon Frisch's idea of a weight system. His work in the area soon proved to be fruitful and influential (see Chapters 2, 3, and 4), and his achievements in turn helped to sharpen his philosophical insight in econometrics.

A major event that launched Haavelmo into a thorough advocacy of the probability approach and therefore into leading a probability revolution in econometrics was the well-known debate around 1940 started by J. M. Keynes regarding Tinbergen's macroeconometric models built for the United Nations (Keynes and Tinbergen 1939–40; Patinkin 1976). Apart from his specific criticisms of Tinbergen's model, many of Keynes's comments touched econometrics to the quick, especially the following points badly in need of improvement: (*a*) the logical link between 'the mazes of arithmetic' of econometric reasoning using mathematical and statistical tools and 'the mazes of logic' of the non-mathematical reasoning in standard economics; (*b*) the position of econometrics in economics, and particularly its limitations, which had been viewed as serious by many economists; and (*c*) the status quo of econometrics itself as a self-contained, systematic subdiscipline. Keynes's paper seemed to bring to a head the growing desire in the profession to systematize econometrics and consolidate its position in economics.

The most comprehensive response to Keynes's criticisms came from Haavelmo in a paper 'Statistical Testing of Business-Cycle Theories' (1943*a*) and a monograph *The Probability Approach in Econometrics* (1944; mimeographed in 1941). The paper was a critique of the deep-rooted prejudice in economics circles against the application of statistical inference based on probability theory, as explained by Schumpeter (1939) and culminating in the Keynes–Tinbergen debate. The monograph provided a 'most comprehensive exposition' of the 'logical foundations of econometrics' (Stone 1946)[8] and was recognized as 'a new

[8] Richard Stone expressed the view that Haavelmo's work resulted from the Keynes–Tinbergen debate (Stone 1946). This was recently confirmed by T. W. Anderson (1990).

milestone' in econometrics (Koopmans 1950: 4), and later as 'the manifesto' of econometrics. It is because of this work that the thorough adoption of probability theory in econometrics is also known as the 'Haavelmo revolution' (Morgan 1987, 1990).

Haavelmo put forward three linked arguments for the probability approach: (*a*) if the common view of economic time-series was extended from one-dimensional to multi-dimensional in terms of its probability distribution, the application of sampling theory was naturally justified; (*b*) if sampling theory could be applied to analyse economic data, the resulting statistical outcome would bear certain significance in empirical estimating and testing hypothetical statements, and would be at least no worse than the outcome obtained from any other inductive or speculative methods; and (*c*) if theories were to be formulated into explicit hypothetical statements, they should by nature be tentative and therefore should be made stochastic, because practically no theories in an exact form could survive statistical tests except for 'very broad and uninteresting statements' (Haavelmo 1943*a*). These arguments were strengthened in the preface to *The Probability Approach in Econometrics*. It began with an analogy of econometric modelling to bridge building—to build a bridge between 'economic theory and actual measurements'. This task directly necessitated 'a theoretical foundation' for econometrics 'based upon modern theory of probability and statistical inference' (p. iii), thus far the most rigorous analytics in formal inductive methods. Previous econometric studies, Haavelmo observed, abounded with confusion caused by attempts to deal with model construction, estimation, and prediction without 'a probabilistic formulation of hypotheses' (p. 10). But implicitly they all rested 'ultimately, upon some, perhaps very vague, notion of probability and random variables', as long as they utilized some statistical tools. So why not adopt the approach explicitly and finally to clear away 'much of the confusion in current economic research' (p. 10) and replace it with the 'class of scientific statements that can be expressed in probability terms' (p. iv).

The Probability Approach in Econometrics exhibits an elaborate arrangement of ideas and arguments throughout its six chapters, tightly knit together by two successive themes: a general theme of justifying the indispensability of the probability approach and a specific theme of formalizing a consistent and generalized modelling procedure using maximum-likelihood and hypothesis-testing principles. The first theme is covered in the first three chapters of the monograph, focusing upon the general strategies for model building, or in Haavelmo's terms, the problems of how to make a 'design of experiment'. The second theme runs from the third chapter 'Stochastical Schemes as a Basis for Econometrics' until the end, comprising the technical procedure of model specification, hypothesis-testing, estimation, and prediction within a probabilistic framework. The third chapter served as the crux of the monograph, in accord with the title.

Haavelmo set forth his justification for the probability approach, in chapter 1, 'Abstract Models and Reality', from the following fundamental problem arising in econometric modelling: how to set up abstract models of economic reality that were operational in respect to economic data. An immediate dilemma encountered by model-builders was concerned with economic variables, the first basic element of econometric models. While a theoretical construct required quantitative definitions of variables as exact as possible, only vague concepts could be found in reality, or, in his words, 'ambiguities' were unavoidable 'in classifications and measurements of real phenomena' (Haavelmo 1943a: 4). The problem was traced to a failure to distinguish the elements of a threefold classification involving a contrast between 'observational' variables and 'theoretical' variables as representatives of 'true' variables.[9] It was of 'great importance' therefore to draw distinctions between the three, distinctions necessitated by inaccurately measured data and passive observations, and to express them explicitly in model construction and specification. They involved setting up a tentative theoretical model, circumscribing the number of 'objects in real economic life' that were of interest, in such a way that relationships fitted out from real economic data were able to be 'identified with those in the model' via the 'a priori hypotheses' implied in it. Further contemplation led to another difficulty, in addition to the conceptual complexity of variables, i.e. how to select variables and choose specific relations between them

---

[9] Haavelmo's classification of 'observational', 'theoretical', and 'true' variables seems to correspond closely to that of Schumpeter's 'random', 'theoretical', and 'historical' variables (Schumpeter 1939: ch. V).

to set up the tentative model, which formed the topic of chapter 2, 'The Degree of Permanence of Economic Laws'. It was very difficult to find high degrees of permanence or stability in the empirical relations corresponding to the theoretical relations proposed for a variety of reasons: first, misfit of economic theories to reality due to the *ceteris paribus* premiss, upon which most economic relationships were formulated, but which could never be satisfied by observed data; secondly, poor 'reversibility' of economic relations, i.e. the fact that economic time-series data arose from 'one-way' historical processes and did not belong to the type 'which would result from the designs of experiments prescribed in economic theory' (Haavelmo 1943*a*: 18); thirdly, inevitable simplification in theorizing about economic activities in terms of a selected number of economic variables and the relations between them (see Chapter 2); and fourthly, the difficulty in picking out individual economic relations that were constant or stable over time from 'the simultaneous action of a whole system of fundamental laws' (p. 38) latent beneath the observations. All these led to two conclusions concerning theoretical models: they should be 'blurred' or augmented by random factors to narrow the gap from reality so as to become more accurate from the applied viewpoint; they should be retained when they failed to get support from data evidence, and not rejected. Naturally, the probability scheme was the best resource for fulfilling these statements.

In chapter 3, Haavelmo demonstrated at length how economists should adapt themselves to a rigorous probability setting in formulating their theories. But prior to that, he discussed the practical meaning of probability. In his view, 'the question is not whether probabilities exist or not, but whether—if we proceed as if they existed—we are able to make statements about real phenomena that are "correct for practical purposes"' (p. 43). He observed:

Much futile discussion has taken place in regard to the question of what probabilities actually are, the type of events for which probabilities 'exist', and so forth. Various types of 'foundations of probability' have been offered, some of them starting from observable frequencies of events, some appealing to the idea of a priori belief or to some other notion of reality. Still other 'foundations' are of a purely formal nature without any reference to real phenomena. But they have one thing in common, namely, that they end up with a certain concept of probability that is of a purely abstract nature. For in all the 'foundations' offered the system of probabilities involved are, finally, required to satisfy some logical consistency requirements, and to have these fulfilled a price must be paid, which invariably consists in giving up the exact equivalence between the theoretical probabilities and whatever real phenomena we might consider. In this respect, probability schemes are not different from other theoretical schemes. The rigorous notions of probabilities and probability distributions 'exist' only in our rational mind, serving us only as a tool for deriving practical statements (p. 48)

This extremely pragmatic and epistemological outlook provided Haavelmo with an open mind to different, even apparently conflicting interpretations of probability. He acknowledged both the 'frequency of occurrence' and 'a measure of our *a priori confidence* in the occurrence of a certain event' as common-sense interpretations of probability (Haavelmo 1943*a*: 48), though he seemed to favour the latter interpretation for the reason that 'for economic time-series . . . a repetition of the "experiment", in the usual sense, is not possible or feasible' (p. 48). Whatever the interpretation, the main point that Haavelmo wished to put forward remained unchanged, i.e. economists should specify explicitly 'the stochastical elements of our economic theories already in the "laws" of behaviour for the single individuals, firms, etc.' in probabilistic terms, before deriving 'the average market relations or relations for the whole society, from these individual "laws"' (pp. 51–2). He further supported his point by discussions on the impact of error terms or disturbances on different relations in economic models with interrelated equations (i.e. SEM). He illustrated this with two examples. The first was a model of investment–profit relations, which he used to show the relative nature of a split between 'systematic' influences and 'disturbances' with respect to different economic relations of interest, in other words, the disturbance in one relation might well become part of the systematic influence in another in an SEM (pp. 54–5). The second example was a model of household income-spending relations, which he used to show the different model derivations that one would arrive at by interpreting the exact equations nested in stochastic equations respectively as 'if-there-were-no-errors equations' and as 'expected-value equations'. It was revealed that the expectations or average relations derived explicitly from stochastic equations differed more often than not from the error-omitted exact equations, corresponding to the stochastic equations, which many had attempted to interpret as equivalent to average relations. Thus, the necessity of model specifications explicitly in probabilistic terms was established. To amplify his point, Haavelmo advocated that economists should broaden their view of narrowly defined 'statistical experiments' to think of economic experiments not as desired or planned experiments but as the type carried out by *'Nature*, and by which the facts *come into existence'* (p. 50), while economists 'merely watch as passive observers' (p. 51).

Based upon these arguments, Haavelmo set about formalizing the basic and general techniques required in econometric modelling mainly by means of the joint probability distribution theory, the maximum-likelihood method, and the Neyman–Pearson theory of hypothesis-testing. Here, he tried to centre conceptually the whole modelling procedure on hypothesis-testing, taking estimation and prediction as particular forms and steps of hypothesis-testing. But his technical adaptations of statistical tools apparently fell short of this goal. Beneath the technicalities, however, it is clear that while uncompromising in his stand for the probability approach, Haavelmo was deeply convinced that the right starting-point for applied modelling was Frisch's structural method embedded in the SEM framework. Such a strong faith in a structural SEM has, in retrospect, diminished considerably the significance of the probability approach (see Chapter 2). Actually, all Haavelmo's technical innovations were undertaken within the SEM framework. These innovations will be dealt with in detail later in the respective chapters.

Haavelmo's 'penetrating analysis initiated the developments in methodology' (Hood and Koopmans 1953: 118) accomplished in the mid- and latter half of the 1940s by workers of the Cowles Commission striving to establish an econometric theory that would have 'caught up with economic theory' (Koopmans 1945). Their achievements, summed up in the Commission Monographs 10 and 14 (Koopmans 1950; Hood and Koopmans 1953), were mainly extensions of the basic techniques that Haavelmo developed under his second theme. It was obvious from the two monographs that Haavelmo's probability approach and the presentation of a joint probability distribution of an SEM were to a large extent treated as equivalent. This was embodied in the fundamental role of the maximum-likelihood method assigned by them in their work. The development of the limited information maximum-likelihood (LIML) estimation method remained the main achievement of the Cowles group (see Chapter 3). Its second achievement—identification theory in terms of order and rank conditions—was quite independent of any probability theory (see Chapter 4). The issue of model choice with respect to statistical inference was ignored (see Koopmans 1950: 44; also ch. 2). Based upon the assumption of given structural models, the Cowles workers spared little effort in devising hypothesis-testing methods (see Chapter 5). Through their work, the influence of Haavelmo's approach was reduced to a spectrum of estimation, identification, testing, and specification, each of which was to grow increasingly independent of the others as the technical complications involved became more numerous.

1.4 ALTERNATIVE APPROACHES

Koopmans's and Haavelmo's attempts were not unparalleled. Concurrently, there were at least two others who supported and endeavoured to adapt probability theory into econometrics. One was Herman Wold, and the other was Gerhard Tintner.

Wold's first book, *A Study in the Analysis of Stationary Time Series*, came out one year after Koopmans's 1937 book (Wold 1938). It was a statistical theory book in a strict sense, and the justification of probability theory in it was related to establishing a more adequate foundation for time-series analysis in general. Nevertheless, it had a close bearing on econometrics because many unsolved econometric problems were concerned with time-series data (cf. Morgan 1991).

Wold traced back and examined carefully the previous methods of time-series analysis stemming from Yule and Slutsky, with particular attention to the business cycle studies of Frisch, C. F. Roos, and Tinbergen. Wold revealed the fact that inference based on conventional time-series methods of periodic analyses using functional simulations of cycles without the probabilistic perspective (e.g. periodograms or difference equations) was often 'incorrect, qualitatively as well as quantitatively' (Wold

1938: 95). He argued that the correct approach would be to put linear regression analysis of time-series 'under the heading of the stationary random process . . . from the viewpoint of the theory of probability' (p. 3). Enlightened by the axiomatization of probability theory by two Russian statisticians, Khintchine and Kolmogoroff, in the early 1930s—a formulation that has since been accepted as standard in the present-day teachings of econometric techniques—Wold set, as 'the chief purpose' of his book, 'bringing the schemes [of linear regression] into place in the theory of probability, thereby uniting the rather isolated results hitherto reached' (p. 29). Wold demonstrated the 'fundamental, active role' played by random elements in linear regression analyses and the indispensability of probabilistic treatments of time-series through a hypothetical set-up of distribution functions. A very important view that Wold developed was to interpret an observed time-series as belonging to a random process, i.e. 'as a sample value of the corresponding distribution in an infinite number of dimensions' representing the universe (p. 4). He devoted the whole book to formulating a more generalized procedure of stationary time-series analysis based on the above concepts (see Chapters 2 and 3).

Wold's introduction of probability concepts and theory actually went further than that in Koopmans's 1937 book. He was motivated by the desire to explore random time-series for an appropriate representation of their latent dynamic structure and means of analysis rather than simply estimating given representations (see Chapter 2). However, the significance of this was not recognized widely, and the book was scarcely referred to in economic circles at the time,[10] perhaps because of its highly statistical nature. Interestingly, Wold's viewpoint did not seem to appeal to Haavelmo, who had cited Wold's book as early as 1939. This was probably due to Haavelmo's dismissal of time-series decomposition techniques from the firm basis of an SEM.

Soon after his 1938 book, Wold became involved in applied time-series studies in demand analysis. The applied experience, plus his earlier theoretical research into stochastic processes,

---

[10] In an interview, Samuelson recalled when talking about Wold's 1938 book, 'It was not a famous book. But some kind of researchers like myself recognized it as an important book'; 'A lot of what is in Box and Jenkins' book was already in Wold's 1938 book' (Qin 1988a).

shaped his 'recursive systems' outlook on the world. When the work on simultaneous-equations modelling by Haavelmo and the Cowles group came out, Wold found himself in rivalry with them (see Chapter 6). In his justification of the recursive approach, Wold extended his outlook on the fundamental role of probability theory in econometrics with the following three arguments: (a) probability theory, and particularly the law of large numbers, allowed for the randomness of individual behaviour and therefore relaxed the postulate of 'minute rationalism' in economic theory; (b) the theory of stochastic processes provided econometrics with a general framework of recursive systems for economic models of a dynamic nature; and (c) such probability models could be estimated using regression analysis based upon sampling theory which was supported by probability theory (Wold and Juréen 1953: 70–4).

While Wold went on to spell out his viewpoint from pure probability theory to support his statistical approach to applied economic problems, G. Tintner traced the general problem in economics from applied studies up to pure probability theory. Different from Wold, Tintner's interest in probability theory was concentrated on its validity and interpretability in economics. This was probably due to the fact that Tintner started his career at the Austrian Institute for Trade Cycle Research, where he was trained to take an economic viewpoint in handling econometric problems, mainly those inherent in economic time-series. Tintner was convinced, from his empirical studies of prices in the business cycle, that 'flexibility' exerted a precondition which invalidated many mathematical formulations in the form of deterministic functions except those statistical formulations that could best capture the mutability of economic time-series (1935, 1940a, 1940b). He also realized that analysis employing merely statistical tools would not carry any conviction 'without sufficient theoretical foundations' in either economics or probability theory (1938a). Inspired by the 'certainty equivalent' attitude in economics around the issue of expectation (cf. Hamouda and Rowley 1988), Tintner saw the feasibility of using probability concepts as 'a general connection between the economic theory of expectations and the statistical theory of errors' (1938b). He first expressed the notion of uncertainty in economics, especially with respect to future expectations, in terms of probability principles (1938*b*). Then he connected these principles to methods in economic time-series analysis (1938*a*).

Tintner based his justification for probability theory upon the stochastic nature of economic behaviour of rational individuals. He achieved this in three steps. First, he classified the factors in utility maximization into 'controllable factors' and 'uncontrollable factors'. Secondly, he separated the errors correspondingly into the first kind arising from adapting the controllable factors to the optimum and the second kind from mistakes in forecasting the uncontrollable factors. Thirdly, he attributed the first kind of errors to the component of random residuals and the second kind to that of random fluctuations in the analysis of common time-series decomposition (Tintner 1938*a*). Subsequently, he maintained (1940*a*) that the first kind of random errors should be dealt with by the variate difference method, into which he made a painstaking enquiry (Tintner 1940*b*),[11] and that the second kind could be handled by the methods proposed by Wold (1938). Since probability theory underlay both types of method, its acceptance came inevitably with studies of the randomness in economic time-series. It was inherent in the importance of these studies, as seen from his argument:

A thorough analysis of the random element in economic time-series is very important for the following reason: Any statistical comparison of time-series or their components or characteristics must be based on the theory of probability on which all statistical methods necessarily rest. But it is impossible to get any comparisons between characteristics of economic time-series that are valid, from the point of view of probability, without having at least an idea about the order of magnitude of the random element involved. . . . Hence, whereas the random element itself is probably not very important for economics, its importance arises from the probability nature of every statistical comparison and hence also of the comparison of certain characteristics of economic time-series. It must be the basis of tests of significance and of statistical tests of hypotheses. (Tintner 1940*b*: 6)

The acceptance of probability theory brought Tintner to the concepts of probability, and he devoted a section of his 1940 book to them (section A, ch. III). He discussed both the frequency

---

[11] This work (Tintner 1940*b*) was completed in 1939. It was published as Monograph 5 of the Cowles Commission for Research in Economics.

definition of von Mises and the axiomatization by the Russians already mentioned in Wold (1938). But his discussion did not arouse as much attention as his adoption of the variate difference method. In particular, it met immediate criticism from Haavelmo because of the underlying philosophy of viewing the random elements as 'additive'. Haavelmo (1941) wrote:

In modern economic dynamics a simple scheme of additive random elements ... takes a secondary place as compared with the schemes where the random elements form an integrating part of the fundamental system of dynamic relations. Random events, whether they be 'from outside' or resulting from characteristic random spreads in the behaviour of different individuals, firms, or groups, usually strike deep into the very structure of economic movements, they change velocities, accelerations, and so forth; they create new initial conditions.

Unlike Wold, Tintner was apparently won over by the works of Haavelmo and the Cowles Commission. He praised them highly as having taken an encouraging step forward in advancing probability theory in relation to statistical inference (Tintner 1949). He abandoned his research in economic time-series analysis by the variate difference method, and went into what he felt required further expansion following the Cowles Commission's work, namely, a reform of economics by probabilistic thinking. He stressed the need for 'a "pure" theory of induction which would permit us to evaluate ultimately the degree of confirmation of given statistical hypotheses without any pragmatic considerations'. To achieve this end, Tintner believed that the key was to establish 'a new theory of probability, which forms a part of an ambitious system of inductive logic', since many previous concepts of probability used in statistical inference were too pragmatic to meet the above requirement. He suggested that Carnap's theory of probability 'may point the way to a satisfactory solution of many philosophical and practical questions connected with statistical inference', because it distinguished and allowed for two concepts of probability: 'probability$_1$' relating to 'the degree of confirmation' and 'probability$_2$' relating to 'empirical frequency'. Further, he was convinced that the first concept—the degree of confirmation—formed the foundation of probability upon which a future theory of testing statistical hypotheses should be based in econometrics (Tintner 1949, 1952).

'From a philosophical and epistemological point', he attributed the unsatisfactory results of current econometrics to its being based solely upon the second concept of empirical frequency (1952: 17). He then pinpointed the roots of the problem, namely, the deterministic nature of economic theories. He devoted much of his subsequent research to this area (cf. Tintner and Sengapta 1972).

Both Wold and Tintner's efforts were largely overshadowed by the increasing acceptance of the approach developed by Haavelmo and the Cowles group, despite the fact that Wold's stand on the objective probability notion and his use of classic statistical methods were actually very much in tune with mainstream econometrics, and that Tintner's proposition of the probability notion of 'degrees of belief' was quite in step with the thinking of the majority of the economic profession at the time (see also Marschak 1954). In fact, discussions on the probability approach appeared to be out of date once the use of probability theory was taken for granted in econometrics. Interest in the two notions of objective probability and subjective probability remained in abeyance until the emergence of Bayesian econometrics from the 1960s onwards (cf. Qin 1991).

1.5 An Incomplete Revolution

As pointed out in Section 1.3, Haavelmo's probability approach was embodied in two themes: a general theme of 'randomizing' economic and hence econometric thinking, and a specific theme of systematically adapting into econometrics the modern theory of statistics based upon probability theory. Essentially, his general theme contained two messages: (a) economists should apply stochastic rather than deterministic methods from mathematics in their formalization of economic theories, and (b) such theories should allow for the possibility of certain checks by observable data information mainly of a non-experimental type. What Tintner endeavoured to do after the Cowles group's contribution was mainly to carry on the first message. Other pioneer attempts along the same line included the classical works of, for example, Neumann and Morgenstern (1947) and Arrow (1951). New theories thus developed since the late 1940s brought in probability-based concepts, such as 'game', 'decision', 'rational expectation', etc., which were to play fundamental roles in modern economics. But they became increasingly the sole interest of theoretical economists.

To most econometricians, Haavelmo's specific theme alone already seemed sufficient to serve as the foundation for what they adopted from mathematical statistics. As described in Section 1.3, Haavelmo tried to combine the following to implement this theme: (a) Frisch's structural method; (b) Fisher's maximum-likelihood principle; and (c) Neyman–Pearson hypothesis-testing approach. It turned out that his attempt, later that of the Cowles group, was successful only with the first two, not with the three together, at least in technical terms if not in epistemological terms. The ML principle founded upon probability theory provided Haavelmo and the Cowles group with an insightful representation of the joint behaviour of random variables interrelated in some structure postulated by economic theory, and a series of measures to handle it. More importantly, this vision of joint distribution was consistent with and complementary to the standard equilibrium viewpoint in economics, a crucial reason for them to gain dominance in econometrics. Here, Wold served as a contrast because he took the 'sequence' analysis of the non-mainstream Swedish School as his economics foundation (cf. Morgan 1991), even though the statistical methods that he applied were similar.

However, problems would arise as soon as the hypothesis-testing scheme was added to the combination of Frisch's structural method with the ML principle. A fundamental difficulty was where exactly the principle of hypothesis-testing should be placed to function, and how much weight it should be given, in regard to the postulated theoretical model, within the structural method framework. This difficulty virtually hindered Haavelmo from making more concrete progress with his general theme, particularly with the second message contained in the theme. The Cowles group simply dodged the difficulty by explicitly leaving open the issue of model choice (see Chapters 2, 5, and 6). Consequently, characteristics from data analysis were left with no formal place to feed back their effect (see Chapter 3).

The incongruity of the Neyman–Pearson approach with the other two implied, at root, a conflict between the view of taking the postulated theoretical model as 'deterministic', i.e. absolutely true or correct, and that of treating it as indeterminate and tentative. The main stem of econometrics formalized after Haavelmo and the Cowles group's contribution was built upon the assumption that the economic theory concerned was known. Thus the revolutionary essence of Haavelmo's probability approach was not completely carried through. The approach was carried through only to the extent that the stochastic nature of economic activities, and hence the necessity of reformulating their theoretical counterparts in terms of probabilities, were formally recognized by the econometric profession. Issues concerning the uncertainty of economic theories *per se*, and particularly their impact on econometric modelling were not yet widely recognized nor formally tackled. In other words, what was widely accepted by most econometricians was merely probability theory as the pillar of statistical methods applied to given structural models derived from deterministic economic theories added with random errors.

For years after Haavelmo's 1944 book, the significance of the probability approach was mainly reflected in the use of these statistical methods. His discovery of least-squares 'bias' (see Chapter 3), and his advocacy of ML specification and estimation methods were, and still are, commonly regarded as his central contribution to econometrics (see Koopmans 1945; Stone 1946; and Epstein 1987). For example, in recalling the Cowles workers' contribution following Haavelmo's book, T. W. Anderson spoke of 'this new approach, first using probability in modern statistical inference in economics', as 'more precisely the simultaneous-equations approach' (Phillips 1986). Restricted by the simultaneous-equation approach, econometric theorists allocated a minor part of their attention to studying the statistical features of economic data with respect to their economic implications (see Chapter 3). On the other hand, econometric practitioners did not find it essential to follow the formal specification procedure of the approach in their applied work of measuring known economic theories. This aspect was interestingly illustrated by the following quotations from Haavelmo's comment and M. R. Fisher's response in a symposium, published in *Bulletin of Oxford University Institute of Statistics* in 1957, on Fisher's model of British household saving behaviour (1956):

Haavelmo: It is clear that such [Fisher's modelling] procedures must have as their foundation some stochastic specification of the 'universe' from which the survey data are drawn. It seems, however, that the practice in sample survey projects is to omit such precise stochastic specifications. . . . The idea that an explicit specification of the stochastic model is necessary may not be shared by all econometricians. For my own part I have found it almost unavoidable to go into this matter in some detail, in order to interpret some of the results presented in Dr Fisher's article. (Haavelmo 1957)

Fisher: While in general sympathy with Haavelmo's attitude and attack on these problems [about specification of stochastic models], I find myself unable to divorce so completely theoretical specification from empirical examination. . . . The use of such [Haavelmo's] specifications has in the past often led to the retention of too great generality in models. The most conspicuous advance of these new theories has been their dependence on very restrictive assumptions which are the more capable of contradiction. (Fisher 1957)

Haavelmo and some of his contemporaries were not ignorant of the weakness of their approach at work. They attributed it mainly to the lack of well-formulated economic theories. Subsequent development along Haavelmo's probability approach was made mostly in formalizing theories with consideration of uncertainty in economics, and in inventing better statistical techniques for matching data to given theoretical models in econometrics. A good epitome of the situation was the title of the three-volume work *Uncertainty and Estimation in Economics* by D. G. Champernowne (1969). A clearer description of it concerning the role of probability theory could be seen from the following quote: 'The field of economic enquiry wherein the orthodox statistician is most at home is that which uses the tool of the sample survey . . . The design and analysis of such sampling enquiries has been highly developed, and it is in this rather minor branch of applied economics that the theory of probability is in fact most directly useful' (Champernowne 1969: 5).

The rest of the book gives a detailed account of how textbook econometrics came into being in such circumstances. There, the incompleteness of Haavelmo's probability revolution can be better appreciated from the uneven development of abundant estimation and identification theories and techniques on the one hand (Chapters 3 and 4), and of sparse testing and model-specification theories on the other (Chapters 5 and 6). In particular, the difficult problem of how to formulate and reformulate theoretical models with respect to data information is revealed in the continuous controversies over modelling strategies (see Chapter 6), and in the growing gap between actual econometric practice, which remained *ad hoc*, problematic, and considerably deterministic, and the theoretical research, which narrowed down and moved further into certain technical aspects of individual econometric modelling steps.

2

Model Construction

All the efforts involved in setting up the probability foundation
were spurred on by and aimed at building models that could
bridge economic theories with data. So were the efforts spent
on formalizing the processes of estimation, identification, and
testing, as described in the following chapters. However, the
concept of a 'model' did not exist at the time of the earliest
econometric attempts. During the pre-model stage, econometric
practice was mainly concerned with measuring approximately
certain economic laws by descriptive statistics for the purpose
of either predicting the future or specifying those laws, or both.
This was gradually modified from two angles, due probably to
the number of unsatisfactory results and seemingly persistent
discrepancies between the laws and the observations. One was
the conceptual separation of statistical laws from economic laws.
The other was the shift of use from descriptive statistical tools
to those of statistical inference. Both entailed the eventual
creation of a separate entity, a 'model', which was more manœuv-
rable and more modest than a 'law'. Upon its creation, a model
came to serve as the vehicle to confront, with data, economic
theory specified in a measurable and testable form. It also
furnished applied economists with a basis for schematizing their
empirical studies. Models thus made up the substance of econometrics.

Models were further classified into theoretical and statistical
ones soon after the birth of the concept. The former was applied
to models derived directly from a priori theories, and the latter to
models formed through data-fitting. It was soon recognized that
most theoretical models were incomplete for econometric purposes,
whereas statistical models could turn out nonsensical with respect to economic interpretation. Consequently there emerged a
structural modelling procedure, in which model building was

schematized into a process of starting from a structural model given by theory and then estimating the structural coefficients from data. Such a definite, structurally based strategy in turn helped to unravel the econometric modelling practice into a relatively well-ordered routine of model formulation, specification, identification, estimation, and testing. A systematic theory of econometrics was thus brought into being.

This chapter recounts the emergence of models, the common criteria and principles used for model choice, and the generalization of model construction as econometrics focused on the structural modelling procedure. Section 2.1 reviews the pre-model period; Section 2.2 looks at the emergence of models and the structural method of model construction.[1] The first generalization efforts of the model-building strategy and criteria are dealt with in Section 2.3. The chapter concludes with the establishment of the structural modelling procedure.

2.1 ECONOMETRIC MEASUREMENT WITHOUT MODELS

The concept of 'model' seems to have come into econometrics in the early 1930s. But conscious attempts at econometric model building did not appear till the second half of the 1930s.[2] Before then, statistical enquiries had taken place in demand analysis, production theory, and business cycle studies. A common practice was to put economic theories into some mathematical formulations, and then to measure the coefficients against real data by statistical means. Results of this kind developed first in the field of demand analysis, associated with the names of Moore, the Working brothers, Ezekiel, Schultz, and others (cf. Morgan 1990). Developments in estimating production functions, led by Douglas and Cobb, were in the making as an extension of the above statistical approach to demand analysis (e.g. see Cobb and

---

[1] Most of the historical events covered in these two sections have been described in more detail by Morgan (1990). Only the aspect concerning model-building principles of these events are reported here in order to present a full picture of how the strategy of structural model construction evolved.

[2] It has been found so far that the earliest use of the term 'model' occurred when Frisch discussed business cycle 'models' at the Lausanne Meeting of the Econometric Society in 1931 (cf. Staehle 1933: 82). It is generally considered that Tinbergen was the first to apply the concept to building a Dutch model in 1936 (see Magnus and Morgan 1987; Morgan 1990).

Douglas 1928; Douglas 1934). When there were no well-established theories available, as was often the case in the field of
business cycle studies, a historical approach was usually preferred, in which the formulations depended heavily upon data-
fitting results. The general purpose of most of these applied
studies was to 'in part verify pure theory, in part suggest
revisions of statement, and in part suggest new laws' (Persons
1925).

One direct origin of formulating non-mathematical economic
statements in mathematical forms could be traced back to
the Lausanne School during the late nineteenth century (e.g.
cf. Debreu 1986). However, the efforts of the empirical economists of the early twentieth century differed significantly from
those of the tradition of the Lausanne School. Economists of the
Lausanne School utilized mathematics mainly as a kind of
formal logic to enhance the rigour of theoretical statements. The
products came from purely deductive reasoning about human
intentions; whereas those empirical economists tried to refine
these products by integrating them with data, i.e. the observed
outcome assumed to come from those intentions. Initial attempts
revealed two major weaknesses of the 'intention-based' neoclassical theory for practical purposes. One was its heavy dependence upon unrealistic *ceteris paribus* assumptions. The other
was a general lack of the dynamic perspective. As a result,
empirical formulations in applied econometric studies went
beyond, and were demarcated from, the exact formulations of
neoclassical theory. This was reflected in the use of terms such
as 'statistical laws', 'schemes', and 'equation systems', for these
empirical formulations, before the term 'model' was actually
used.

Miscellaneous problems were noticed and discussed in working out empirical formulations in those early days. Essentially,
they centred on two basic issues: (*a*) how to decide which
variables should be included, and (*b*) how to choose the equation
forms. Beneath these issues lurked two fundamental problems:
(*a*) What standpoint should modellers take, in making the above
two types of decisions, between the existing economic theory
and the observed data? (*b*) What criteria should they abide by
to justify their decisions? It was chiefly these latent problems
that produced labyrinths for econometricians.

Empirical extensions of theoretical statements emerged prim-arily in the field of demand analysis. A procedure of formulating 'statistical laws' was developed by Moore and summarized by Schultz (1930, 1938). In this procedure, economic theories were regarded as 'general hypotheses', and model building as choice of auxiliary assumptions to the hypotheses through the selection of appropriate equation forms. The selection was considered to comprise the first two issues mentioned above, i.e. 'to decide what variables to include in the equation and what functional relationship to assume among the variables' (Schultz 1938: 136). The initial principle for variable selection was economic theory, supplemented by some dynamic considerations (e.g. a time factor). It meant to start modelling from simple theories formed from *ceteris paribus* reasoning, and to process the selection through trial data fittings by gradually increasing the number of vari-ables. This implied a simple → general approach. The choice of functional forms was then the research focus of the procedure, involving 'a delicate balancing of several factors': '(*a*) The simplicity of the curve . . . relative to the state of analysis and to the practical end in view'; '(*b*) The fecundity of the curve'; '(*c*) The fit of the data'; '(*d*) The facility with which the con-stants of a curve may be computed'; '(*e*) The *a priori* validity' (pp. 139–40). However, with few statistical tools in support, these criteria often turned out to be still too broad for judgement in practice. Even Schultz admitted that the fitness of the data had to rest ultimately on 'aesthetic' considerations (p. 140), indicating a considerable degree of arbitrariness in the actual choice of 'a rational formula' among 'many different equations' representing the same data over time 'equally well' (Schultz 1930: 88).

The non-uniqueness of functional forms led to an immediate problem: how to interpret, or justify, the forms in terms of economic theories, or in other words, how to make the chosen forms correspond with the theories. In those early days, two main categories of formulation were frequently used. They were both derived from static regression (Frisch and Waugh 1933; cf. Schultz 1933). The first was 'partial time regression method' (i.e. static regression in levels plus a time-trend term):

$$y_t = a_0 + a_1 x_t + a_2 t. \tag{2.1}$$

The second was 'individual trend method' (i.e. static regression in detrended variables or 'growth rates'):

$$\frac{y_t}{y_{t-1}} = b_0 + b_1 \frac{x_t}{x_{t-1}} \qquad (2.2)$$

or

$$(y_t - ct) = b_0 + b_1(x_t - dt) \qquad (2.2')$$

where a, b, c, d were coefficients.

Schultz interpreted the first type as a 'short-time, *reversible*' scheme and the second as a 'long-time, *irreversible*' scheme, on the basis of whether or not the values of variables in levels could be recovered once the coefficient estimates were obtained (1930: 39). Frisch and Waugh disagreed with such interpretation mainly from the consideration of theoretical correspondence. They pointed out that regressions made on both formulations (2.1) and (2.2') would actually lead to '*identically* the same results' with respect to the coefficient estimates, i.e. $a_1 = b_1$, and thus the same estimated relationship between y and x. They hence argued that the two formulations 'differ only in the technique of computation used in order to arrive at the results' (Frisch and Waugh 1933). The actual long-run and short-run distinction lay only in the fact that (2.2') did not specify the separate effect of t on y as (2.1) did. This could be obtained by combining (2.1) and (2.2'):

$$(y_t - ct) = a_0 + a_1(x_t - dt) + (a_1d - c + a_2)t = b_0 + b_1(x_t - dt).$$

Frisch and Waugh maintained that it was meaningless to discuss which method was superior unless the chosen regression expression was 'referred to a given theoretical framework', specified a priori 'which sort of influence it is desired to eliminate, and which sort to preserve'. They further expounded that 'an empirically determined relation is "true" if it approximates fairly well a certain well-defined theoretical relationship, assumed to represent the nature of the phenomenon studied'. They denoted such a specified relationship 'a structural relation' (Frisch and Waugh 1933). Later on, the term 'structural', modifying either a relation, a coefficient, or a model of economic behaviour to be studied, acquired a central place in econometric modelling.

Frisch and Waugh's critique shed light upon the danger of equating regression relations indiscriminately to theoretical

relations, and upon the need to look closely at the correspondence problem, propelling the separation and formalization of
the identification issue (see Chapter 4). Frisch and Waugh's
paper also showed the necessity of clearly specifying structural
relations prior to coefficient estimation, irrespective of whether
there was a firmly received theory. This brought the issue of
model construction in statistical demand analysis into line with
that in business cycle modelling, where the struggle to find and
establish structural relations had been much more in evidence.

A key obstacle in business cycle studies was the lack of well-
established economic theories to back model formulations. Since
short-run movements formed the central concern, the early
studies here tended to be more data-based and less unified in
terms of model-formulating rules than in demand analysis. Two
important strands of research methods at the time were periodic
analysis and business barometers.

Henry Moore was responsible for developing the method of
periodic analysis (1914, 1923). Essentially, the method employed
harmonic analysis and Fourier series as the functional form to
mimic the 'rhythmic phenomena' of economic cycles. Moore set
up three conditions to justify his functional choice: (*a*) the
function chosen should represent data as fully as possible; (*b*) it
allowed description of a causal relationship; (*c*) it could depict
the essential characteristics of periodicities. He believed that the
method of periodograms based on harmonic analysis satisfied
these three conditions (Moore 1914: 137–8). As for the choice
of variables, Moore tried to pick up factors which formed clearly
a one-way causal chain over time, e.g. weather → agricultural
production → business cycles in his business cycle theory. It is
noticeable that Moore's strategy here corresponded closely to
his viewpoint in applied demand studies, namely, a priori knowledge should be used to guide the variable choice on the principle
that the chosen variables were significantly related by a causal
chain, while the selection of functional forms should depend
upon visual inspection of the data. Moore's strategy was followed in many econometric studies long after periodic analysis
became obsolete (e.g. see Davis 1941*a*).

In contrast, the method underlying the Harvard barometer,
pioneered by Persons, modelled business cycles from quite a
different perspective (Persons 1916, 1922–3) (see also Samuelson

1987). Since short-run forecasting was given priority over long-run causal explanations, the method relied heavily on data-fitting, especially in variable selection. Here, variable selection played a more important role than the choice of functional form, which assumed simple linear functions, as long as they produced satisfying short-run local results. In Persons's words, the major concern of the barometer method was to find out 'what statistical series should logically be combined to secure a barometer of general business conditions', and 'what series have variations precedent to the variations in the business barometer thus obtained and, therefore, offer a reliable basis for forecasting business conditions' (Persons 1916). Roughly, Persons's selection strategy comprised the following four steps: (*a*) take into account all the data series that might contribute to business cycles, select one as a standard (e.g. wholesale prices), and detrend all the data series; (*b*) pick out series that show strong relations to the cycles by correlation analysis and, in particular, use serial and autocorrelation analyses of each series and its first-order differences as checks for the selection; (*c*) combine all of the selected series that fluctuated concurrently with the standard series into a business barometer; and (*d*) select those series fluctuating one lag ahead of the barometer to form a forecasting device. The resulting type of model was what is now called a 'leading indicator':

$$y_{t+1} = a + bx_t. \tag{2.3}$$

Noticeably in this model type, the causal direction was indicated solely by one-lagged variables, in contrast to the models with simultaneous relations between variables derived from theory. This again manifested the preference of statistical outcome to theoretical reasoning in Persons's strategy. This strategy was later inherited largely by the National Bureau of Economic Research.

The method of harmonic analyses was soon in disfavour for being too rigid to depict the volatility of business cycles, as described in Chapter 1, whereas the method of business barometers was questioned mainly on account of its theoretical ground. Both ran further into serious statistical problems with the publication of G. Yule's two influential investigations. The first looked into the problem of nonsense correlations between time-series (Yule

1926), and the second into the problem of periodic analysis of disturbed series (Yule 1927). Yule used constructed series of given curves in both studies. In his 1926 paper, he pointed out that spurious correlation arose from the fact that most of the time-series available were only small samples of very long uncorrelated curves. He classified time-series into the four types of 'random', 'oscillatory', 'conjunct', and 'disjunct'. He suggested that a way to detect nonsense correlations in the 'conjunct' (autocorrelated) case was to see whether each series had 'random differences' or 'conjunct differences', the latter of which 'formed the dangerous class of series, correlations between short samples tending towards unity' (i.e. belonged to 'non-stationary' series in the present terminology). In his 1927 paper, Yule demonstrated that harmonic analysis might be misleading for time-series containing 'true disturbances' rather than additive measurement errors. In this case, he proposed to use the form of linear-difference regression equations for data description:

$$y_t = \sum \beta_i y_{t-i} + \varepsilon_t. \tag{2.4}$$

This formed the origin of autoregressive processes or autoregressions (AR).

Yule's 1927 critique was reinforced by E. Slutsky, who put forth the idea that cyclic time-series might be generated by a summation of random causes (Slutsky 1937). In particular, Slutsky showed, also by artificially constructed series, that autocorrelated series were liable to be such random summations. The works of Yule and Slutsky exerted a great impact on early econometricians by highlighting the danger of inferring causal relationships fitted directly from time-series data, due to the probable lack of independence between different variables, or between the present and lagged values of the same variables in the data sample. Many of them took Yule's and Slutsky's message as a 'taboo' against applying statistical techniques to economic time-series analysis, and hence were 'scared away' (Haavelmo 1944: 17).

2.2 EMERGENCE OF STRUCTURAL MODEL CONSTRUCTION

As seen from the previous section, a dilemma was implied in the early empirical studies in both demand analysis and business cycle analysis. If one started from theory, one might well find available economic theory far from adequate for the purpose of econometric measurement; but if one started from data, one could run into the danger of making spurious inference about economic causalities. It thus became imperative for econometricians to build a more soundly based and systematic procedure of model construction. As already described, signs of systematization increased following the founding of the Econometric Society in 1931. In terms of model construction, these included (*a*) general acceptance of economic theory as the yardstick for variable choice, supplemented by statistical estimation results; (*b*) widening use of discrete, mainly linear, difference equations as the basic equation form; and (*c*) growing attention on a complete system of interdependent relations in modelling. All these led to the formation of a structural method of model construction.

During the early days of econometrics, Frisch had kept a most cautious and critical eye on the economic interpretability of any applied studies, as could be seen from his 1933 critique of Leontief's demand–supply estimation method, to be described in Chapter 4, as well as from his other paper of the same year, jointly with Waugh, described in the previous section. Yule's and Slutsky's results convinced him that any mathematical and statistical methods trying to capture the time-shape of data by smoothing them were susceptible to adding artificial fluctuations to the data and therefore dangerous. He thus maintained that economic time-series were actually 'created by an *economic structure* which functions in such a way that the random disturbances to which it is exposed, are cumulated approximately by a linear operator' (Frisch 1936) (Frisch conceived the idea of linear operators in the late 1920s; see Morgan 1990). With these insights, Frisch rejected the existing 'mechanical decomposition' method,[3] i.e. to characterize time-series variables by decomposing them into trend, seasonal, cycle, and irregular fluctuation. He sought to replace it with 'the structural decomposition' method, i.e. specifying the economic theory of interest in the basic equation form of 'linear cumulators' (i.e. linear

---

[3] This method lingered on through the 1930s, mostly with the old Cowles Commission in Colorado, and was summarized in Davis (1941*a*), till the work on simultaneity by the Cowles Commission in Chicago appeared.

dynamic equations), prior to statistical analyses, to serve as a guideline (Frisch 1936) (see Chapter 1). Furthermore, Frisch recognized the importance of setting up a complete system in order to capture the impact of any shocks to an economy in motion, or to study any functions of economic dynamics. Combining considerations for empirical feasibility with his firm stand on theoretical priority, Frisch settled on the model form of a '*weight system*' (e.g. a system of linear equations), defining how each factor of interest (from theory) contributed to the total outcome observed. Statistical theory came in to furnish methods for measuring the magnitudes of the 'weights', and then evaluating '*various types of theoretical schemes*'. This process could be carried out repeatedly. 'Only through a combination of these (economic and statistical) theories together with an intensive utilisation of actual data' could 'a realistic explanation of economic phenomena . . . be arrived at' (Frisch 1936). This new structural method suggested putting more weight on theory formulation in econometric model construction. It exerted a strong influence on the subsequent developments in mathematical economics.

Frisch's structural method was best exemplified by his paper 'Propagation Problems and Impulse Problems in Dynamic Economics' (1933*c*). Combining the two ideas: '(1) the continuous solution of a determinate dynamic system and (2) the discontinuous shocks intervening and supplying the energy that may maintain the swings', Frisch designed a structural model ('a theoretical set-up' in his words and a 'rocking-horse' model as it was later called), using mixed difference and differential equations to relate consumption, production of capital goods, and 'the carry-on-activity'. The way in which the model was formulated paved the way for later macroeconometric modelling. In particular, it showed that (*a*) an econometric model should be designed in such a way that it went deeper than merely mechanically approximating the cyclic pattern in the data, to present an economically meaningful mechanism capable of explaining the generating process of the 'time-shape' of cycles; (*b*) such systems (models) should be aggregative and closed (the number of equations being equal to the number of dependent variables), comprising dynamic structural relations of interest (in the form of mixed difference and differential equations); and

(c) 'much of the reasoning' for constructing the system should be undertaken 'on *a priori* grounds', relatively independently of the 'statistical determination' of structural parameters (Frisch 1933c). This last point was illustrated by the fact that Frisch did not perform any actual statistical estimation after he had built his rocking-horse model. Instead, he simply used guessed figures for those parameters, because they could as well serve his real purpose—to study the dynamic features or the time-shape of his construct. The study was carried out by transforming the evaluated structural model into one 'final equation', i.e. a difference equation in terms of one major variable of interest. The final equation differed from any statistical equations of the autoregressive form in that its parameters were derived rather than estimated from data, though it took the same mathematical form as an autoregressive equation.

Considering model formulation in the above a priori manner, Frisch came to view problems arising a posteriori from data-fitting as 'inversion' problems (Frisch 1936). He pointed out two 'fundamental' ones: one concerning the prospect of finding a means 'to determine the shape of the weight curves' uniquely from available data (i.e. the identification problem, see Chapter 3), and the other concerning the possibility of isolating individual effects of each independent factor in the same equation (namely, the 'multicollinearity' problem in Frisch 1934). Frisch thought that these problems could be circumvented by his 'confluence analysis' (Frisch 1934), together with the technique of 'bunch maps' (cf. also Hendry and Morgan 1989, and Chapter 3). The technique followed essentially the same principle for variable selection as that used by Moore and Schultz, i.e. the simple → general route of modelling. Noticeably, it allowed for some data-based variable choice only within the scope delimited by economic theory, which was called by Frisch the process of 'statistical construction of econometric functions' (Frisch 1934: 9). In order to differentiate this statistical construction from pure theoretical relations, he invented the concepts of 'reducibility' versus 'irreducibility', and of 'coflux' versus 'super-flux' for the identifiability of equations (see Chapter 3), so as to show the contrast as well as the correspondence between them caused mainly by the simultaneity feature of economic variables. A deeper concept that Frisch put forward to explain the differentiation was 'autonomy', referring to the invariance of individual theoretical relations with respect to each other over time (cf. Aldrich 1989). The 'degree of autonomy' was used to indicate how successfully the structural relations of interest had been verified by data by means of confluence analysis, and thus implied a key criterion for structural model building (Frisch 1938).

At the European Meeting of the Econometric Society in 1936, Frisch summarized the above main ideas into 'an ideal programme for macrodynamic studies' following the structural method:

A. *Theoretical inquiry.* (1) Define your variables. (2) State the structural relations which you suppose to exist between the variables. (3) Derive a number of confluent relations, which lead to confluent elasticities, showing the response of one variable in a certain sub-group to another when all the rest are held constant. (3a) Use these relations for reasoning about variations compatible with the subsystem. (3b) Consider the response of the system to exogenous shocks: a dynamic analysis leading to criteria of stability. (3c) Consider how the whole system will evolve in time. B. *Statistical inquiry.* (4) Obtain some final equations. A final equation is a confluent relation which is reduced to its smallest degree of freedom, and in which the coefficients have a statistically uniquely determined meaning. Never try to fit to the data anything but a final equation. (5) One also may scrutinise the data, and derive empirical formulae by the statistical technique now known as 'confluence analysis.' In particular a final equation may be tested in this way. (6) If the final equation contains only one variable, and is linear, construct the corresponding characteristic equation and consider its roots. They will determine the time-shape of the evolution that would ensue if the system were left to itself. When we have found in this way how the system *would* proceed through time, we do not expect actual history to move like that, for this history is affected by a stream of erratic shocks. The actual time-shape will now be a weighted average extending over the shocks, the weights of the average being those given by the system as it would proceed in isolation. (7) Fundamental inversion problems: (7a) to determine the system of weights from a given time-shape; (7b) to determine the shocks. (8) Attempt a forecast using the weights determined by the inversion, and assuming—in the absence of better information—the future shocks to be zero. (Brown 1937: 365–6)

Much of Frisch's 'ideal programme' was first put into practice by Jan Tinbergen. However, Tinbergen did not undertake the structural method when he started his applied macro-model-building career around the mid-1930s. As a pioneer practitioner, he had placed much weight on data inspection in model construction, at least as much as on economic theory if not more, when he built the first macroeconometric model (a model of the Dutch economy) in 1936 (Tinbergen 1937). Tinbergen believed that acceptable applied models came from proper combinations of economic theories and empirical findings. In principle, he resorted to economic theory for the choice of possible variables and their relationships, and to statistical calculations for the choice of actual equation forms. Yet in practice he often relied on statistical results for his final decisions (this could be seen from several of the equations of his Dutch model). Actually, Tinbergen initially disapproved of restricting the empirical modelling process by theoretical formulations. He had classified the earlier applied modelling practice into the 'historical' method (i.e. correlation analysis) and the 'structural' method (i.e. direct measurement of theoretical parameters). He argued that 'in general, since data at our disposal do not permit following the structural method, the historical method has been chosen' (1935). He made an interesting analogy between model building and 'kitchen work' (1937). But he soon reversed his argument and dismissed the historical method as being not only 'superficial' but also problematic both in theory and in practice (Tinbergen 1938b).[4]

In spite of his conversion to the structural method, Tinbergen retained much of his 'kitchen work' style in his two-volume masterpiece *Statistical Testing of Business-Cycle Theories* (1939). However, he became more cautious about the economic meaning of both his practice and its description. He acknowledged that econometric models should be based on 'a priori considerations', but viewed them broadly so as to include both 'economic theory' and 'common sense' (1939: ii. 10). Tinbergen adopted static relations, whenever possible, in correspondence with the relevant theoretical relations. Wherever a priori considerations were found inadequate, he resorted to the principle of 'the highest

---

[4] Frisch's 1938 memorandum seemed to have exerted strong influence on Tinbergen's change of argument. Tinbergen later also credited much of the influence on his early way of thinking of macroeconometric modelling to Frisch, Marschak, Staehle, and other economists (Magnus and Morgan 1987).

correlation' as before. This could be seen from his use of the growth rate and leading indicator equation forms. As for the dynamic feature, Tinbergen shared much of Frisch's view of linear, weight equations as the appropriate equation form, but abandoned the particular form of mixed difference and differential equations, in favour of purely discrete equations for practical reasons. In particular, he settled on the equation form of 'distributed lags' as a simple and handy form.[5] One-lag equations of the following form (sometimes mixed with static regressions or leading indicators) appeared most frequently in his 1939 model:

$$y_t = a + b_1 x_t + b_2 x_{t-1} + e_t. \qquad (2.5)$$

Statistical fitness seemed to be his ultimate criterion for equation choice. The only additional measure that he took was to cross-check the variables primarily selected with the technique of Frisch's bunch maps, as a safeguard against multicollinearity. Tinbergen estimated all the equations separately using the ordinary least squares (OLS) without further consideration. He was actually not so much concerned with the statistical characteristics of equation forms as with the representability of the economy through the overall behaviour of the model (e.g. in terms of the final equation), produced by the designed mechanism of an interdependent equation system, or in his words, 'the result of a complete series of successive causal connections' (Tinbergen 1940). Correspondingly, he elaborated the two aspects of causality and completeness with respect to model construction.

1. The causal connections of interest were denoted by first distinguishing 'between *exogen* and *endogen* movements' ('the former being movements during which certain data vary, while, in the latter, the data are supposed to be constant') (Tinbergen 1935); he then concentrated on the 'endogen' movements conditioned upon the 'exogen' movements. This led to the corresponding differentiation of the chosen variables into 'endogenous' and 'exogenous' ones, with 'exogenous' denoting variables to 'be considered as given even in the most general economic problems'

---

[5] The concept of 'distributed lags' was first introduced by I. Fisher in discussing the movement of money supply in the 1920s; see Alt (1942) for a detailed account of its early development.

and 'endogenous' denoting the remainder (Tinbergen and Polak 1950).

2. The concept of completeness was defined as a necessary requirement of a model to have 'as many relations as there are variables to be explained'. He further explained that 'the word "complete" need not be interpreted in the sense that every detail in the complicated economic organism is described. . . . By increasing or decreasing the number of phenomena, a more refined or a rougher picture or "model" of reality may be obtained' (Tinbergen 1939: ii. 15).

This led to another important criterion of model construction, namely, models 'must be simplified' representations of reality (Tinbergen 1938b). Tinbergen classified three types of simplifications. First, 'simplifications in economic structure', i.e. using the macro- rather than micro-analysis approach. Second, 'simplifications in time structure', usually by reducing the number of distributed lags. Third, 'simplifications in mathematical form of relationships' mostly through the use of linear formulae (1938b). However, there followed no specification of the rules for judging whether the actual simplifications made were valid, except the completeness requirement. Otherwise, Tinbergen simply left the simplification process open, first, to 'the economist' 'to exercise his judgement' 'at liberty' (Tinbergen 1939: ii. 15), and then to the econometrician to accomplish through 'trial and error' (p. 21).

Around the time that Tinbergen was constructing his US macro-model, a US disaggregate model was developed by the Industrial Section of the US National Resources Committee (NRC) (Means 1938).[6] Remarkably, many ideas concerning model building in this model appeared similar to those in Tinbergen's 1939 model, although the two models differed dramatically in terms of the model contents, form, and purposes. The NRC model was described as being set up by first disaggregating the economy into eighty-one industrial segments and then establishing 138 relationships through the following steps: (a) choose variables in each segment and establish hypothetical causal relationships among them according to theory and common

---

[6] I learnt about Means's model from Frederic S. Lee of Roosevelt University, who kindly sent me a copy of Means (1938).

knowledge; (*b*) prepare the relevant data; (*c*) select equation forms by means of the then 'standard correlation techniques' of both graphical and numerical analyses; and (*d*) 'revise and improve the hypothesis in the light of the results obtained' through 'repetition of the steps' (p. 77). However, it was admitted by Means (1938) that the empirical results had the final say whenever they differed clearly from logical considerations. Interdependence formed the focus of the model, but was completely overlooked in the statistical analysis. Therefore, the correspondence problem or the differentiation of theoretical relations from statistical ones did not even appear. These might account partially for the fact that the NRC model exerted little impact on econometrics either theoretically or practically. It was almost totally ignored in the econometric literature.

2.3 FORMALIZATION OF
STRUCTURAL MODEL FORMULATION

Tinbergen's ingenious modelling work soon became the 'model' for applied modellers, yet his remarks on model building were largely working summaries of his experiences. The task of formalization of the structural modelling procedure was undertaken first by Koopmans, and then by Haavelmo.

As mentioned in Section 1.2, Koopmans introduced Fisher's sampling approach and the ML method into Frisch's framework (Koopmans 1937), prior to Tinbergen's two volumes. Convinced by the works of his predecessors that 'causation, determination are concepts outside the domain of statistics' (p. 57), Koopmans endeavoured to unravel the modelling process into three separate steps of model specification (including identification), estimation, and distribution, following Fisher's approach. In Koopmans's view, the concept of '*specification*' formed a more precise description and a more rigorous treatment of Frisch's a posteriori 'statistical construction' activity. Following Fisher, Koopmans designated specification as 'the choice of mathematical form of the population' (p. 3), adopting five rules of Fisher's specification. They were listed to clarify the relationship of specification with theory (I) and data (II), and the appraisal criteria of specification (III, VI, and V). He suggested that these rules should be used to 'serve as a basis for discussing the specification problem with regard to the application of sampling theory to regression analysis of economic time-series' (p. 10):

I. In the specification should be implied all a priori knowledge on the nature of the data which is relevant to the estimation of the required parameters. . . .

II. In specifying the parent distribution such a posteriori information as to its form should be worked up as may be extracted from the sample itself with a reasonable degree of reliability and is relevant to the estimation of the required parameters. . . .

III. Extension of the specification by the introduction of additional assumptions not imposed by the rules I and II should be avoided as much as possible. . . .

IV. The specified form of the parent distribution should be neither so general nor so complicated as to make mathematical treatment of the problems of estimation and distribution too cumbersome and intricate or even impossible. . . .

V. In so far as the specification extends beyond the elements supplied by the rules I, II and III, the accuracy of estimation of the required parameters should not be very sensitive to an inexact fulfilment of the additional assumptions. (pp. 8–9)

Rules I and II highlighted the role of model specification as the juncture of theory and data, and of theory formulation and measurement (estimation). Notice that the emphasis in Rule I on the inclusion of all 'a priori knowledge' implied that the common practice of ad hoc pre-model analysis and comparison of theories ought ideally to be brought explicitly into the model specification. Correspondingly, all a posteriori information should be exploited in the specification of the distribution function (Rule II). These entailed that generality be the primal requirement for the specification, as followed by Rule III. But generality had to be counterbalanced with the requirement of simplicity due to technical constraints, mainly with respect to estimation (Rule IV). The limit of compromise between generality and simplicity was set in Rule V, which suggested that any simplification which would violate Rule III should be carefully adopted on condition of the stability of parameter estimates.

Koopmans devoted one chapter of his book to specification with respect to econometric modelling. He emphasized that the validity of any results of statistical studies depended upon the adequacy of the specification in representing 'the essential

features of the object of inquiry'. Accordingly, it was crucial in
the process *'that no relevant determining variable was omitted
from the set of variables'*. Formulae specified short of this
generality requirement 'may lose their meaning, even if they
happen to suggest a very accurate estimation of the regression
coefficients' (Koopmans 1937: 63). He argued that Fisher's
specification procedure was well suited to Frisch's errors-in-
variables formulation, since, in effect, it only imposed distributional assumptions on the error terms and not on the distribution
of the systematic parts of the variables (true variables). Furthermore, assumptions imposed in the specification could be viewed
as hypotheses, the validity of which might 'be tested from
the data' (p. 62). However, the purport of Koopmans's discussion on specification was to support his technical development
of the weighted regression method (see Chapter 3). Therefore,
when he illustrated his whole point at the end of his book by
an empirical model previously built by Tinbergen, what he
demonstrated was merely the part of the specification procedure
closely connected with the estimation step, namely, that of
how to impose distributional assumptions on the error terms,
rather than the complete process defined by the five rules that
he had stated.

Apparently, Koopmans's discussion on specification and the
five rules, and particularly the importance of generality in
specification, escaped broad recognition. The reference to Koopmans's 1937 work made in Tinbergen's 1939 work centred only
around Koopmans's weighted regression method and the idea
about specifying the distribution of the error terms (Tinbergen
1939: 32-3). The general neglect may also be due to Koopmans's
failure to introduce the whole approach of probability theory,
as described already in Chapter 1. Nevertheless, Koopmans's
contribution to model specification seemed to be well ahead of
its time.

Tinbergen's 1939 model enhanced Koopmans's knowledge of
econometric modelling. Meanwhile, he felt the impending
necessity of improving Tinbergen's work for close theoretical
scrutiny, as it immediately aroused much questioning. In response especially to Keynes's criticism, Koopmans set to formalizing the logic of Tinbergen's method in a paper 'The Logic of
Econometric Business Cycle Research' (1941). In this paper,

modelling was stated to start from a 'general working hypothesis' of main causal connections derived from economic theory, and, at the same time, 'not contradicted by the data'.
Moreover, the general working hypothesis should be supplemented by 'additional information' for reducing its multiple
implications, so as to allow for 'conditional' inferences. The
additional information was identified with Tinbergen's three
types of simplifications, i.e. to make choices of equation forms
and variables, as well as to separate the chosen variables into
exogenous, lagged, and random etc. Again, five principles were
listed for making these specifications: (a) the principle of statistical censorship, requiring that 'the additional information should
not imply statements which can be unconditionally rejected
because they are contradicted by the data'; (b) the principle of
scientific economy, i.e. 'no statement be included that could be
derived from the data with the help of the other statements
included', so as to ensure that 'the additional information is
truly complementary to the data'; (c) the principle of a solid
basis to leave 'a high degree of plausibility' to the model; (d) the
principle of a sufficient basis, as a counterbalance but secondary
to the third principle, to provide 'sufficiently specific' information for 'quantitatively definite positive conclusions'; and (e) the
tentative requirement (not a principle!) of mathematical simplicity for 'manageability' in practice, but this 'as an end in itself
has little justification in the long run'. The first two principles
were assigned to the part of statistical analysis in modelling, the
third and fourth mainly to economic reasoning.

It is interesting to compare these principles with those rules
adopted in Koopmans, 1937. The responsibility of statistical
studies appeared to have been upgraded in model specification,
but the bulk of economic theory was moved into the model
formulation process in the form of general working hypotheses
prior to specification. Thus it became largely exempted from
statistical falsification, which was directed mainly to statements
implied in the additional information. This suggested a significant move towards the theory-based measurement stance, without explicit regard to any active role of possible data-based
discovery of theory. On the other hand, the definite requirement
for scientific economy was new. It bore noticeable resemblance
to the present concept of 'parsimonious encompassing' (cf. Hendry

and Richard 1982, 1987). However, the role of simplification was remarkably downgraded. On the whole, the change from the five rules to the five principles embodied a turn from simply copying statistical theory to adapting it into an organic part of the emerging econometric theory of model formulation.

A more thorough adaptation was due to Haavelmo as part of his campaign for the probability approach. The experience in handling the identification problem and developing Frisch's confluence analysis (see Chapter 4) led Haavelmo to pinpoint a severe loophole in previous piecemeal applications of statistical methods to a priori formed economic theory, intrinsically of the Walrasian type: there lacked a proper correspondence between the interdependence of economic relations and their statistical treatment. With his knowledge in probability theory and statistics, he turned to the concept of 'a joint probability distribution' of all the variables as an immediate and fundamental solution to form a representation of the corresponding statistical interdependence.

In his two classics (1943b) and (1944), Haavelmo provided a full justification for his joint distribution specification of general economic models. The key message underlying his arguments was that a system of equations was only a theoretical representation for the economic theory free of the *ceteris paribus* condition; and hence that, in practice, 'a design of experiment' should be attached to the theory in such a way that the resulting hypothesis in statistical formulation would be also rid of the *ceteris paribus* condition, consistent with the system-of-equations representation. Thus, a logical gap existed in the common practice of applying estimation (and mainly regression) techniques directly to mathematical formulations of theory. The step of model specification was essential, after the selection of variables and their possible links, to make clear the statistical characteristics of how the observed values of the variables were generated, especially their interactive nature. In fact, the formulation–measurement procedure always contained implicit specification. For instance, OLS, the most frequently used estimation method, contained a *de facto* specification of merely assuming a marginal distribution to each variable. The problem with it was that such a specification often contradicted the characteristic of interdependency described so frequently in economic theory. Explicit specification was thus indispensable. In particular, the interdependency should be expressed by a joint probability distribution of all the variables, commonly in the form of a likelihood function. This could be achieved by imposing certain probability distributions on the error terms, as Koopmans had pointed out. But taking a decisive step further than Koopmans, Haavelmo demonstrated that 'the *parameters* (or some more general properties) of these distributions' amounted to 'certain additional characteristics of the theoretical model itself', and that they 'describe the *structure* of the model just as much as do the systematic influences' of the explanatory variables (Haavelmo 1944: 51). Mathematically, the influence was exerted through transformations of the system, 'by which to derive the joint probability distribution of the *observable* variables'. Consequently, estimation of the structural parameters became that of the parameters of the specified joint probability law. Haavelmo remarked that these facts were 'obvious to statisticians' but 'overlooked in the work of most economists who construct dynamic models to be fitted to economic data' (Haavelmo 1943*b*). The argument of joint distribution specification formed the cornerstone of Haavelmo's probability revolution (e.g. it is referred to as 'the Haavelmo distribution' by Spanos 1989). Many even regarded the probability approach as equivalent to joint distribution specification, as already described in Chapter 1.

Haavelmo's modelling criteria reinforced, in essence, Koopmans's specification rules, or principles, III to V. Generalization of econometric modelling theory was an obvious task of Haavelmo's 1944 monograph. In that work, he tried to convey his basic ideas and theories in mathematical and statistical terms without imposing any particular equation forms (not even linearity). However, he was not unaware of the dilemma resulting in practice from the simplification requirement. In fact, he devoted a whole section to 'the question of simplicity in the formulation of economic laws'. Interestingly his major concern here fell on variable selection. He suggested that the variables which could be simplified out should either have little potential influence on the specified variables, or otherwise show little change over time. Here, Haavelmo brought in Frisch's concept of the degree of 'autonomy' as the yardstick for valid simplifications. He stated that 'the principal task of economic theory is to establish such relations as might be expected to possess as high a degree of autonomy as possible' (Haavelmo 1944: 29). 'Autonomy' served as the essential guideline in both modelling and model evaluation in Haavelmo's programme (cf. Aldrich 1989). It was used to denote those theoretical relations which were validated in the sense that the parameters were found uniquely estimable and highly constant over time, and which were fundamental in the sense that they would remain invariant in face of any *hypothetical* variations' that occurred in other theoretical relations (Haavelmo 1944: 29). But, in spite of his profound discussion of the notion, Haavelmo did not offer any definite means as how to measure the degree of autonomy in practice. He admitted that the notion was 'highly relative', and that to find 'autonomous relations' was 'a matter of intuition and factual knowledge', 'an art', 'not an analytical process' (pp. 29–31). He briefly related the construction of autonomous structural relations to the hypothesis-testing scheme by referring to it as 'making fruitful hypotheses as to how reality actually is' (p. 31). But since the scheme was not well combined with the bulk of his theory, this more objective idea was eventually left unfulfilled (see Chapter 5).

2.4 Maturity of Simultaneous-Equations Model Formulation

Haavelmo's joint distribution specification was immediately recognized as a 'principal advance' (Koopmans 1950). It fulfilled the founding work for the simultaneous-equations model (SEM) approach. The SEM specification demarcated econometric model construction from merely formulating economic theory in mathematical terms, and therefore led to econometrics parting company with mathematical economics, which had been defined under the same name of 'econometrics' when the Econometric Society was founded. Econometrically, by setting up a counterpart to the purely theoretical systems-of-equations approach of a traditional Walrasian type, the specification helped to consolidate econometric modelling upon the basis of general economic theory. Economic theory in turn helped to establish the central position of an SEM as the general structural model form in the econometric formalization. In the process, the position of the structural modelling procedure was consolidated.

Haavelmo's joint distribution specification was immediately applied to the case of linear equations by Mann and Wald (1943). They specified a system of simultaneous, stochastic, linear difference equations made of a vector of random variables x_t and its lags:

$$A_0 x_t + A_1 x_{t-1} + \ldots + A_r x_{t-r} = \epsilon_t \qquad (t = 1, \ldots, T) \quad (2.6)$$

(ϵ_t: a vector of successively independent random disturbances, and r: the largest lag). They presented basic solutions to (2.6) using the methods of maximum-likelihood specification and estimation (see Chapter 3). This formula was soon extended by the Cowles Commission by classifying x_t into y_t, a vector of dependent variables, and z_t, a vector of explanatory variables:

$$B_0 y_t + B_1 y_{t-1} + \ldots + B_r y_{t-r} + \gamma_0 + \Gamma_0 z_t + \Gamma_1 z_{t-1}$$
$$+ \ldots + \Gamma_r z_{t-r} = \epsilon_t$$
$$(t = 1, \ldots, T). \qquad (2.7)$$

The equations in (2.7) were actually a combination of the two generalized forms of autoregression and distributed lags (ADL). Most of the Cowles contribution was made on equipping the joint distribution specification of (2.7), by means of the maximum-likelihood principle, with identification criteria and ML estimation methods (see Chapters 4 and 3). Model (2.7) has since been commonly recognized as the most generalized linear structural model in orthodox econometrics. This image was backed up by the close correspondence of (2.7) to the general equilibrium model in economics, and by the basic assumptions about the error terms being zero mean, homoskedastic, and non-autoregressive in the joint distribution specification of (2.7). The generality, in turn, rendered model (2.7) the appearance of absolute truth, which was just required of the structural modelling approach. Under the approach, the generality was further consolidated in the establishment of the general way, in moving from model specification to identification and estimation, of going from the structural form to its corresponding statistical form, referred to as 'the reduced form':

$$y_t = P_1 y_{t-1} + \ldots + P_r y_{t-r} + q_0 + Q_0 z_t + Q_1 z_{t-1}$$
$$+ \ldots + Q_r z_{t-r} + v_t$$
$$(t = 1, \ldots, T). \tag{2.8}$$

This modelling route gradually crowded out the route from structural equations to final equations, in which the dependent variables were derived as functions of all their previous values. Again, this showed that the aspect of measuring theoretical interdependency among variables was accorded a great deal more attention than the aspect of studying the dynamic features of individual variables in the econometric formalization.

The transformation from a structural model to its reduced form exposed the need for a separate step, designated as 'identification', with respect to the parameter solvability of (2.7). To secure the solvability, a certain number of additional a priori restrictions often had to be imposed on (2.7). Such impositions actually implied the loss of the assumed generality of an SEM over its reduced form, but this was tightly shielded by the very step of identification (see Chapter 4). At the time, what this step brought to immediate attention, in terms of model construction, was the practical question of 'when is an equation system complete for statistical purposes'. The question actually formed the title of a paper that Koopmans wrote separately in Cowles Monograph 10. In that paper, Koopmans redefined not only Tinbergen's notion of completeness, but also the distinction between the concepts of endogenous and exogenous variables (Koopmans 1950: 393–409).

As with Tinbergen's definition, Koopmans defined a complete model as one with the number of equations equal to the number of endogenous variables. The key then lay in the separation of endogenous and exogenous variables. The common practice so far was to assume the separation a priori according to the particular 'purpose of exposition', or the economic theory of interest, irrespective of the a posteriori statistical analysis. Koopmans looked into both of the a priori and a posteriori prerequisites of exogenous variables. He classified the former into two types of variables, one non-economic ('departmental') or 'wholly or partly outside the scope of economics' and the other 'causal', i.e. one which would 'influence the remaining (endogenous) variables' but would not be 'influenced thereby'. The causal type could be further divided into those which were 'strictly' free of the influence of endogenous variables and those which were only 'approximately' free (Koopmans 1950: 393–4). He then explained exogenous variables in the a posteriori case as those which were not only unaffected by the endogenous variables but also independent of the error terms, i.e. the case in which the complete structural system with parameters α's and variables x's:

$$\phi_i(\alpha_{i1}, \ldots, \alpha_{iQ_i}; x_1(t), \ldots, x_N(t); x_1(t-1),$$
$$\ldots x_N(t-1); \ldots) = \epsilon_i(t)$$
$$(i = 1, \ldots, N; t = 1, \ldots, T). \tag{2.9}$$

could be separated into two sets of equations by dividing the x's into two groups:

$$\phi_i(\alpha_{i1}, \ldots, \alpha_{iQ_i}; x_1(t), \ldots, x_G(t), x_{G+1}(t), \ldots, x_N(t);$$
$$x_1(t-1), \ldots, x_N(t-1); \ldots) = \epsilon_i(t)$$
$$(i = 1, \ldots, G; t = 1, \ldots, T). \tag{2.9a}$$

$$\phi_i(\alpha_{i1}, \ldots, \alpha_{iQ_i}; x_{G+1}(t), \ldots, x_N(t);$$
$$x_1(t-1), \ldots x_N(t-1); \ldots) = \epsilon_i(t)$$
$$(i = G+1, \ldots, N; t = 1, \ldots, T). \tag{2.9b}$$

such that the set of equations in (2.9b) could be disregarded for the subject of study. The mismatch between the a priori and a posteriori requirements led him to the conclusion that 'the concept of exogenous variables must be defined more strictly and narrowly than for some purposes of economic theory' in order to set up a complete model (Koopmans 1950: 399). Combination of both sides brought about the first rigorous econometric definition of exogeneity. As a result, the range of qualified exogenous variables was found to be significantly reduced. So Koopmans turned to the concept of 'predetermined variables', a term used to denote all the lagged variables as well as current exogenous variables in the theoretical sense. Under certain assumptions, he proved that predetermined variables possessed the same properties as those exogenous variables defined in the statistical sense. In order to bring out the newly defined exogenous variables in model specification, Koopmans made use of a 'conditional distribution function'[7] to condition

---

[7] It is interesting to note that Haavelmo had used the formulae of conditional expectation in supporting his argument for the joint distribution specification. But

the probability density of the endogenous variables upon all the predetermined variables (p. 402). This produced a succinct way to contrast the econometric concept of exogeneity with those old ones judged by mere economic considerations, because a transformation in the specification of the joint distribution function of the error terms into the product of the conditional distribution of the error terms upon exogenous variables and the marginal distribution of these exogenous variables was valid only for the econometrically exogenous variables.[8] This way of conditional specification actually indicated the possibility of subjecting the economically exogenous variables to statistical tests. But this point was overwhelmed, at the time, by the firm faith of the Cowles group in the pillar of economic theory. Instead, Koopmans used it to further divide (2.9a) into two sets of equations:

$$\phi_i(\alpha_{i1}, \ldots, \alpha_{iQ_i}; x_1(t), \ldots, x_G(t); x_{G+1}(t), \ldots, x_N(t);$$
$$x_1(t-1), \ldots, x_G(t-1); \ldots) = \epsilon_i(t)$$
$$(i = 1, \ldots, g; t = 1, \ldots, T). \tag{2.10a}$$

$$\phi_i(\alpha_{i1}, \ldots, \alpha_{iQ_i}; x_{g+1}(t), \ldots, x_G(t); x_{G+1}(t), \ldots, x_N(t);$$
$$x_1(t-1), \ldots, x_G(t-1); \ldots) = \epsilon_i(t)$$
$$(i = g+1, \ldots, G; t = 1, \ldots, T). \tag{2.10b}$$

Koopmans maintained that the specification of exogeneity amounted to 'two successive reductions of the size of the original equation system' (2.9). The first was that the equations in (2.9b) 'connecting only exogenous variables are omitted'. The second reduction was that the subsystem (2.10b) '"explaining" the pre-determined variables is omitted' (p. 407). Hence, model (2.10a) was regarded as complete for statistical purposes. However, Koopmans neither discussed its distinctions from the original complete system, particularly the effect of the two reductions

apparently he failed to incorporate the idea of conditional distribution explicitly in his theoretical framework.

[8] Conditional specification was soon adapted as a subsequent step to the joint distribution specification, expressing all the endogenous variables by means of a conditional probability distribution function of these variables jointly upon all the exogenous variables in the specification (e.g. cf. Christ 1951; Klein and Goldberger 1955). It was regarded as an advantageous means to 'make the model narrower' with respect to the distributions of the endogenous variables (Hood and Koopmans 1954: 118).

upon the generality of the original model, nor explored the conditions for the two reductions. The job was not followed up until the joint investigation by Engle, Hendry, and Richard (1983) over twenty years later.

Apparently, it is not accidental that Koopmans did not pursue further these modelling problems. Since the central task of the Cowles Commission was to formalize the statistical methods applicable to econometric analyses, given economic theory, they consciously left open the issue of how to put particular economic theory into a particular structural model. They were aware of the non-uniqueness generally existing in structural model formulations, and referred to the problem as 'multiple hypotheses'. It was stated frankly in both the Cowles research proposal and Monograph 10 that the issue of model choice by means of statistical testing on 'multiple hypotheses' was 'deliberately postponed' and outside the scope of their ongoing studies (see Marschak 1946; Koopmans 1950: 44–5).

The problem of model choice became acute as soon as researchers of the Cowles group set their foot in the applied field. Of the first few applied models, e.g. Haavelmo's consumption model and Klein models I–III, the starting structural models were seldom sufficiently general or complete. Normally, assumptions had to be added so as to get any economic models into statistically 'well-defined' models for the structural → reduced-form transform (Haavelmo 1947) (cf. also Girshick and Haavelmo 1947). The techniques produced by the Cowles group could not come into effect until such a transformation was attainable (see Chapter 6).

By assuming this attainability, however, estimation took the central stage. The evolution of this topic forms the theme of Chapter 3. The related issue of identification is to be traced in Chapter 4. Stories of how some applied econometricians found themselves far outside the assumption in actual modelling practice are put off to the later chapters.

3

Estimation

Estimation can be seen as the genesis of econometrics, since finding estimates for coefficients of economically meaningful relationships has always been the central motive and fulfilment of applied modelling activities. These were first recorded in the works of American agricultural economists, statistical economists, and statisticians early in this century (cf. Epstein 1987; Fox 1989; Morgan 1990). As neither the entity of 'model' existed nor was the modelling process systemized at the time, estimation would represent the principal efforts of 'measurement', and therefore denote a much broader and vaguer task than is understood nowadays. The main desire was to get certain economically meaningful quantities from data to implement certain economic theories of interest, whereas little attention was spared to aspects of estimation in the usual sense of mathematical statistics. This connotation gradually dwindled and converged from the 1930s onward towards the statistical sense of estimation, i.e. how to obtain the optimal estimates of parameters in different circumstances and how to evaluate the optimality of different estimates in line with various statistical criteria. The convergence was accompanied by the formation of the structural modelling procedure and the advent of the probability revolution. During the course of formation, the aspect of establishing economic meaningfulness was implicitly assigned to a priori structural model construction; the aspect of ensuring the attainability of unique parameter estimates was classified under the name of identification; the aspect of verifying a posteriori the theory of interest was designated to testing; and the aspect of empirical discovery from data was left mostly unattended. Estimation became separated out just as one of the basic steps along with model construction, identification, and testing. Subsequent research activities in estimation were confined to technical development of new optimal estimators for increasingly complicated model forms.

Section 3.1 describes the early developments in estimation methods centring around the least squares (LS) principle; how this led to the maximum-likelihood (ML) method in a simultaneous-equations system is the content of Section 3.2; Section 3.3 turns to look at special problems in the context of time-series analysis; other developments concerning errors-in-variables models are summed up in Section 3.4; the final completion of basic estimation theory of orthodox econometrics takes up Section 3.5.

3.1 FROM LS TO ML ESTIMATION BEFORE HAAVELMO'S REVOLUTION

When econometric practice first appeared early this century, estimation covered an all-inclusive process of actual data exploration to find some interpretable and economically significant relations and attach approximate values to the coefficients. The basic ideas were somewhat simple: operational knowledge in economics could be eventually embodied, through careful statistical studies of actual economic data, in estimated quantitative relations expressing economic theories. Estimation, therefore, was concerned with the possibility of obtaining numerical values for the coefficients in the anticipated economic relations, much more than with investigation of the statistical reliability of the findings. Considerations of economic measurement dominated the judgement of 'the goodness of fit'; or in other words, evaluation of estimates was vaguely mixed up with the possibility of finding parameters of economic significance. The statistical aspect was apparently assumed to have been looked after by statisticians who had invented such estimation tools as ordinary least-squares (OLS) and correlation analyses of single equations. Simple regression by the LS methods was used widely and almost indiscriminately. Time-series constituted the main type of data being studied. Empirical estimation results came out particularly from the fields of demand–supply analyses and business cycle studies (cf. Morgan 1990). The preliminary results exhibited certain limitations of simple regression with the OLS, and hence invoked critical discussions on the methods of estimation. The principal ones which could be sorted out included:

1. The problem of regression choice. As described in Chapter 1, variables and their relations were very much considered in a non-stochastic world in the early days. Thus, when the direction of regression was reversed, the resulting OLS coefficient estimates would differ from those derived from the original regression estimates. An immediate solution, suggested by Moore, was to guide the choice by economic theory. A more persuasive explanation, provided later by Schultz (1925), treated the problem in terms of measurement errors and attributed it to different degrees of measurement errors in different data series. The simplest form of his model is:

$$Y_t = \alpha + \beta X_t \qquad (3.1)$$

$$Y_t = y_t - e_t \qquad (3.2)$$

$$X_t = x_t - d_t. \qquad (3.3)$$

Y_t and X_t being the observed values of the true y_t and x_t, and e_t and d_t their measurement errors (assuming $E(e_t) = E(d_t) = E(e_t d_t) = 0$ for simplicity). Under this model specification, the problem of regression choice arose because normally neither e_t nor d_t vanished, as assumed by OLS regression. Schultz proposed to solve the problem by replacing OLS regression with orthogonal regression, i.e. assigning equal weights to e_t and d_t by assuming the ratio of their variances $\sigma_e^2/\sigma_d^2 = 1$, which resulted in the coefficient estimate lying between the two OLS estimates of the two regression directions. To overcome the weakness of scale dependence of orthogonalization in Schultz's method, Frisch (1929) suggested the method of diagonal mean regression, i.e. choosing the ratio to be a certain constant so that β became the geometric mean of the two slopes of the simple regressions.

2. The problem of correspondence between the estimated relations and the relevant economic theories. This was first found in demand studies where estimated results were not always guaranteed to correspond to the a priori specified theoretical relations, and eventually led to the development of identification theory (see Chapter 4). This problem at the time aroused an awareness of the effect of the simultaneity of economic relations, or the interdependence of economic variables. Various solutions proposed all resorted essentially to additional information outside the original model design. In the errors-in-variables context

like the above model, the parameters α and β were obviously not uniquely estimable without any information about the ratio of the error variances. Naturally, new estimation methods were needed.

3. The problem of nonsense correlations, elucidated first by Yule (1926), as already described in Chapter 2. Yule's results informed early econometricians that it would be precarious to take any significant statistical relations blindly as causal relations, since the former did not necessarily imply the latter, and that many of the commonly used estimation methods would be invalidated when the time-series used exhibited serious serial correlation. Yule's warnings appeared to result in excessive caution in some early econometricians, who were already questioning the supposed randomness of economic data, creating a reaction against the purely statistical approach of time-series analysis.

All these problems suggested that it was often oversimplifying to measure economic relations merely by means of regression and LS techniques. From a non-probabilistic outlook of economics, the root problem was then ascribed to data inaccuracy. Hence, errors-in-variables models of the above type were widely adopted around the end of the 1920s, and theoretical discussions on estimation became quite sceptical of the standard Fisherian statistical approach for its random variable assumption. Most estimation studies in econometrics were geared towards the invention of new techniques specially appropriate to the errors-in-variables model form at the start of the 1930s. The actual statistical problems relating to the optimality of estimation procedures were overshadowed by considerations of the measurement error problem in the context of a single equation and of the identification problem in the context of a system of equations. Formal estimation theory in line with statistical theory did not emerge until the systematic adoption of the probability approach, under which these issues were able to be unravelled and sorted out for separate investigation.

An outlier to the above position was found in an early paper by Tinbergen (1930) on the determination of supply curves in the presence of demand curves. Tinbergen developed (perhaps unintentionally) the method of indirect least-squares (ILS) estimation by transforming the theoretical relations into what are now called the reduced-form equations, estimating parameters of these equations by OLS and then solving the theoretical parameters using the reduced-form parameter estimates. Tinbergen did not discuss the properties of his ILS estimates since his main attention was directed towards the solution of simultaneous problems, especially in relation to identification (see Chapter 4). He probably took it for granted that the statistical qualities of ILS were the same as those of OLS, being already taken care of by statisticians.

Even econometric theorists were too afflicted with the jungle of problems now known as identification, measurement errors, multicollinearity, model choice, and so forth, to heed the possible statistical non-optimality of the OLS and ILS methods when applied to economic time-series and in a simultaneous context. As already described, a leading figure to combat the jungle was R. Frisch. It was because of concern about the above problems rather than about the statistical properties of the estimators used that Frisch rejected the simple and direct application of the OLS method. This was best seen from his critique of Leontief's method of demand analysis (Frisch 1933b), where 'the least squares minimizing procedures' were discarded at the outset of the paper solely for identification reasons (see Chapter 4). Based on the belief that there existed exact economic relations in a Walrasian system, Frisch (1934) devised his own method of confluence analysis and the bunch map apparatus based on the errors-in-variables explanation (see Hendry and Morgan (1989) for a more detailed explanation).

The basic idea of the bunch map analysis actually followed that of orthogonal regression, i.e. there was a 'true regression line' lying somewhere within the boundary of the elementary regression lines. The techniques involved therefore were quite simple: preparing a set of all the possibly relevant variables to the question, doing elementary regression by OLS in all the possible directions for all the possible combinations of two or more (normalized) variables out of the set, and graphing all the coefficient estimates in diagrams (i.e. bunch maps) for comparison and judgement. A smaller set of variables of real interest was then chosen according to the degrees of convergence shown in the bunch maps, and the 'true' coefficients were obtained by taking geometric means of all the corresponding elementary regression results (a kind of generalized diagonal regression).

Notice that estimation here comprised a broad three-step process starting from a prepostulated domain for the structural model set by theory: local OLS estimation of every regression direction → variable choice → true parameter calculation. The process would normally proceed iteratively.

The general problem of estimating regression coefficients when all the variables were subject to errors had actually been formally dealt with by some statisticians before Frisch's confluence analysis. But it was probably C. F. Roos, who, exclusively for econometric purposes, first attacked this technical problem in line with the statistical criterion of 'best-fit' in a paper devoted wholly to the estimation issue (1937) (the paper was presented at the 1936 session of the Cowles Commission Seminars). Roos followed the 'best-fit' criterion of the OLS principle in establishing his results. He put forward a general form of weighted regression to locate a best-fit line among all the elementary LS best-fit lines for single equations,[1] and stated conditions for the solutions to be independent of the choice of the coordinate system. He ascribed his enquiry to Schultz's (1925) orthogonal regression, and sought to choose the direction of LS minimization by the relative importance of the error of each variable, which was expressed in terms of a weight. Roos pointed out that his method included OLS, Schultz's orthogonal regression, and other previous results as special cases.

Further formalization of the weighted regression method was carried out by Koopmans (1937). As described in the previous two chapters, Koopmans undertook the job of formalizing Frisch's ideas into the Fisherian framework. In doing so, he introduced into econometrics Fisher's classification of model specification (including identification), estimation, and distribution. The classification enabled Koopmans to expose the major weak points in Frisch's estimation method, namely, the indistinctness of actual sample estimates and their hypothetical population values, and the lack of rigour in using the estimated results, and to overcome them with rigorous statistical procedure.

---

[1] The method is explained in early econometric textbooks such as Klein (1953), where a succinct footnote is worth quoting: 'The term "weighted regression" indicates that the sum of squares or quadratic form to be minimized has components weighted inversely to the size of error variance and covariance' (p. 293).

Koopmans employed Fisher's statistical approach and the maximum-likelihood (ML) method to deduce the method of weighted regression following van Uven's analysis (1930) (i.e. a two-step procedure to obtain the extreme values). The approach brought in explicitly, for judgement of estimates, the standard optimality criteria of 'unbiasedness' and 'consistency', the latter being a new criterion to econometricians for the best-fit, in cognizance of the relationship of sample data to the underlying theoretical population. Although Koopmans did not discuss these properties at length, the estimators that he obtained showed clear superiority over Frisch's bunch map estimates from the viewpoint of statistical consistency in the population and of clearer probability specification of the error terms. Yet, the method of ML in Koopmans (1937) was mainly confined to estimation. Another weak point lay in the assumption that the ratios of the variance–covariance matrix of the errors were known before estimation (see Chapter 4). Studies following the track of Koopmans's weighted regression were carried on by Tintner, who proposed to use the variate difference method to estimate the variance–covariance matrix before the regression (Tintner 1940*b*, 1944) (see Section 3.3). But his proposal was pointed out to be logically inconsistent (see Haavelmo 1941; also Klein 1953). By then, researches in this area had already been overwhelmed by Haavelmo's advocacy of the probability approach, and the development of simultaneous-equations estimation methods in the errors-in-equations model.

Koopmans's synthesis of Fisher's and Frisch's methods heralded a big leap forward in systematizing econometric methods. The acceptance of the concept of sample estimation elucidated the hidden fact that several intermediate logical steps, e.g. the step from sample to population, were required to fulfil the task of bridging general theory with concrete data. Once the loopholes in the old practice of relating statistical estimates directly to theoretical parameters were uncovered, the purpose of estimation became focused upon the distributional properties of sample estimators, with the objective of obtaining the *best* inference about the characteristics of the hypothetical population for certain given theoretical relations specified a priori. But on the other hand, the scope of the estimation task shouldered by econometricians was considerably diminished, since (*a*) technically, the invention of various estimators fell largely into statisticians' field of interests; (b) econometrically, a considerable portion of interest was separated out from estimation into model specification and identification; and (c) methodologically, claims that could be made on the basis of the estimates, once explicitly recognized as merely sample results, became rather modest relative to the general theoretical inferences concerning population regularities.

A short time after Koopmans's (1937) book, the famous Tinbergen model came out (1939). In his two-volume report of the model, Tinbergen devoted only a small part to statistical properties of his estimation results. This left much room for later developments. The developments branched roughly in two directions, one based upon the simultaneous-equations form and the other upon time-series recursive form. The next two sections trace the story of estimation along these two directions. As the scope of estimation in econometrics converged to the standard statistical domain, most of the later developments were increasingly technical, concerning the logical consistency and optimality of estimators for various model forms used in empirical work. Intrinsic conceptual problems relevant to the whole modelling procedure were however often disguised underneath the technicalities.

3.2 ML ESTIMATION OF SIMULTANEOUS-EQUATIONS SYSTEMS

The first overt rejection of the least-squares estimation method in a simultaneous-equations system was made by Haavelmo in his preparation for the probability revolution. Somewhat different from Koopmans, who was mainly concerned with the impreciseness of applied economists in using statistical methods, Haavelmo was more concerned with their carelessness in linking statistical results with economic theory. Haavelmo first noticed that there were problems in the OLS method for single-equation estimation in a simultaneous-equations model, when he delved into the problem of how to get parameter estimates of a final confluent relation (i.e. a final equation) derived from a system of structural relations (Haavelmo 1938).[2] He pointed out two problems

---

[2] Haavelmo delivered the main idea of his 1938 paper to the 1936 Oxford Meeting of the Econometric Society.

of the method: (*a*) it neglected the 'multidependencies' among the structural relations; and (*b*) multiple errors might be brought into the final equation coefficients if they were derived from structural coefficients estimated separately. Haavelmo's immediate solution was to start estimation from the final equation by means of some 'mean regression' such as Frisch's diagonal regression. He soon discovered, however, the limitation of the classical regression methods in a discussion on how to fit the dynamic pattern of a variable affected constantly by irregular shocks (Haavelmo 1939). He used a linear difference equation to represent the true (theoretical) variable and its lags. Assuming that the variables were affected by shocks at every time-interval, the corresponding stochastic difference equation for the observed variable and its lags would equate to a complicated moving average of the error series with the unknown difference-equation parameters in the coefficients. Haavelmo observed in this case that 'if the hypothesis of shock maintenance is accepted as true we are therefore in general not justified in fitting a theoretical relation to the observed series by means of the least-squares method' (Haavelmo 1939). Noticeably by then, Haavelmo had put aside measurement errors in the variables in his model, perhaps because he felt that they were trivial in comparison with the random shocks and would make the already complicated stochastic dynamic scheme even more complicated to handle. In fact, he tried to simplify the general stochastic scheme by reducing the moving average error series into one error term in each equation under investigation. This encouraged the use of the errors-in-equations form in favour of the errors-in-variables form in econometrics.

Tinbergen's 1939 macrodynamic model as well as Frisch's critique of Tinbergen's modelling (1938) must have stimulated Haavelmo, for he quickly turned to the identification problem in the situation when the observed dynamic data were the result of simultaneous movements of all the structural relations (see Chapter 4). The investigation apparently enhanced his interest in the estimation problems of simultaneous-equations systems. As he shifted into the probability approach and grasped the insight of the principle of joint distribution of variables in model specification, Haavelmo finally saw the kernel of the problem of applying the OLS method to simultaneous-equations systems.

It produced estimates of parameters different from the parameters of interest specified in the structural model. This discovery finally cleared the path for the maximum-likelihood approach.

Haavelmo's discovery was explained in both *The Probability Approach in Econometrics* (1944)[3] and 'The Statistical Implications of a System of Simultaneous Equations' (1943*b*). The latter started with the following simplest simultaneous-equations model:

$$Y = aX + \varepsilon_1 \tag{3.4}$$

$$X = bY + \varepsilon_2, \tag{3.5}$$

where ε_1 and $\varepsilon_2 \sim N(0, V)$, $V = \begin{bmatrix} \sigma_{11}^2 & 0 \\ 0 & \sigma_{22}^2 \end{bmatrix}$.

If X were to be used to explain Y, the common practice with the OLS method applied separately to the first equation, an investigator would believe:

$$E(Y \mid X) = aX. \tag{3.6}$$

However the reduced form for Y turned out to be:

$$Y = \frac{\varepsilon_1 + a\varepsilon_2}{1 - ab} \tag{3.7}$$

and the correct conditional expectation allowing for simultaneity should be:

$$E(Y \mid X) = \frac{\sigma_Y}{\sigma_X} \rho_{XY} X = \frac{b\sigma_{11}^2 + a\sigma_{22}^2}{b^2\sigma_{11}^2 + \sigma_{22}^2} X. \tag{3.8}$$

ρ_{XY} being the correlation coefficient of X and Y. Obviously applying OLS to (3.4) and (3.5) separately would result in estimates of parameters different from the parameters allowing for the simultaneity consideration.[4] Haavelmo generalized the model form in his later discussion.

---

[3] The problem was demonstrated by an example contrasting sharply with his abstract formulation of identification theory in the book. Haavelmo also pointed out that the OLS method could be applied separately to the reduced form, i.e. Tinbergen's ILS method.

[4] Frisch's (1933*b*) paper presented a derivation that was very close to disclosing this problem (see Epstein 1987). But there were three fundamental differences between his model and Haavelmo's model: (*a*) Haavelmo's model transcended

Haavelmo imputed the wrong use of the OLS method to two reasons: the illusive 'notion that one can operate with some vague idea about "small errors" without introducing the concepts of stochastic variables and probability distribution', and the insufficient specification of 'only the marginal probability law' for each random variable even if one accepted 'the notion of probability and random variables'. He maintained that only by bringing out explicitly the statistical implications of the simultaneous-equations model (i.e. all the random variables were specified as jointly distributed) could one find correct methods of estimation. The essence was to consider the simultaneous-equations system 'as a system of transformation, by which to derive the joint probability distribution of the observable variables from the specified distribution of the error terms' and to formulate all the parameter estimators 'on the basis of this joint probability law of all the observable variables involved in the system' (Haavelmo 1943b). His statements made it clear that estimation should proceed in logical consistency with model specification. Somehow his message became simplified later into one that the OLS would produce systematic bias in the simultaneity context—referred to as the 'Haavelmo bias'.

To solve the problem, Haavelmo turned to the principle and method of ML. The method allowed a transformation of the structural equations into the joint distribution function of the random disturbances so as to get an expression of the joint distribution of the observable variables. The ML estimators of the unknown structural parameters in the expression were derived by maximizing this joint distribution function (to make the probability density the largest). These estimators formally extended econometricians' criteria of 'goodness of fit' from only the sample data at hand to aspects of the sample–population relationship (e.g. from the property of unbiasedness to that of consistency). The appealing properties of ML estimators took up a great part of the attention of the Cowles researchers. Consequently, Haavelmo's probability revolution was treated as

the particular demand–supply content of Frisch's model; (b) Haavelmo's model was based in a probabilistic setting; (c) Haavelmo stressed the joint distribution of X and Y by putting X deliberately on the left-hand side of the second equation, an expression closer to the errors-in-variables model than to Frisch's model.

almost equivalent to his discovery of the OLS problem[5] and his advocacy for ML estimation. The implication of his argument for logical consistency between model estimation and specification was neglected till much later.

The task of rigorous statistical treatment of ML estimation of a closed model of linear stochastic difference equations was carried out by Mann and Wald (1943). Their paper made a notable impact on the estimation theory in econometrics. In view of the great difficulty encountered by R. L. Anderson (1942) and Koopmans (1942), in deriving the exact distributions of ML estimates, Mann and Wald turned to tackle the problem from the asymptotic standpoint and provided the first rigorous results. Their work led to the general acceptance of a set of common statistical criteria. They were basically consistency and efficiency, as well as unbiasedness. The asymptotic concept became especially influential, because it not only circumvented the technical difficulty of obtaining exact sampling distribution functions in various circumstances, but also shifted the focus on sample analysis from samples to the underlying populations.

Mann and Wald's main contribution was the proof of the consistency and asymptotically normal distributions of the ML estimators for the model form set out as equation (2.6) in the previous chapter, i.e.:

$$A_0 x_t + A_1 x_{t-1} + \ldots + A_r x_{t-r} = \epsilon_t \quad (t = 1, \ldots, T),$$

under the assumptions that the model was stationary and the vectors $(\epsilon_{1t}, \ldots, \epsilon_{rt})$ were mutually independently and identically distributed with finite higher moments. They showed that the classical regression method of OLS generally failed to produce consistent estimates except in the cases of either a single equation or the structural coefficients being stringently restricted in certain ways (in all these cases OLS estimates were always deducible from the ML estimates). The ML method thus displayed its superiority over the classical regression methods. It was also observed that ML estimation of the system was conditional upon the identifiability (see Chapter 4) of the system,

---

[5] Tinbergen admitted when recalling this period of history that 'the Haavelmo discovery was the most important thing for me. I immediately felt that he was right' (Magnus and Morgan 1987).

which was often doubtful unless there was additional a priori information available to set up sufficient restrictions on the values of some coefficients. Otherwise, the reduced-form results would be the best possible that one could get from estimation. They also showed that estimation via ILS, if the system was identifiable, would involve some loss of estimation efficiency.

Mann and Wald's work on the simultaneous-equations system could be seen as a complementary extension of Haavelmo's discovery of the OLS problem. One of their noteworthy generalizations was that they based their investigation explicitly on a dynamic model in terms of difference equations. But they did not focus as much consideration on dynamics as on the interdependency of economic variables. Thus, their results encouraged the concentrated attack on simultaneous-equations estimation problems by the Cowles workers, leaving aside the problems concerning time-series.

There were certain jobs left undone in Mann and Wald's treatment, e.g. the conditions of the required a priori information (i.e. identification theory), the full description of the properties of ML estimation and its computational problems, and the problem of sample size. It was in these directions that the ensuing work of the Cowles Commission progressed (see Koopmans 1950; Hood and Koopmans 1953).

The problem about the conditions of the required a priori information was formally separated out and dealt with under the title of 'identification' (see Chapter 4). Another 'most fully discussed' topic besides identification in the Cowles Monograph 10 was concerned with the properties of the ML methods in the simultaneity context (Koopmans 1950: 4). With an independent identification procedure in mind, Koopmans *et al.* were able to rearrange Mann and Wald's model into one with explicitly classified endogenous variables and exogenous variables (see equation (2.7) of the previous chapter). Under similar assumptions to Mann and Wald, the methods of ML estimation of the structural parameters were spelt out in great detail, following essentially the same basic ideas as adapted by Haavelmo (1943*b*). The relationship of the method to the amount of a priori information was stressed in addition to the usual discussion of the consistency and other asymptotic properties of ML estimates in different cases. The approach was designated as 'information-preserving maximum-likelihood method' to denote its efficiency in utilizing all the a priori information. It later became commonly called 'full-information maximum-likelihood' (FIML) estimation.

Computational problems of the FIML estimator were highlighted for applied work because of its non-linearity and large matrix calculations in the face of the quite limited computer capacity at the time. Alternatives for simplifying these estimators were explored along the lines of utilizing at one time only that part of information related directly to specific equations of interest in the system. Research done along these lines brought about the methods of 'limited-information' estimation. A method following directly from the ML principle was suggested by Girshick,[6] and formalized by Anderson and Rubin (1949, 1950), known as the method of 'limited-information maximum-likelihood' (LIML) (see also their papers in Koopmans, 1950; Hood and Koopmans, 1953). The method was analogous to the idea of ILS. Maximization was carried out on the likelihood function only over that part of the reduced-form equations of the structural model which corresponded to the endogenous variables appearing in the structural equations of interest. In doing so, LIML proved itself to be a more feasible method for applied work by trading off a certain degree of efficiency of FIML for much lighter computational as well as specification burdens (i.e. a fully specified complete system was no longer necessary). The first application of the method was carried out by Girshick and Haavelmo in an attempt to estimate the demand relations for food (1947).

All the results of ML estimation developed by the Cowles workers were based on large sample assumptions. Although they were not unaware of the fact that 'the practical usefulness' of all the desirable asymptotic properties would 'diminish' (Koopmans 1950: 42) once the samples became small, little was done about it due probably to the enormous technical difficulties. Hurwicz contributed a limited study in this respect. He examined the bias of the LS and ML estimators of the single-equation multitemporal model for finite and small-sized samples. The signific-

---

[6] In a letter to the Commission in Dec. 1945, Girshick put forward an idea which clearly suggested LIML (see Epstein 1987).

ance of the biases found by him presented 'urgent need for more intensive study of the small sample properties of estimates', and especially the 'approximate sampling distributions' in the commonly 'autoregressive time-series' of economic data (Koopmans 1950: 367). There were two other papers which set the prelude to small sample studies (cf. Phillips 1983). One was by Haavelmo (1947) in a study concerned with measuring the marginal propensity to consume. Notably, he applied the method of ILS rather than ML for estimation in that paper. Finite sample properties of estimators such as BLUEs ('best linear unbiased estimators') were discussed as of comparable importance to asymptotic properties. The other paper was by Anderson and Rubin (1949), where the theoretical derivation of LIML was first given. They based their deduction of the confidence regions of the LIML estimates on small sample theory, and proposed an approximate small sample test of restrictions as well.

On the whole, the LIML method was probably the most important contribution to estimation theory by the Cowles Commission. It succeeded in showing how econometricians should view and deal with single economic relations which were thought to constitute a system of interdependent relations. More broadly, the ML approach marked the establishment of a theoretical foundation for the estimation procedure. Later developments were to concentrate upon devising various estimation methods either easier to calculate or with less stringent assumptions.

3.3 ESTIMATION WITH SPECIAL CONCERNS FOR TIME-SERIES DATA

The problem of estimation under simultaneity was solved in principle by the Cowles group. But they left untouched a number of issues pertaining to applied models, which violated one way or another the basic assumptions of the Cowles type of model form. One of the crucial issues was related to the serial dependence between successive observations of a time-series variable.

Combating serial correlation (i.e. linear serial dependence) was a major job of time-series analysis, which actually had a longer history than the ML methods for multivariable estimation.

Application of the theory of time-series analysis to economic data went back to the very early days of econometrics. But early developments in this area were relatively primitive, muddled, and intermittent compared to those along the simultaneity route. Moreover, the estimation side was largely overshadowed by discussion of choice of model formulations, as seen in Chapter 2.

It has already been stated that econometric estimation stemmed from the attempts to characterize economic time-series data. Hence time-series analysis, in its very first developments, embraced nearly the entire domain of econometric practice. This is discernible in Davis (1941a, 1941b). A narrower view of time-series analysis emphasized the dynamic aspect of data. The main methods at the early stage were harmonic analysis using Fourier series and simple correlation analysis such as the business barometers. Both resorted to the OLS method for statistical estimation. Subsequent discussion in econometric circles during the 1930s centred around the appropriate way to model the dynamics represented in time-series data. The LS principle was still taken as the single estimation tool-supplier without dispute. Actually, serious attempts to develop the appropriate ways to do time-series estimation were being made in mathematical statistics peripheral to the econometric circle.

The development was concentrated upon a model scheme called 'linear autoregression (AR)' originated by Yule (1927) (see equation (2.4) in Chapter 2). Various techniques were invented to surmount the key difficulty of how to form the best possible estimators in the presence of serial correlation. Although the principle of LS was used for most of the cases, these developments contrasted strikingly with developments in econometrics taking place at the same time. From the beginning, the time-series methods were rigorously derived from sampling concepts. Distributional properties of the regression estimators were carefully examined in most cases in conjunction with statistical tests.

In his 1927 paper, Yule set up a second-order autoregressive model, approximated it with the autocorrelation coefficients, and used the method of LS to estimate the model. This method was generalized by G. Walker (1931) and formed what was later known as 'Yule–Walker estimates' of the partial autocorrelation function (Yule–Walker equation). In the early 1930s, A. C. Aitken, in trying to fit polynomials to data, established a method of estimation for a general linear regression equation where the regressors could be treated as either weighted or correlated with the errors (Aitken 1934–5). He decided that the squared residuals to be minimized according to the LS principle should be weighted by the variance–covariance matrix of the errors in this case and derived his estimator as OLS transformed by the matrix. His method amounted to using the symmetric and positive definite property of the variance–covariance matrix to transform the original equation into one with zero covariances, so as to make LS applicable. Aitken's method, now referred to as 'generalized least-squares' (GLS), had apparently remained unnoticed by econometricians for a decade.[7]

The problem of serial correlation in time-series received growing attention after the 1940s, noticeably led by the establishment of the first statistical test, the von Neumann ratio (see Chapter 5). The watershed in estimation was made by Mann and Wald (1943) (already described at length in Section 3.2), with their formulation of estimators for autoregressive equations. It should be borne in mind that the general view on the role of model estimation had become relatively settled in econometrics by this time. Econometricians' attitude toward time-series, therefore, was somewhat different from that of the statisticians, who regarded the lack of independence in time-series samples as a distinct feature of the data. To many econometricians, this was treated as a problem of the data samples and certainly a serious technical problem from the standpoint of estimating or statistically inferring the structural parameters of any particular models, since such a problem had never been the concern of economic theory formulation and specification in a general way (see Chapter 6).

It was from the econometric viewpoint that Mann and Wald developed their AR estimator. They endeavoured to tackle dynamics, simultaneity, and stochasticity together with 'the general theory of ML estimates' (Mann and Wald 1943). But, as mentioned in Section 3.2, their generalization of ML over LS was

---

[7] The earliest paper, found so far, which cited Aitken's 1934–5 work is by Tintner (1944).

not as influential in the time-series aspect as in the simultaneity aspect, since their chief interest, as well as that of the Cowles workers, was in simultaneous-equations estimation. Serial and autocorrelations were ruled out by assumption in the major results in Cowles Monograph 10 (Koopmans 1950). They were only briefly discussed in Part Two of the monograph assigned to 'Problems Specific to Time-Series'. But hardly any substantial advance was made there, and definitely nothing with respect to estimation in time-series analysis. From this perspective, it looked almost delusive to see the strong claim of Monograph 10 on dynamics, while the real emphasis was on simultaneity. The subsequent Monograph 14 altogether discarded the part of time-series discussions (Hood and Koopmans 1953).

The theoretical achievements by the Cowles group encouraged econometricians in other places to strive in the same direction. The first econometric device for estimating parameters acknowledging the presence of serial correlations was worked out by G. H. Orcutt and D. Cochrane at the Department of Applied Economics (DAE) of Cambridge University (cf. Gilbert 1988). Orcutt became interested in the autocorrelative property of time-series as compared to random series around 1940. With a physics background and a strong knowledge of computing machines, he set out to tackle the problem by experimental means of data simulation, or 'Monte Carlo' studies. In the late 1940s, he joined a DAE's project of developing 'methods for the satisfactory handling of time-series and, in particular, relatively short time-series such as are normally available to the economists' (DAE 1951). Since he was greatly excited by Tinbergen's 1939 work when it first came out, Orcutt started his investigation by experimenting with the time-series used in Tinbergen's US model (Orcutt 1948). He found that autocorrelations existed quite commonly in many economic time-series, and that in consequence would affect the efficiency of the OLS estimator. Together with D. Cochrane, Orcutt worked on how to find the appropriate model form for economic time-series (Cochrane and Orcutt 1949; Orcutt and Cochrane 1949).[8] Maintaining the struc-

[8] D. G. Champernowne was also working on a similar problem independently at the time (e.g. Champernowne 1948). Orcutt recalled that he became aware of Champernowne's work some time after he had started on the DAE's project (Qin 1988*b*).

tural model stance, they arrived at the explanation that all the economic time-series 'could be considered as generated from autocorrelated processes', and they believed that it was 'the sample autocorrelation property', rather than 'the true auto-correlation problem', that mattered in the analysis (Cochrane and Orcutt 1949). This led them to shifting the target of analysis from the independence between the present and lagged variables, as in the works of Yule, and Mann and Wald, to the inde-pendence between the error terms, since as a sample problem, 'the significant factor in the analysis is the autocorrelation of the error term and not the autocorrelation of the time-series themselves' (Cochrane and Orcutt 1949). Based on the model form of a first-order AR in the error terms:

$$y_t = \alpha_0 + \alpha_1 x_t + u_t \qquad t = 1, \ldots, T \qquad (3.9)$$

$$u_t = \beta u_{t-1} + \varepsilon_t \qquad |\beta| < 1; \ \varepsilon_t \sim IN(0, \sigma_\varepsilon^2). \qquad (3.10)$$

Orcutt and Cochrane showed that the OLS residuals tended to be biased towards a random series when the error terms were actually autocorrelated. Since the OLS estimator lost efficiency in the presence of autocorrelation, they elaborated Aitken's GLS into a two-step estimation procedure later known as the Cochrane–Orcutt estimator. The idea was to obtain a GLS estimator based on OLS residuals and then to estimate α_0 and α_1 using the estimated β. An iteration could be easily pursued by reperfor-ming the two steps on the new set of residuals of the second step till convergence. This was called the 'Cochrane–Orcutt iterative procedure'. Alternatively, the method could be viewed as making a transformation ('autoregressive transformation') by substituting the above second equation in the first. At the time, Orcutt and Cochrane's work immediately won wide recog-nition in econometrics as a systematic improvement in the estimation of AR processes. Their view about the important role of autocorrelation of the errors of time-series strengthened the growing attitude of treating the existence of serial correlation as an unfortunate 'complication' of economic data among econo-metric time-series analysts.[9]

[9] The word 'complication' was used by Tintner in his influential textbook (1952). Note that he participated in the research project of the 'Analysis of Time-Series' at DAE during 1948–9 (DAE 1951).

Although based on the LS principle, the actual computation of Cochrane–Orcutt estimators was still an onerous task for the computers then available. This stimulated developments of new time-series estimators, which would ease the computational burden. One such development was made by J. Durbin, who was jointly responsible with G. S. Watson for developing the powerful D–W test for residual autocorrelation soon after the Cochrane–Orcutt results (see Chapter 5). Durbin proposed later an alternative procedure to Cochrane and Orcutt's method (1960b) (see also Durbin 1960a). He chose to regress y_t directly on x_t and their lagged terms—a method based on a transformation of the two equations (3.9) and (3.10), instead of on the residuals. Durbin insisted that the rationale of his estimation method was similar to Cochrane–Orcutt's method, except that it was computationally simpler when the numbers of exogenous variables and autoregression order were not very large.

3.4 OTHER ESTIMATION METHODS FOR ERRORS-IN-VARIABLES MODELS

Before the Cowles work dominated in econometric theory, substantial developments were still made in analysing errors-in-variables models. The major ones concerning estimation were methods of instrumental variables (IV), principal components, and canonical correlation. The first one was designed to do away with the requirement for the assumedly known variance–covariance matrix in achieving consistent estimation, and later became an extremely powerful and general method. Whereas the latter two, aiming to help with variable choice through estimation, soon drew in their horns.

3.4.1 Instrumental Variables[10]

In 1940 Wald introduced a new method for estimating bivariate equations with errors-in-variables. He summarized the previous methods up to Koopmans (1937) and Allen (1939), and pointed out their common shortcoming of dependence on a priori know-

---

[10] For earlier cases of what were later recognized as applications of IV methods, see Epstein (1987) and Morgan (1990).

ledge about the variance–covariance matrix of the error terms. To circumvent this, Wald proposed to split up the observed sample into two subsamples so as to apply the geometric principle of a generalized two-point form for consistent estimation of the parameters (under the assumption of no correlation between the measurement errors and between the values of the individual error series). Wald stated that the key rule of his method was to make the subdivision independent of the errors. The idea amounted to solving the estimation problem by carefully creating new variables to help remove the dependence of the original regressors on the errors, but Wald did not seem to recognize the generality of his method.

Concurrently, Olav Reiersøl, a former research assistant of Frisch, worked on developing new estimation methods for Frisch's confluence analysis. Abandoning the impasse of finding first the variance–covariance matrix of the actually unobservable errors, Reiersøl turned to grapple directly with the observed part of the true variables and employed the lagged moments of the observed values of the variables to help achieve estimation (1941). Subsequently, he generalized his idea in a thesis entitled 'Confluence Analysis by Means of Instrumental Sets of Variables' (Reiersøl 1945), where the method got its name 'the method of instrumental variables (IV)'. He stated that the method of IV was actually very flexible, and that Wald's 1940 method, the method of using lagged regressors (he termed the original regressors 'investigation variables'), or through moving averages or differencing devices could all be interpreted as IV applications. He made it clear in terms of rigorous conditions and theorems that any variables which were highly correlated with the 'investigation variables' on the one hand, and ideally uncorrelated with the disturbances of those variables on the other, could be used as IV, and that application of IV provided a systematic approach to estimating either simultaneous-equations models or lag-regression models in the framework of errors-in-variables. The generality of the method was however severely obscured by the errors-in-variables framework at that time, when the errors-in-equations model form prevailed. Moreover, Reiersøl stated the IV method in a way almost incomprehensible to many people, so that his ideas were rarely understood fully then, even by his colleagues in the Cowles Commission, whom he visited in 1947 and for whom he worked in the summer of 1949.[11]

R. C. Geary was, at the time, one of the few who did understand the significance of Reiersøl's method. In fact, he developed similar ideas independently and proposed to attack the problem of estimating parameters in errors-in-variables models by means of higher (than one) order moments because of their properties of semi-invariance under linear transformations of the variables (1942, 1943). When Reiersøl's results came out, Geary immediately realized that their methods had identical essence, namely, to utilize additional information through constructing a certain set of IVs. He pursued this direction, and verified that the IV method furnished consistent parameter estimates for errors-in-variables equations and, in particular, for autoregressive equations with large samples (Geary 1949) (the research was done at DAE during 1946-7 (DAE 1951)).

3.4.2 Principal Components[12]

The method of principal components was closely associated with the estimation of errors-in-variables models. It was first devised by H. Hotelling in the 1930s in connection with factor analysis in psychology (1933). It was designed to reduce a set of variables to a number of independent components which were fundamental for characterization of the original set. This was achieved through analysis of the covariance matrix of the original set of variables via its characteristic roots. The method was soon extended to the context of errors-in-variables by M. A. Girshick (1936), who showed that the principal components could help find the variance estimates of a regression equation, and that these estimates would be equivalent to ML estimates if the variables were normally distributed. Koopmans referred to Hotelling's principal component method in his 1937 book, but he used it very cautiously and only as a computational device.

---

[11] Two papers on the IV method are found among the Cowles Commission unpublished documents: 'A Note on Geary's Papers' by T. W. Anderson (1946), and 'Confluence Analysis when the Model Contains both Shocks and Errors' by Reiersøl (Discussion Papers: No. 306, 1947). They show that the Cowles people were not ignorant of the method, but possibly did not grasp all its implications.

[12] Discussions here are restricted to the applicability of the method to econometric estimation. See Tintner (1952) for its wider use in economics.

The earliest trial to apply the method to econometrics was undertaken by R. Stone in modelling the blocks of transactions of US data (1947). He managed to reduce seventeen variables to three principal components (income, rate of change of income, and a time-trend) with the method. The result confirmed his a priori expectations based on economic theory. A serious dilemma was immediately discovered with this application (see the discussions following his paper), namely, that the a priori theoretical knowledge, if correct, considerably reduced the significance of the method; and on the other hand, the intention of statistical discovery was hampered by the fact that economic time-series seldom satisfy the assumptions of the method. In addition, it was very difficult to see the exact economic meanings of the principal factors after heavy mathematical derivations. In an era when the prevalent conviction was that estimation could only be done correctly in conjunction with theoretically well-specified structural models, and when various techniques consistent with this idea were being promoted, Stone's ambition to discover 'a set of "inner variables"' from data by the method of principal components was stillborn.

On the other hand, Stone's work induced Geary to dig into the relationship between principal components regression and the classical multiple regression method (e.g. Koopmans's weighted regression method (1937)), because both were dependent on the technique of characteristic roots. Geary's enquiry resulted in a formal equivalence of Koopmans's method and the principal components method (1948). This result appeared to make redundant the application of principal component regression.

3.4.3 Canonical Correlation

The method of canonical correlation, due also to H. Hotelling (1936), was developed in close relation to the method of principal components. The method was designed to show the interrelations between two sets of variables by maximizing the correlation between two linear combinations of the variables in each set.

The first experiment with the method in econometrics was pioneered by F. V. Waugh (1942), who applied it to finding the canonical correlation between prices and consumption, and between quality indexes of different agricultural commodities.

While he was clearly aware of the fact that the method could easily lead to nonsense results unless backed up by economic reasoning, Waugh still argued for its use in helping to reduce the number of relevant variables to a moderate size, as was often required in the field of applied microeconomic analyses.

Later, Tintner (1950a) established formal relations between canonical correlation, principal components, weighted regressions, and discriminant analysis within the general framework of multivariate analysis. However, by then, all the methods aiming at variable reduction through statistical devices had fallen into disfavour through comparison with the growing enterprise of structural modelling procedure. With the formalization of identification theory, the view prevailed that variables should be selected a priori by economic theory (see Chapter 4). Therefore, there was little purpose in taking pains to develop statistical methods to this end. Furthermore, the available methods of principal components and canonical correlation required certain conditions in fulfilling such a task, which were often violated by economic data. As the errors-in-variables formulation faded away with the prevalence of the errors-in-equations formulation, the methods of IV, principal components, and canonical correlation were crowded out of the central concerns of estimation theory. Although Hotelling's papers on both methods were referred to in Cowles Monograph 10, they were merely made use of in the development of computational procedures rather than in estimation. These methods later extended their lives in econometrics by conforming to the structural modelling procedure, during which much of the motivation behind them disappeared.

3.5 From ML back to LS,
Completion of Estimation Procedure
for Simultaneous-Equations Systems

There was a resurgence of the LS principle after the Cowles elaboration of the ML principle and methods. Although the LIML method reduced the computational burden of the FIML method considerably, its application then still faced computational problems and required stringent assumptions. The majority of applied studies stuck to the LS methods despite the logical beauty of the Cowles results. Ironically, even Haavelmo, one of the earliest ML advocates, had turned back to LS in his applied work in the midst of the Cowles workers' clamour for estimation consistency, as mentioned in Section 3.2. The Cowles ML approach was further challenged by Wold's opposition to the simultaneous-equations model form in advocating the recursive model form. Trying to rehabilitate the status of LS methods, Wold, together with Juréen, proved the equivalence of LS estimation with FIML estimation in a recursive system when the disturbances of different equations were independently and normally distributed. Their method followed Aitken's GLS method and Cochrane–Orcutt results (1953). Klein (1955) immediately pointed out that their model form actually was a special case of the simultaneous-equations system. The dispute soon centred on the issue of model construction, leaving aside the estimation aspect (see Chapter 6).

A decisive breakthrough came in the invention of what is now referred to as the 'two-stage least squares' (2SLS) method by a Dutch econometrician, Henri Theil (1953), and then independently by R. L. Basmann (1957), a young American scholar. With this development, the statistical optimality of LS estimators was formally restored for simultaneous-equations models.

Theil's approach could be viewed as a development of ILS. He discovered that the crux for legitimate use of LS in the simultaneous context was to find ways to transform the original system into one with mutually independent error terms, and hence to establish approximate independence between the regressors and the error term in each equation. He managed to achieve this by making use of the second moment matrices resulting from applying LS to the reduced form of the original system. He named his method 'two-round' estimation since it used LS on an LS transformation of the model. Theil also showed the mathematical equivalence of his method with the LIML method.

Basmann approached the problem from a more generalized angle. He started off from a simple but general linear regression form:

$$y_1 = Z\alpha_1 + e_1, \tag{3.11}$$

where $y_1 = (y_{11}, \ldots, y_{N1})'$; $Z = (z_{th})$, $t = 1, \ldots, N$, $h = 1, \ldots, n$; $\alpha_1 = (\alpha_{11}, \ldots, \alpha_{1n})'$; $e_1 = (e_{11}, \ldots, e_{N1})'$. (Notice that Z and e_1

were not assumed to be independent.) Basmann pointed out that consistent LS estimation amounted to constructing estimators:

$$\alpha_1 = Ay_1 = \alpha_1 + Ae_1 \tag{3.12}$$

such that the probability limit of Ae_1 vanished for a special choice of the transformation matrix A. The classical method of OLS, he explained, provided the correct A directly because of the independence of Z from e_1. In the case of simultaneous-equations systems, such a matrix had to be searched for. Basmann made use of the property of non-correlation of the exogenous variables with the error terms and constructed the transformation matrix with the exogenous variables and the OLS estimates of the endogenous variables regressed on all the exogenous variables (i.e. the reduced-form regression). By doing so, he arrived at the same method as Theil's, namely, enclosing an OLS procedure in his 'generalization of the classical method of least-squares' (or GLS). Basmann also proved that his estimators possessed the same optimal properties as those of LIML estimators.

The appearance of 2SLS highlighted the use of another method in simultaneous equation estimation: the method of instrumental variables developed by Reiersøl and Geary in the context of errors-in-variables models. Actually, the applicability of IV methods to simultaneous-equations systems was already recognized independently of 2SLS both from the side of errors-in-variables and from the side of simultaneity.

The former aspect was reflected in J. Durbin's succinct survey 'Errors in Variables' (1954a). Durbin stated in relation to estimation (a) that the method of IV could be used to estimate both the errors-in-variables model and the autoregressive and simultaneous-equations model; (b) that the ML estimators of the simultaneous-equations model could be converted into IV estimators when the system was extended to multiple regression equations; and (c) that a simultaneous-equations model without measurement errors was in effect a special case of the general errors-in-variables model. Unfortunately, Durbin's survey did not attract much attention initially, probably due to the diminished interest in the errors-in-variables model amid the triumph of the simultaneous-equations modelling in the errors-in-equations framework.

From the side of the SEM, evidence showed that the Cowles workers had perceived partially the association of IV with LIML before Durbin,[13] though they failed to realize its actual implication and full advantages. This was best seen from an early econometric textbook by Klein (1953). The method of IV was described in the book as 'a related technique' 'to the limited information method' (p. 122), and put under the subheading of 'Limited Information Estimates' for single-equation estimation in the context of simultaneous-equations models. Klein explained that the idea of using instrumental variables was to obtain consistent LS estimators by transforming the original model with some carefully chosen exogenous variables and predetermined variables. However, the advantage of generality implied in the choice of IV was not recognized. Instead, IV was interpreted as having 'arbitrariness' especially in the case of overidentification. The method was thus disfavoured in comparison with LIML. Klein's (1953) description of IV clearly explained why the Cowles people had missed this easy passage to LS via IV in the search for simpler estimation methods to FIML, which resulted in LIML.

Theil's 2SLS reminded Klein (1955) at once of IV, and he conceived a new interpretation of Theil's theory in terms of the method of IV. He pointed out in formal proofs that Theil's method was in fact 'the same thing as the method of instrumental variables, using a particular linear combination of instrumental variables and leaving no room for arbitrary selection', which had been regarded as problematic in the case of overidentification. However, Klein's increasing interest in empirical econometric modelling distracted him from further theoretical enquiry into the statistical properties of IV. The task was taken up by J. D. Sargan (1958, 1959) quite independently of Klein's discussion.

It was interesting to note that Sargan learnt the method of IV from Geary (1948), following closely the time-series analysis

[13] In a letter to the author on 11 January 1988, Klein wrote, 'There is no doubt at all that the instrumental variable method was well known and discussed at the Cowles Commission during 1945–7. We discussed it in connection with Wald's method of fitting equations when both variables are subject to error. We also discussed it in connection with Geary's paper on errors of observation, which was published a bit later.'

tradition. This standpoint apparently offered him a broad perspective, when he decided to enquire further into the IV method. He was especially interested in the relationship between it and Anderson and Rubin's LIML method (cf. Phillips 1985). Sargan grasped the similarity of ideas implied in the IV methods proposed by Geary and Reiersøl, and the LIML method. He saw that the method of IV was a more general approach than commonly recognized. Inspired by Durbin (1954), he realized that IV could be used to estimate models which combined measurement errors in the Cowles framework on the one hand (1958), and extend the framework to the time-series formulation on the other hand (1959). The major task of Sargan's work on IV was to dispel the misbelief of arbitrariness in the choice of IVs. He developed his arguments using a generalized simultaneous-equations model with measurement errors (1958), and later with autocorrelated errors (1959). He proved that the existence of choice for IV indicated generality of the method rather than arbitrariness, by showing (*a*) that there existed an optimum IV estimator, which could be obtained by means of Hotelling's canonical correlation since the best IV should be designed with maximum correlation with the original variables and minimum correlation with the error terms; and (*b*) that the optimum IV estimator was equivalent to a LIML estimator, and was of wider use in that the former could use either predetermined variables or exogenous variables outside the model, whereas the latter could not use outside variables and were often biased in the presence of large measurement errors. Sargan also provided a summary, based on his own experience, concerning the application of the method of IV in actual empirical work.

As mentioned above, Sargan employed the technique of canonical correlation in obtaining the optimum IV. The technique was soon adapted to a larger scale in the simultaneous-equations framework (e.g. in Hooper 1959). It was suggested that canonical correlation methods should be used to calculate the correlation coefficients between the explanatory variables and all the dependent variables in simultaneous-equations estimation, since in a strict statistical sense, regression should always be complemented by some measurement of the extent to which the estimated systematic relationships could explain the movement of the dependent variables. Note that the adaptation of canonical correlation into econometrics this time served solely for the purpose of estimation, instead of variable reduction, for which it had first been designed.

On the other hand, the method of principal components, which had been consigned to limbo, was revived in the 1960s when the technique was recommended to tackle the problem of multicollinearity, following a proposal by a statistician Kendall (1961), e.g. in Johnson *et al.* (1973). But like the case of canonical correlation method, the inspiration of empirical discovery from data by statistical means, for which that method had first been introduced into econometrics, had already disappeared.

The basic theory of estimation had been completed by the end of the 1950s. The principle of ML had provided estimation with a solid theoretical foundation, linking it with model formulation, specification, and identification into a logically consistent modelling process. In particular, the concept of FIML provided the general logic for the whole procedure of parameter estimation for a system of interdependent variables, while the concept of LIML clarified the logic of estimating single relations with a simultaneous-equations system lying underneath. The principle of IV, on the other hand, had furnished the general guidelines for approaching estimation problems in various circumstances. Finally, the methods developed around the LS principle in combination with the IV method had pointed out ways that could always be sought out in econometric practice to reduce the estimation procedure into some simple LS formulations. Theoretical developments in the subsequent decade largely played the role of supplementing and substantiating the technical aspects of the basic estimation theory.

However, the problem concerning the correct choice of estimation methods in applied modelling had not yet been solved, because the choice turned out to depend largely upon the correct choice of model forms. Debates over this issue will be described in Chapter 6. Prior to that, there are two other issues, which lie actually between the two choices, to be reported: the issue about the possibility of finding the correct coefficient estimates for given structural relations (Chapter 4) and the issue about the use of these estimates for inferring the correctness of the relations (Chapter 5).

4

Identification[1]

The issue of identification stemmed from the quest to know the attainability of economically meaningful relationships from statistical analysis of economic data in early estimation attempts. It arose out of the 'correspondence' problems 'between economic activity, the data that activity generates, the theoretical economic model and the estimated relationship' (Morgan 1990: 162). There were actually two layers of the correspondence in question: the correspondence of the estimated statistical relationships with the theoretical relationships of interest, and then the correspondence of the statistically estimable theoretical relationships with the relationships generally recognized as 'true'. As the issue was separated out from the realm of estimation to form the topic of identification, the second layer was detached from it and fell into the realm of hypothesis-testing. When identification theory was eventually formalized, its purpose became focused on essentializing the conditions under which a certain set of values of structural parameters could be uniquely determined from the data among all the permissible sets embodied in a mathematically complete theoretical model, usually composed of a simultaneous-equations system. These conditions are most commonly known as the order and rank conditions in the context of linear, simultaneous-equations models in present-day econometrics textbooks. On the other hand, the emergence of identification theory played a key role in the formal establishment of the structural approach of orthodox econometrics, through its links to model testing and model specification. Only, this aspect of the theory has been appreciated far less in the textbooks. This chapter traces the formalization of identification theory around two interwoven themes: how the identification

[1] This chapter is based on Qin (1989).

problem was perceived and described in connection with the other issues in modelling; and how the problem was formalized and tackled with mathematical and statistical means. Section 4.1 outlines the early appearance of the identification problem and some *ad hoc* solutions for particular cases and model forms before the mid-1930s; Section 4.2 centres upon the initial systematic work on the issue around 1940; Section 4.3 is devoted to the contribution of the Cowles group; the completion of the theoretical framework and its overlaps with other modelling issues form the subject of Section 4.4.

4.1 TAKING SHAPE[2]

As seen from Chapter 3, correspondence problems constituted the main concern in estimation discussions during the early days of econometrics. Conceptually, there were serious apprehensions among early econometricians concerning whether statistical estimation could lead to the desired relationships derived from non-mathematical economic theory, and whether statistical estimation could help to discover true economic relationships, possibly through verification of some hypothetical theories. Technically, the lack of a guaranteed unique solution was discovered quite early on from empirical demand curving-fitting, i.e. a definite demand curve could not always be found from the regression results. For example, the problem was discussed in the works of Lehfeldt, Lenoir, and Moore as described in Morgan (1990). The issue of identification emerged as a combination of this technical difficulty with the former conceptual aspect of the correspondence problem and gradually settled on the possibility of uniquely determining the parameter values of an a priori theoretical model from statistical estimation. Meanwhile, the issues concerning the 'truth' of the relationships of interest remained with the bulk of applied econometric modelling, aiming at verifying the theory provided it was identifiable.[3]

---

[2] There is a chapter on the early development of correspondence (identification) problems in Morgan (1990). The present chapter makes frequent references to Morgan's work in respect to those very early facts.
[3] See Ch. 5 on hypothesis-testing for this aspect of locating true theoretical relations with respect to reality. It was several decades later that this aspect of

In fact, early discussions of the identification problem were in a muddled state, because terminologies varied and also because it was often treated in conjunction with other modelling problems. Although early applied workers seldom failed to take note of the problem since the day when Moore had mistaken his unintentionally estimated supply curve of pig-iron for the intended demand curve (1914), their opinions over the cause of the problem differed and the methods proposed were *ad hoc* (see Morgan 1990). The problem was most often discussed in the context of using one set of quantity and price time-series data to estimate the theoretical theme of an interdependent system of supply and demand equations. The simplest case would be:

$$D = \alpha_0 + \alpha_1 P \qquad (4.1)$$

$$S = \beta_0 + \beta_1 P \qquad (4.2)$$

under the assumption of constant elasticities. As denoted commonly, D (demand), S (supply), and P were the (usual) log forms of the actual quantities and price. In statistical estimation, the theme became:

$$D = \alpha_0 + \alpha_1 P + u \qquad (4.1')$$

$$S = \beta_0 + \beta_1 P + v, \qquad (4.2')$$

where u and v were errors. Obviously, only the coefficients of one equation could be estimated in the above model and there was a difficulty in deciding to which equation the one fitted regression line should correspond. At the time, there was no dispute over the attribution of this difficulty to discrepancies between theory and practice, or a problem of identifying 'statistically determined demand curves' 'with theoretical demand curves' (Working 1925). Disagreements came with the further explanations and prescriptions. Many assigned the problem to an estimation problem caused by inaccurate data, and concentrated on classifying and handling the data, as for example in the works of the Working brothers. Their prescription was that the regression line be identified with the curve which exhibited

correspondence problems was discussed again under the term of 'identification' in economic time-series analysis (see Box and Jenkins 1970). However, identification theory thus defined falls outside the period of examination here.

far less shift or 'variability' than the other (i.e. Variance(u) being much smaller than Variance(v) or vice versa). But indeterminacy would clearly arise in the case of equal shifts or no shifts of the two (e.g. see Schultz 1930). This led to the suggestion of using additional information to make up for the data insufficiency (e.g. Wright 1928).[4] Such a suggestion implied that the trouble was due to an inadequately formulated theoretical model rather than estimation of inaccurate data. For instance, the demand and supply curves could be determined if the model was specified as:

$$D_t = \alpha_0 + \alpha_1 P_t + u_t \tag{4.3}$$

$$S_t = \beta_0 + \beta_1 P_{t-1} + v_t \tag{4.4}$$

$$D_t = S_t. \tag{4.5}$$

Such type of models appeared in the works of Moore and Ezekiel (see Morgan 1990), and later became known as the 'cobweb' model.

This approach was elaborated by Tinbergen in 1930. As mentioned in the previous chapter, Tinbergen actually derived the reduced form of a two-equation demand-and-supply model in his ILS estimation. By doing so, he was able to illustrate how extra information was required to calculate the theoretical relations of demand and supply respectively from the estimates of the statistical (reduced-form) relations. He added new variables to the two theoretical equations separately to achieve the unique solution of all the theoretical parameters from the reduced-form parameter estimates.

Theorization of the identification problem started in the 1930s, and soon became a central topic in the whole formative movement of econometrics.[5] This was due, on the one hand, to the intimate connection to economic theory that early econo-

---

[4] To solve the problem, Wright (1928) devised a method called 'path analysis', which essentially employed instrumental variables as the additional information (see Epstein 1989). It also preceded Simon's method of causal ordering in the 1950s (see Sect. 4.4). However, the method received little notice in econometric circles.

[5] Samuelson recalled, 'The problem of identification that arose in the early 1930s in connection with demand–supply curves also arose in the late 1930s after the Keynesian revolution, in connection with the question of how to measure a saving schedule and an investment schedule. . . . There was lots of confusion in people's minds. Identification was a very lively topic at the time' (Qin 1988a).

metricians were keen to have with their statistical analyses. On the other hand, the identification problem seemed to offer a tantalizing way to rid economic theory of its unrealistic *ceteris paribus* pillar. At the same time, enquiries into the problem cultivated the division between the aspect of correspondence with respect to a priori formulated theoretical relationships, and that of correspondence with respect to 'true' relationships. They also helped to draw increasing attention to the statistical representation of the interdependency property in economics, which led eventually to the simultaneous-equations modelling.

R. Frisch was the forerunner in the formalization of identification theory. He was among the first to view the identification problem as arising from the desire to 'approach a statistical material with the object of determining numerically the constants of certain theoretical laws that we have worked out *a priori*' (Frisch 1933*b*). As stated in the previous chapters, Frisch set up a structural modelling procedure, in which the identification problem was classified into one of the 'two fundamental inversion problems', i.e. the problem of how to obtain unique estimates of the structural parameters of interest in a linear model form of a 'weight system' (Frisch 1936) (the other problem was essentially concerned with 'multicollinearity'). From the 'inversion' angle, Frisch tended to tackle the two problems together, or even ascribe identification to multicollinearity, in developing his statistical methods.

As described earlier, the errors-in-variables model formed the basis for Frisch to contrive his apparatus of confluence analysis (Frisch 1934). In the errors-in-variables context, Frisch's explanation for the cause of the identification problem was: theoretical ('true') variables were latent and behaved in accordance with a certain deterministic mechanism of often interdependent nature; people could only get indirect observations of them with some errors, e.g. measurement errors; and these errors might block the way to discover the mechanism statistically. Therefore, he turned his investigation to the identification condition of a single bivariate equation with errors in variables of the simple form:

$$Y_t = \alpha X_t + \beta \qquad (4.6)$$

$$X_t = x_t - \varepsilon_t \qquad t = 1, \ldots, T \qquad (4.7)$$

$$Y_t = y_t - \delta_t, \qquad (4.8)$$

where X, Y were the 'true' latent variables, x, y their observed values, and ε_t, δ_t their measurement errors. Frisch reduced the identification condition for α and β, i.e. the condition of α and β being uniquely estimable, to having known variances and covariance, i.e. the variance and covariance matrix, of ε_t and δ_t. His diagonal regression method of estimation was based upon this condition (see Chapter 3). Using the same explanation, Frisch criticized as 'fundamentally unsound' Leontief's method of estimating simultaneously demand and supply curves, for it might end up with coefficients 'determined essentially by the random disturbances in the material' (Frisch 1933b, cf. Morgan 1990, ch. 6). In this paper, Frisch extended the above model to a general two-equations simultaneous system, on the basis of a simple demand–supply model, and imposed certain assumptions (as a kind of precondition) about the values of the variances and covariances (the shifts) of the error terms to ensure the model identification. This method simply formalized the *ad hoc* practice of watching the different degrees of shifts in data developed by E. J. Working and others.

These assumptions were retained in Koopmans's attempts to accommodate Frisch's diagonal regression with Fisher's ordinary regression theory in establishing his weighted regression method (Koopmans 1937) (see Chapter 3). However, Koopmans was aware of the unreality in assuming that the ratios of the variances and covariances of the disturbances in his model were '*a priori* given', just for the purpose of ensuring the estimability of the parameters (p. 61). Leaving the problem open, Koopmans chose to put the imposition of such an assumption in the section of 'specification'.

Subsequently, R. Allen (1939) demonstrated that assuming as given the values of two of the three parameters—the standard deviations of the two variables' errors and their correlation coefficient—was a condition for consistent estimation of a two-variable linear regression equation. By 1940, it was generally accepted to be a 'common feature' that 'the fitted straight line [of variables subject to errors] cannot be determined without a priori assumptions (independent of the observations) regarding the weights of the errors' (Wald 1940). In order to circumvent these unrealistic assumptions, Wald contrived a *de facto* IV estimator to create the required amount of additional information (see Chapter 3, Section 4). Reiersøl (1941) proposed to achieve the identifiability of structural coefficients through the less arbitrary rank condition on the matrix of second moments of the disturbances under certain assumptions, in an effort to improve Frisch's confluence analysis. Both Wald's and Reiersøl's results strengthened the position of treating identification as part of estimation. However, by then the major interest in econometric modelling had been moving away from the errors-in-variables model towards simultaneous-equations models with errors in equations.

Tinbergen's pioneering work in applied macro-modelling in the late 1930s enhanced Frisch's interest in seeking a general solution to the identification problem in a simultaneous-equations system. Instead of making assumptions about the fluctuation (variances and covariances) of the data, Frisch sought to establish certain general conditions of identification, and in so doing he brought about a substantial advance in understanding and handling the problem (Frisch 1938).

Although the term 'identification' was never mentioned, nor was the problem singled out completely, the ideas conveyed in Frisch's 1938 paper contained many of the basic principles of the identification theory, and greatly motivated its formal emergence. For example, in the famous Cowles Monograph 10, Koopmans, Rubin, and Leipnik acknowledged that 'the first systematic discussion of the problem of identification was given by Frisch' in his 1938 paper (Koopmans 1950: 69). The ideas in this paper can be summed up in the following way. First, Frisch advocated a thorough enquiry about the 'delicate' connection between 'the relations we work with in theory and those we get by fitting curves to actual statistical data' (p. 2). He put forth a number of definitions to facilitate the enquiry, the most noticeable of them being 'structure' (see Chapter 1). Next, Frisch examined particularly the mathematical property of coefficient determinability in the form of a general linear lag-equations model. He designated the case when coefficients could be uniquely determined 'irreducibility' and the converse 'reducibility'. He chose the exponential function to specify the x's (variables) of the lag-equations, and worked out a general criterion for reducibility in terms of the rank condition of a matrix whose elements were deduced from the exponential function. Then he classified all equations into 'coflux' equations and 'superflux' equations according to the irreducibility and reducibility of their coefficients with respect to the set of x's involved. Finally, Frisch put forward a very important notion about the nature of passive observations, namely, 'the investigator is restricted to observing what happens *when all equations in a large determinate system are actually fulfilled simultaneously*'. He observed that such passive observations in consequence precluded investigators from discovering these equations 'unless they happen to be coflux equations' (p. 15).

Noticeably, Frisch still attributed the identification problem to a data problem. He saw that lack of identification occurred frequently with structural models of simultaneous-equations systems, and that the mathematical nature of identification was coefficient determinability (reducible or irreducible). However, he considered the cause of indeterminability being that the data series were only passively observed and might be highly correlated. His rank method was designed to examine essentially whether the data exhibited multicollinearity. Although it premissed implicitly a certain configuration of the structural model concerned, the method was not devised to locate that model feature separately. In his non-mathematical discussion, Frisch did notice that statistically discovered equations should be coflux equations (implying that they were always identifiable in principle), and that coflux equations were not always the desired structural equations, whereas he failed to incorporate this point into his rank condition. The condition was applied indiscriminately to both structural and statistical (reduced-form) equations alike.

4.2 Initial Systematization

A formal identification theory for a general simultaneous-equations system was on the edge of realization after Frisch's 1938 memorandum. An insightful breakthrough was made by Marschak (1942) in an article entitled 'Economic Interdependence and Statistical Analysis' in memory of Henry Schultz (written in March 1940). Marschak put the whole identification issue explicitly in the context of variable simultaneity. He believed that 'the single empirical equations are less useful or necessary for the empirical analysis of the system' (p. 136). He observed 'that complete clarity on the [identification] subject is certainly still far from universal and that a systematic and elementary treatment may be of some use if only to point out where the unsolved questions seem to lie' (p. 140). Drawing upon the analyses of both the a priori information methods and the reducibility method by previous econometricians, Marschak raised two questions concerning the identification of a system of *m* equations with unrestricted functional forms: (*a*) Which equations in the system had 'the relatively stable parameters' (or were 'identifiable')? (*b*) What were the conditions making possible the 'evaluation' of the parameters in those identifiable equations? Marschak pointed out that although the answer to the first question depended on additional sources of information, e.g. variable variability, they often implied making extra assumptions additional to the information contained in the data used in deriving the equations. He then stated that the answer to the second question rested on 'the nature of the theoretical system itself', because 'whatever the number of observations as compared with the number of parameters', it was possible that 'some of the sets of the observation equations become dependent and therefore indeterminate' (pp. 140–4). He employed the vanishing of a Jacobian determinant (each element of which was a partial derivative of one of the equations with respect to one of its parameters) to examine this indeterminacy. To distinguish those additional restrictions from the nature of a model, Marschak classified his discussion on the two questions under two separate headings: 'Variate Parameters' and 'Lost Dimensions'.

Evidently, Marschak came quite close to the heart of the identification problem despite his inexact description of the whole concept. He narrowed down the scope of enquiry set by Frisch, and outlined the subject more explicitly. He subdivided identification into two separate issues: one, which he took as identification and was assigned to model formulation, was essentially related to what was later known as the order criterion of identification; the other, assigned to estimation, was to the rank criterion. In his view, while additional information was needed irrespective of the number of observations, it was not always sufficient to possess only such information for identification, without imposing other conditions on the system itself. Marschak's analysis carried in embryo the ideas of formalizing two separate (necessary and sufficient) identification conditions, as in the standard identification theory of present textbooks, which was about to emerge.

Concurrent with Marschak's solutions to identification, Haavelmo worked out a formal mathematical explanation for the identification problem in a paper called 'The Problem of Testing Economic Theories by Means of Passive Observations', which was delivered at the 1940 Cowles Commission conference. Noticeably, this title suggested that Haavelmo's early conception of the problem was connected to the testability as well as the estimability of economic theory from data. He explained the problem as arising from the question: 'Can we measure economic structure relations (e.g. individual indifference surfaces or other "behavioristic" relations) by means of data which satisfy simultaneously a whole network of such relations, i.e. data obtained by a "passive watching of the game" and not by planned experiments?' Haavelmo went directly to structural models of 'exact equation systems' in the following general form of m equations, n variables, and k parameters:

$$f_i(x_1, \ldots, x_m, x_{m+1}, \ldots, x_n; \alpha_1, \ldots, \alpha_k)$$
$$i = 1, \ldots, m \qquad\qquad (4.9)$$

under the assumption that (4.9) had a unique solution for m variables $(x_1, \ldots, x_m)$ for given sets of the α's:

$$x_i = \phi_i(x_{m+1}, \ldots, x_n; \alpha_1, \ldots, \alpha_k) \qquad i = 1, \ldots, m. \quad (4.10)$$

Haavelmo then put the identification problem into one of seeking the 'sufficient conditions for the uniqueness of the α's with respect to the [observed data] set $S(\alpha^0)$'. One of such conditions that he found was the linear independence among the first derivatives:

$$\frac{\partial \phi_i}{\partial \alpha_1}, \frac{\partial \phi_i}{\partial \alpha_2}, \ldots, \frac{\partial \phi_i}{\partial \alpha_k}, \qquad i = 1, \ldots, m \qquad (4.11)$$

for all values of the α's. This approach to the problem bore an obvious resemblance to Frisch's approach shown in his 1938 memorandum. The most remarkable point was that Haavelmo retained Frisch's viewpoint of a deterministic structural model even though he had by then moved considerably towards a probabilistic stand, as shown in Chapter 1. The only difference was that Haavelmo excluded statistical relations in his discussion of identification conditions.

Haavelmo extended his idea in the above paper in his 1944 monograph (Haavelmo 1944). His insightful discussion on the probabilistic viewpoint furnished him with a general logical base for his earlier explanation that the main cause of the identification problem was due to the passive position of economists with respect to economic phenomena, and the stochastic nature of the generating mechanism of economic data. Haavelmo elaborated this further: in order to test whether observational variables correspond to theoretical variables, a theoretical model was needed, with which 'a corresponding system of quantities or objects in real economic life' must be identified through observed relations, to define 'one particular theoretical structure of the economy' (p. 8); however, economists did not have the power to control and manipulate economic performance so as to get their desired amount of observations to enable them to do this; therefore, an explicit set of conditions was needed specifying in what circumstances the desired identification was guaranteed; furthermore, the fact that an economic structure was not forever invariant suggested that it was desirable for economists always to know the structures, and hence to have an identification theory, to enable them to produce from observations better explanations of the causes of facts and better predictions of the future.

Haavelmo treated the identification problem formally in the fifth chapter of the monograph. There, he undertook 'a very general discussion of one central problem in identification: the formulation of conditions under which all structural relations of the system can be identified' (Koopmans 1950: 70). Haavelmo ascribed the identification problem to the 'problem of confluent relations (or the problem of arbitrary parameters)', which had 'particular significance in the field of econometrics, and relevant to the very construction of economic models' and which formed one of 'the two fundamental problems of estimation in economic research' (the other one was the problem of best estimates). He considered the solution to identification as 'a problem of pure mathematics' (Haavelmo 1944: 91–2). His mathematical deduction followed essentially the procedure of his 1940 paper. He started from a general function similar to (4.9), with an additional assumption that all the x's were independent variables. The identification problem was transformed into determining the least number k of parameters the values of which could be uniquely obtained (assuming that there could be more than k parameters). Haavelmo then went through the same route of employing the inverse functions (4.10) to convert the determination of k into the condition that a corresponding Jacobian determinant (made of the elements of (4.11)) should be non-vanishing in order to obtain a non-singular mapping from the parametric space on to the state space. Determination of this condition was related to that of the number of linearly independent functions by an extension of the Gramian criterion, which was thought to be a common and feasible way in practice. Haavelmo's derivation shaped the way for the eventual systematization of identification theory by Koopmans *et al.* (see the next section), who believed that their own work could be obtained 'as a specialization of Haavelmo's results' (Koopmans 1950: 70).

Haavelmo concluded his discussion with an illustration of his theorems by a simple supply–demand model (Haavelmo 1944: 99–102). He first transformed his structural model into a reduced form (without calling it such) and then set up indirect estimation equations of the structural parameters and the joint probability density function of the endogenous variables, all in terms of the transformed (reduced-form) parameters. Without checking, he inferred that there existed a one-to-one correspondence between the seven original (structural) parameters and the seven transformed (reduced-form) ones, and hence the former would be identifiable if the latter were shown to possess unique values. So he applied his condition of linear independence to the derivative functions of the reduced-form parameters and verified that all of them were determinable in general with respect to the variable data set.

The illustration reveals that apparently Haavelmo still muddled up the model aspect with the data aspect of the identification problem. He did not seem to realize the property that the reduced-form parameters should always be uniquely estimable in theory. His application of his theorems amounted essentially to checking what is known as the rank condition of identification. Since the multicollinear problem had not then been un-ravelled from the identification problem, Haavelmo was natur-ally drawn more towards the data aspect than the model aspect of identification (cf. Aldrich 1991).[6] This explains why he chose to discuss the problem in the chapter on estimation.

A clearer view of the relation between structural forms and reduced forms with respect to the model aspect of identification was provided by Mann and Wald in a general system of linear simultaneous equations (1943). Mann and Wald still considered the problem under the category of estimation. They realized that reduced-form parameters could generally be evaluated uniquely, while problems arose in determining parameters of the 'original' (structural) equations. They found it 'impossible to have con-sistent estimates for all the unknown parameters' when two (structural) systems were not distinguishable in form from each other on the basis of empirical observations. In such cases, they suggested that reduced forms should be used because the reduced-form parameters were generally always estimable from the observations. To demonstrate the advantages of the reduced-form method, they gave examples using two models discussed a little earlier by Haavelmo (1943b). Haavelmo's first model was a general stochastic system:

$$Y = \alpha X + \varepsilon_1 \qquad (4.12)$$

$$X = \beta Y + \varepsilon_2. \qquad (4.13)$$

His second model was an investment and consumption system:

$$u_t = \alpha r_t + \beta + \varepsilon_{1t} \qquad (4.14)$$

$$v_t = k(u_t - u_{t-1}) + \varepsilon_{2t} \qquad (4.15)$$

$$r_t = u_t + v_t \qquad (4.16)$$

(u: consumption, v: investment, and r: total income). Haavelmo used the models only to demonstrate the inconsistency of the least-squares estimates in contrast to the consistent maximum-likelihood estimates. He neglected the identification aspect of

[6] I thought that it was 'misleading' of Haavelmo to check identifiability on the reduced form instead of the structural form, since reduced forms were always identifiable by the textbook identification criteria (Qin 1989). Later, Aldrich (1991) rightly points out that Haavelmo was not unjustified in doing so, with respect to the fact that the multicollinearity problem was still entangled in the identification problem at the time.

the models. Mann and Wald showed that the first model was unidentifiable unless additional knowledge was available or assumed, such as the identical variances of the errors, because there were four unknown structural parameters with only three reduced-form parameters estimable. In contrast, they showed that the second model had seven reduced-form parameters to be estimated against only five structural parameters. Additional restrictions were needed in this case to prevent excess information being arbitrarily discarded in the process of moving from the reduced form to the original (structural) system. Remarkably, these examples provide a clear-cut picture of the differences between what became labelled as 'under'-, 'exact'-, and 'over'-identification later.

4.3 The First Explicit Formalization

In spite of their innovative endeavour, neither Marschak nor Haavelmo unravelled and solved the identification issue completely. The task was carried on by the Cowles Commission group in the mid-1940s (Koopmans 1950). The major work was accomplished by Koopmans, Hurwicz, and Wald. The initiation of a systematic study of identification as a separate issue was due to Koopmans, who, jointly with Rubin and Leipnik, set up criteria using a priori information to 'determine the identifiability of equations in linear systems'. 'Hurwicz and Wald further clarified the identification problem in logical and mathematical terms' (Christ 1952: 36–7).

Koopmans *et al.* provided the first explication of the nature of the identification problem in terms of the present terminology. They argued that if a linear system of difference equations 'is viewed only as a mathematical specification of the joint probability distribution of the observable variables, it can be written in many different ways' which would be mathematically equivalent, and which they called different 'representations'. If representations had the same probability distributions of variables, they were 'observationally equivalent' and could not be distinguished even employing 'the best that can be expected from statistical methods'. 'The distribution of the variables can be looked upon as determining the set of all observationally equivalent representations of it, and is completely defined by any of these representations. From a mathematical point of view, it is immaterial which representation is employed, except that it will be desirable to choose a simple one. In terms of economics, however, different representations of the same system are not at all equivalent.' From the economic point of view, it was 'important' to have the equation system 'in a form in which the greatest possible number of its equations can be identified and recognized as structural equations', because any one of them, according to theory, could be changed independently (Koopmans 1950: 62–3). They argued further that since identification theory dealt with the unique determination of structural equations or the 'unambiguous definition' of the parameters of these equations to be estimated, identification in fact was 'a logical problem that precedes estimation. It is therefore not a problem in statistical inference, but an a priori problem arising in the specification and interpretation of the probability distribution of the variables. As such it deserves separate classification' (p. 70).

Koopmans *et al.* translated the above ideas into formal mathematical terms. They demonstrated that in order to achieve identification, one had to impose on the general structural system various restrictions according to a priori knowledge and information in addition to those from economic theory. Under the independence assumptions similar to those used by Haavelmo, they first established a number of theorems on the necessary and sufficient conditions for identifiability of one structural equation in the system under linear restrictions (i.e. zero restrictions on single parameters and restrictions of linear dependence on two or more parameters in the same equations). The sufficient condition for a single equation was formulated in terms of the rank condition of a submatrix of parameters (obtained by deleting from the parametric matrix of the system the row of the one equation to be identified), which corresponded to the absent variables in that one equation. This contained an essential and necessary condition concerning the number (or order) of independent restrictions imposed on parameters of that equation. Thus they established the basic rank and order conditions for identification in standard, present-day textbooks. Next, they examined the situation where not all equations of the system could be identified. To achieve identifiability, they suggested the imposition of linear dummy restrictions to supplement the insufficient number of independent a priori restrictions of the structural models constructed according to certain economic theories, provided that these dummy restrictions did not eliminate the observed variables from the original probability distribution. They then extended their analyses to other types of restrictions, such as bilinear restrictions and linear dependence restrictions on the distributions of disturbances. However, no general conditions for these circumstances were derived. Finally, they set out a number of problems requiring further discussion.

Koopmans *et al.* also classified three types of identification as 'unique', 'multiple', and 'incomplete' in terms of a transformation matrix (which represented relations among observably equivalent structures), with respect to part of a model. When the matrix was a unit matrix, the identification was defined as unique in that there were no other structures equivalent to the one identified. The label of multiple identification was applied to cases where there were a finite number of different transformation matrices (to represent a finite number of observational equations). When the number became infinite, identification was said to be incomplete. Both unique and multiple identification were called complete identification. This classification corresponds to exact-, over-, and under-identification respectively in the current terminology.

Although their paper relied mainly on linear algebra, it is not easy to read since it used many complicated symbols, often denoted by several subscripts and superscripts. Wald made an effort to generalize their results (1950). In his very succinct note, he went straight to the mathematical nature of the identification problem bypassing all its econometric content. Although he considered the problem essentially as one of the existence of an inverse function, as Haavelmo had done, Wald apparently viewed identification more from the data and statistical side than from the side of an 'inverted' deterministic equation system. He included in the a priori identifying restrictions not only variable coefficients but also variances and covariances. By putting them together, these variable coefficients, variances, and covariances were treated more as statistical moments of distribution functions than as parameters of ordinary functions. He deduced two lemmas to show the invariance property of certain functions of these moments in undergoing admissible transformations (i.e. transformations that left the a priori restrictions intact). Then he converted the identification problem into one of invariance of certain functions of the moments in such transformations and proved the equivalence of these functions with those in the lemmas. Finally he related the number of unknown variable coefficients to the number of a priori restrictions and established an identification condition in terms of the rank condition of the Jacobian matrix concerned under some assumptions, in a similar approach to that of Marschak and Haavelmo.

Unlike Koopmans and Wald who concentrated on identification conditions, Hurwicz centred his attention on the concept of identification, and expressed it in formal mathematical language, to help in 'clarifying the logic of the identification problems' (Hurwicz 1950: 246). His clarification covered three aspects: the general concept of identification in relation to models, the classification of different degrees of identification, and the function of a priori conditions. Hurwicz maintained that identifiability was an intrinsic attribute of a model 'entirely independent of any sampling aspects of structural estimation' (p. 257). He used the term 'identification power' to denote the attribute (p. 245). He defined a model $\mathfrak{G}_0$ as 'an a priori postulated class of structures S that is a proper subset of the class $\mathfrak{G}$ of all structures', generating the cumulative probability distribution G of the observed variables. Since G could be regarded as 'produced by an operation (usually a transformation) $\mathfrak{F}$ performed on the distribution F of the (non-observable) disturbance', structures, therefore, could be represented as $S = (F, \mathfrak{F})$ (pp. 247–8). However, since in general, G might be generated by more than one structure, structural estimation through G to obtain S depended on the identification power of the particular model formulated.

This approach to explain identification in terms of the identification power of a model has two immediate implications. It is essential to build an identifiable model for the purpose of prediction when the structure is subject to change; and it is important to distinguish identification from estimation: the former is concerned with the possibility of getting a unique S from a G and the latter deals with the problem of how to get the best value of G from a given sample.

Similarly to Koopmans, Hurwicz classified the identification power of a model into the three categories of 'unique', 'multiple', and 'incomplete'. But instead of distinguishing them from the transformation matrix, he directly used the number of structures for the definition, which was closer to the heart of the problem. He described as 'uniquely identifying' models that possessed 'the property that for any element G_1' in the class of all G's generated by the elements of the model, 'there exists *one and only one* S_1' in the model 'such that S_1 generates G_1'. If there existed more than one such structure S_1 generating the same G_1 in the model, but the number was 'finite or denumerably infinite', the model was called multiply identifying (Hurwicz 1950: 249). When the number of such structures became 'nondenumerable infinity' (p. 256), the model was incompletely identifying. As before, uniquely identifying models and multiple identifying models were grouped as models with 'complete identification power' (p. 248).

Finally, Hurwicz turned to distinguish identification from specification. A priori conditions comprising 'identifying restrictions' and criteria were regarded as provisional means to help originally specified but incompletely identifying models to achieve identification. Identifying restrictions were 'additional assumptions' 'with regard to S' for the purpose of 'narrowing down' the model $\mathfrak{S}_0$ to 'a proper subset' of it (p. 248). Criteria established a priori facilitated the originally observably indistinguishable structures in a model to become distinguishable, by partitioning the class of 'all structures into a system of nonoverlapping subclasses' (p. 253).

Hurwicz's distinction was simply a formal way of saying that only those conditions which were added to the usual specification of given theoretical models purely for the sake of securing unique solutions were counted as identification conditions. His definition of 'identifying restrictions' furnished the logical base for the design of overidentification tests by Anderson and Rubin (see Chapter 5). There was no dispute that these a priori imposed restrictions should be tested if possible. However, there was some dispute when the identification issue was further discussed in connection to the question 'when is an equation system complete for statistical purposes?' (Koopmans 1950: 393–409) (see Chapter 2). In trying to answer that question, Koop-

mans discussed the link between identification and the specification of exogenous and predetermined variables, and found
certain equivalence between the two (pp. 408–9). The message
contained in his discussion was provoking. If specifying conditions
for model completion were equivalent to identifying restrictions,
then they should not be taken for granted and exempted from
statistical tests. This was particularly important for the situation
where specification involved adding to structural models uncertain restrictions not implied in the given economic theories
of interest. But the message was deeply concealed by the formalization of identification theory as a separate step posed between
model specification and estimation. With the classification of
identifying restrictions and the technical criteria in terms of
order and rank conditions, the a priori formulated structural
model could safely retain its image of generality and fundament-
ality in estimation and hypothesis-testing, as already mentioned
in Chapter 2.

4.4 FURTHER DEVELOPMENTS

The identification conditions developed so far had been basically
formalized in non-probability mathematics. Their connection to
statistical inference was only lightly suggested in Wald and
Hurwicz's works. On the other hand, development of identification tests entailed a new version of the conditions that should
be consistent with the principle of hypothesis-testing and estimation, and hence with the whole probability approach. Work in
this direction was chiefly pushed forward by Reiersøl, initially
by his explicit formulation of identification conditions in the
context of errors-in-variables models (Reiersøl 1950 (written in
1948)). Reiersøl's model ran like this:

$$y_2 = \beta y_1 + \beta_0 \qquad (4.17)$$

$$x_1 = y_1 + v_1 \qquad v_1 \sim N(0, \sigma_1^2) \qquad (4.18)$$

$$x_2 = y_2 + v_2 \qquad v_2 \sim N(0, \sigma_2^2), \qquad (4.19)$$

where x_i were observed values of the true variables y_i. A struc-
ture was represented by a set of values β, β_0; σ_1^2 and σ_2^2 were
the variances of v_1 and v_2 respectively; $\sigma_{12} = \text{cov}(v_1, v_2)$ and
the logarithm of the characteristic function of y_1: $\psi_{y_1}(t)$.

Reiersøl deduced the distribution functions of the variables and their moments by means of characteristic functions, and determined the identification conditions in four theorems under the assumptions of joint normal distribution of the errors and of independent error distributions respectively. The conditions were found to be closely connected with the distribution form (normal or otherwise) of y_1 and y_2, hence x_1 and x_2, and the conditions of v_1, v_2.

Reiersøl's analysis of the identification conditions called econometricians' attention to the identifiability of the parameters of the distribution functions of the disturbances (e.g. their moments), and consequently to the influence of the stochastic elements embodied in probability models on the commonly accepted order and rank conditions for identification. Reiersøl's results gave an immediate inspiration to Koopmans, who was seeking ways to further generalize the identification issue.[7] Jointly, they established the formal link of the identification concept with statistical inference in a paper 'The Identification of Structural Characteristics' (Koopmans and Reiersøl 1950).[8]

Koopmans and Reiersøl highlighted the statistical aspect of the identification problem with the help of the concept of distribution functions. Previously, this aspect had been obscured to a certain degree, first by regarding the identification problem as arising from 'inversion' of the latent deterministic system of theoretical equations, then by demarcation of the identification analysis from estimation and by the rank and order conditions concerning only the coefficients of variables in simultaneous-equation systems. Koopmans and Reiersøl redefined identification, directly from the statistician's angle, as 'the problem of drawing inferences from the probability distribution of the observed variables to the very underlying structure'. They observed

---

[7] Reiersøl visited the Cowles Commission in 1947. He contributed a paper 'On the Identification Problem in Factor Analysis' to the Cowles Commission Discussion Papers (No. 303) at the same time that Koopmans submitted his draft of 'The Identification of Structural Characteristics' for discussion (No. 304). The second became a joint paper when finally published.

[8] Koopmans and Reiersøl's discussion extended beyond the econometric context. They acknowledged that the same problem had arisen in fields other than econometrics such as factor analysis and biometrics, which seemed to enable them to explore the nature of the problem more thoroughly and to generalize the theory further.

that identification was a 'general and fundamental problem arising, in many fields of inquiry, as a concomitant of the scientific procedure that postulates the existence of a structure'. In their formulation of the identification problem, they adopted the basic concepts set out by Hurwicz and expressed further the probability distribution of the observed variables y conditional on the structure S: $H(y \mid S)$ (equivalent to G in Hurwicz's paper). They also reformulated the concept of specification, according to Hurwicz's model concept, as 'specifying a model which by hypothesis contains the structure S generating the distribution H of the observed variables'. In this context, it became clear where the identification problem had stemmed from. The cause was a twofold one: on the one hand, what statistical inference could do at best was to attain, as closely as possible, 'an exact knowledge' of the distribution function $H(y \mid S)$ from the available sample—'Anything not implied in this distribution is not a possible object of statistical inference'; but on the other hand, while 'a given structure S generates one and only one probability distribution $H(y \mid S)$', the inverse was not true, i.e. there might be a one-to-many correspondence from H to S, e.g. $H(y \mid S) = H(y \mid S^*)$, $S \neq S^*$ for all y. Furthermore, the criteria for model specification excluded generally 'the desire for identifiability'. Thus identification theory came into its own right. In other words, 'identification problems are not problems of statistical inference in a strict sense' (the former: $H \to S$ and the latter: a sample of $y \to H$); but identification theory was to 'explore the limitations of statistical inference' (Koopmans and Reiersøl 1950).

Having sorted out the relations between identification and statistical inference, Koopmans and Reiersøl put forward their general themes of identification theory with noticeable emphasis on identifiability subject to statistical tests. In their formulation, identifiability of (or part of) a model was reduced to identifiability of (or some of) its structural characteristics $x(S)$ which encompassed structural parameters and non-parametric functional forms (following Hurwicz). A characteristic structure was defined as identifiable by a model if it maintained the same value in all structures equivalent to that structure. Each characteristic x thus divided all the structures of a model into 'two mutually exclusive subsets': one uniquely identifiable and the other not. Correspondingly, all the distribution functions $H(y \mid S)$ were divided in the same way. So in principle, identifiability of the characteristics could, in some cases, be achieved through tests of the distribution of the observations, e.g. to test the hypothesis that $H(y \mid S)$ belonged to the subset of identifiable distribution functions against the maintained hypothesis: $H(y) \in$ all S. Particularly, tests could be applied to a priori restrictions (termed 'particular specifications') which further narrowed down the set of distribution functions generated by S. The applicability of statistical tests to 'the pre-statistical analysis of identifiability' manifested the link of identification with statistical inference, in that identification of the characteristics depends not only on the model (necessary condition), but also on the actual components of the structures (sufficient condition), the evaluation of which depended totally on statistical estimation of observed data.

Koopmans and Reiersøl's paper expanded the ground for further research in identification theory in two directions. One was to explore more detailed technicalities of identification conditions in various circumstances. For instance, Koopmans formulated order and rank conditions with respect to reduced-form equations in support of the application of the indirect least-squares estimation method (1949b).[9] Many of the subsequent technical developments around the later 1950s and the early 1960s were the work of F. M. Fisher. For instance, he generalized the rank and order conditions under the cases of non-linear and non-homogeneous identifying restrictions (Fisher 1959). Later, he summarized various identification theorems in a monograph (1966).

The other direction was concerned with the link of identification restrictions to other modelling issues through discussions about how to specify and test these restrictions. This was anticipated by the shift of view from the structural system as a deterministic equation system to a stochastic one characterized by distribution functions. Structural parameters then became parameters or functions of the distribution functions. In his exposit-

---

[9] Koopmans completed this paper after his joint paper with Reiersøl (Koopmans and Reiersøl 1950), though the joint paper was published one year later. Koopmans frequently cited the joint paper in this paper.

ory paper to spread the newly established identification theory, Koopmans reiterated the viewpoint that the identifiability of any parameter should be regarded as 'a property of the distribution of the observations' (1949*b*). This was to say that all parameters should be viewed as parameters of distribution functions obeying certain statistical laws, instead of simply as coefficients of a deterministic simultaneous-equation system. Furthermore, he pointed out that the identifiability of these parameters should be 'subject to some suitable statistical test', and that 'the validity of this important conclusion is not limited to linear models'. This brought him to relate the choice and test of a priori identifying restrictions to the troublesome problem of model choice. Since a set of overidentification restrictions specified a priori could be tested, it should also be possible that any particular 'set of specifications' of a model, e.g. 'exclusion of any variable from any equation', be 'subject to statistical tests' for model choice, as long as the model remained identifiable. This again suggested that there was no essential difference between identifying restrictions and other conditions imposed on models in model building, as far as specification was concerned, and thus sowed suspicion about the significance of separating identification theory from model specification, and about the belief in the generality of structural models as the starting basis for structural modelling practice (see Chapter 6). However, at the time, Koopmans did not lead his discussion that far. Instead, he listed a number of technical difficulties in statistical tests (see Chapter 5).

The link between identifiability of a model and its formulation was subsequently examined by H. A. Simon (1953). Standing basically at a deterministic angle, Simon endeavoured to associate the causal ordering in structural equations or models with the classification of endogenous and exogenous variables, and then with identifiability. He set out from a deterministic structural model of a general linear non-homogeneous equation system, assuming implicitly that the correct structural model was known. The system was partitioned into two subsets: subset A which contained all the equations whose variables possessed unique solutions, and subset B which included the remaining equations. Simon used 'causal ordering' to describe the state of dependency for variables in B to get their solutions via the variable solutions of A, because this would form a number of 'asymmetrical relations'. Concentrating on B, he defined the number of solved variables from A needed in B for obtaining finally a unique solution for B as the order of this 'derived structure'. Consequently, those variables in B whose solution relied upon other variables solved outside B were called 'endogenous' and those other variables 'exogenous'. Then, Simon turned to the relationship between causal ordering and the concept of identifiability. He maintained that it was the desire to search for the logical cause or the structural relationship behind the empirical or non-structural relationship and to make a distinction between the two, 'that lies at the root of the identifiability concept'. He argued that from 'epistemological considerations . . . the conditions under which the causal ordering of a structure is operationally meaningful are generally the same as the conditions under which structural equations can be distinguished from non-structural equations, and the same as the conditions under which the question of identifiability of the equations is meaningful.' He continued that a parallel mathematical relationship also existed between the imposition of identifying restrictions (the order condition) and the causal ordering, e.g. to specify certain coefficients in one equation equal to zero meant to assume away the corresponding variables in that equation and therefore determined the causal ordering of the equation. Simon further connected identifiability and causal ordering by means of linear transformations. He observed that identifiability allowed for only one kind of transformation (multiply a row of the coefficient matrix by a scalar) while exact identifiable structure possessed a unique causal ordering which was 'invariant under any transformations permitted by the *a priori* restrictions'. Hence, 'a knowledge of causal ordering of a set of variables can be used to help determine whether the coefficients of a linear structure governing these variables can be determined.' The only difference between the two was that the conditions for identification were stronger than those for causal ordering because of the data requirement contained in the rank condition of identification.

By linking the desire for identifiability to causal ordering, Simon's statements reinforced the point that model identification in principle amounted to no more than model formulation taking extra care of the possibility of securing a unique solution.

However, there was a discernible difference between Simon's approach and Koopmans and Reiersøl's in bringing identifiability closer to model formulation. Koopmans and Reiersøl compared particular specifications to identifying restrictions so as to bring up the issue of specification testing. In contrast, Simon removed the whole issue farther from statistical tests by associating identifiability with model formulation. In fact, Simon's approach sustained Frisch's vision of the existence of a latent but definite structural mechanism faced with some 'inverse' problems of being located. Although identification ceased to be a serious problem in Simon's framework, the questionable point was transformed to causal ordering, to the principles for arbitrating between endogenous and exogenous variables in constructing structural models. This helped to bring up the later debate over the choice of model form between the Cowles Commission's simultaneity and Wold's recursivity (causal chain) (see Chapter 6).

Indeed, identification seemed no longer to pose serious problems in econometric practice since the formalization of identification theory. Actually, overcaution created by the identification discussion warned applied modellers to avoid model unidentifiability at any cost. Identifiability soon became an important criterion in formulating structural models. Many of the applied models were constructed intentionally to be overidentified. The phenomenon aroused open scepticism, successively from G. Orcutt and T.-C. Liu, over the justifiability or congruence of arbitrarily specified identifying restrictions in those structural models (see Chapter 6). Debates on this issue stimulated subsequent developments of identification conditions for less rigidly specified restrictions. Results following the line of Cowles Commission Monograph 10 could be seen, e.g. in F. M. Fisher's 1965 paper, where zero restrictions on some coefficients were replaced by close-to-zero restrictions to achieve 'near identification', and where the corresponding identification conditions were established (Fisher 1965). But a more thorough and general treatment of the problem came from a different route, initiated by J. Drèze (1962), who proposed a completely stochastic specification of the identifying restrictions using the Bayesian approach and developed the corresponding identification conditions (see Qin 1991).

Noticeably, by the time the work to set up the basic identification theory had been accomplished by the Cowles group and its followers, it was confined explicitly to the unique estimability of the structural parameters of given models. The earlier connotation of testability was formally cut out. But it has been shown in Section 4.4 that many of the further developments contained elements that were inherently related to the testability of structural parameters. The relation appeared to be closer and more direct to model construction than to estimation.

5

Testing

Theory verification through applied studies forms one of the main motives for formalizing methods of model estimation and identification. However, the formative period of econometrics saw only slow progress in transforming this general and pragmatic desire into an operational and formal procedure, in sharp contrast to developments in estimation and identification theories. The statistical theory of hypothesis-testing was accepted without much dispute quite early on as the technical vehicle to fulfil this desire. But during the adoption of the theory into econometrics in the 1940s and 1950s, the achievable domain of verification turned out to be considerably reduced. One main accountable factor is that as soon as 'model' became an independent entity in econometrics, the procedure of 'hypothesis → testing → hypothesis' had assumed the complicated form of 'economic theory → econometric model → statistical testing → econometric model → economic theory'. Much of the formalizing effort, already a small part in comparison to that spent on identification, estimation, and related computing issues, was concentrated on the middle part of the procedure, i.e. econometric model → statistical testing → econometric model. Testing in econometrics proper gradually dwindled into part of the modelling procedure and pertained to model evaluation. It meant devising statistical testing tools or applying available statistical tests to econometric models given the structural model framework. Whereas in the applied field, empirical modellers shouldered the task of discriminating between and verifying economic theories against the model results, and they carried it out in an *ad hoc* and often *non-sequitur* way. This chapter describes how the desire to test diverged into model evaluation in econometric theory on the one hand, and economic theory verification in practice on the other, as econometric testing theory took shape.

As usual, the story begins with the early period prior to the formative movement in Section 5.1. The following section looks at the period in which the theme of hypothesis-testing was introduced, and the first test emerged in econometrics. The last two sections report respectively how model testing in applied econometrics and test design in theoretical econometrics developed and moved apart.

5.1 ANTECEDENTS

Verification of economic theory against data evidence was an inherent motive of the econometric movement. Primarily, it was embraced in the general and pragmatic desire to obtain a correspondence between economic observations and economic theory via (*a*) mapping data with a model, (*b*) interpreting both the results and the model in terms of theory, and (*c*) confirming the theory by forecasting results. This broad idea occurred frequently in the early literature, e.g. in the works of Ezekiel, Gilboy, Moore, Schultz, Working, Wright (for details see Morgan 1988, 1990). In fact, the whole activity of empirical studies was viewed as statistical verification of economic theories. This was especially so in the field of applied demand analyses, where orthodox demand theory was thought to be verified through formulating it into estimable relations free of its *ceteris paribus* assumptions, and then obtaining their estimates. But compared to what are regarded as tests in econometrics today, there were few such statistical tools in use during those early days. Estimation and then identification were the issues of focus, as far as the development of econometric techniques was concerned. Research in test methods was significantly outweighed by developments in estimation and identification methods. Among other things, rejection of the 'random sampling' concept because of the non-experimental nature of economic observations blocked the way to any serious attempts to develop strictly statistical tests, let alone the fact that proper statistical theory of testing was only developed in the early 1920s.

The first signs of formal testing attempts could be seen from discussions of correlation coefficients, standard errors, and, occasionally, the classical significance tests of estimated coefficients attached to regression results in some early econometric literature, as supporting evidence to the goodness of fit. However, it turned out that measured economic relationships, even when confirmed by these test results, could still face rejection by misprediction, and by economists denying the applicability of classical statistical techniques. In particular, two major discussions arose in the 1910s and 1920s, which spurred increasing concerns in developing econometric tests, not only for direct theory verification but also for checking the econometric procedure used for verification. One was on the correspondence problems, which led to the subsequent development of identification theory, as described in the previous chapter. Another discussion, initiated by Yule (1926), unveiled the danger of spurious correlation in analysing time-series by means of ordinary regression. Especially, Yule plotted the different distribution curves of the correlation coefficient, R^2, corresponding to different types (stationary and non-stationary) of time-series artificially constructed, to demonstrate its potentially deceiving nature. The curves made it obvious that the R^2 should be high whenever the data series used in regression are non-stationary.

Yule's R^2 plots did not receive wide attention among econometricians. Classical significance tests were still used in applied studies combined with some *ad hoc* methods to combat nonsense regressions. One such method was to observe the distribution of regression residuals, e.g. serious residual correlations were regarded as an indicator of misspecification. For instance, Ezekiel detected 'spurious correlation' in choosing regressors in a price analysis by inspecting residual correlations combined with Fisher's criterion of statistical significance (1933). But mistrust of the classical methods of standard errors and significance tests was common. Two main reasons could account for that. First, the results of such tests were still susceptible to erroneous conclusion due to the frequent violation, by economic data, of the fundamental assumptions underlying the use of these methods (such as small sample size and serial correlation). Secondly and more importantly, investigators could not effectively distinguish whether a regression was meaningful in the economic sense, when it appeared to be significant or irrefutable statistically (see Frisch 1933*b*, 1934; and Schultz 1930, 1938). In particular, Frisch demonstrated these problems with constructed data, following Yule's approach.

In fact, the search for an appropriate method capable of testing statistical relations for their economic significance absorbed Frisch's main attention during the early 1930s. He used 'numerical examples where the nature of the mechanism is known' to try 'a large number of methods' (Frisch 1936), and wound up with 'confluence analysis' and the method of bunch maps. As stated in previous chapters, confluence analysis associated with the bunch map method was essentially an estimation–identification apparatus, through the use of which an economically meaningful relationship was thought to be able to be selected. In the method, Frisch derived certain coefficients from variances, covariance of variables, and their correlation coefficients to indicate 'regression spreads' and the 'scatterances' in the confluence analysis (Frisch 1934). Interestingly, Frisch referred to those coefficients as 'test-parameters'. However, no critical regions were defined to enable these 'test-parameters' to perform as genuine statistical tests. The actual model selection was made by visual discretion, based on the changes in the degrees of tightness or explosiveness of the bunches drawn according to the 'test-parameters', as regressions were made on an increasing number of regressors. The method was thought to have 'furnished the correct criteria for the nonsense of the regression equation' (p. 192), though it suffered from a lack of precision. Frisch was not unaware of this weakness, for he set up a criterion for ideal tests in conclusion: 'The ultimate test of significance must consist in a network of conclusions and cross-checks where theoretical economic considerations, intimate and realistic knowledge of the data, and a refined statistical technique concur' (p. 192).

The unavailability of such an ultimate test led Frisch to the position that it was safer to set up models justifiable by economic theory in the first place than to start from statistical models to test the validity of the theory. This was implied in his advocacy of the 'structural method'. The method brought an additional step of a structural model into the originally direct verification of theory by statistical analysis. Many econometricians were convinced of the correctness of the structural method. They became devoted to working out models that embodied the theory of interest on the one hand and were statistically estimable on the other. This helped to focus their technical interest on estimation and identification problems from the mid-1930s, as already described in Chapters 3 and 4. The resulting research, in turn, led to a growing demand for adapting new statistical tools to deal with the complications created by corresponding economic data with theory through the structural model. Hence, there developed a quest for a formal procedure of evaluating structural models in econometrics.

The quest was encouraged technically by frequent interactions between econometricians and statisticians in the 1930s, as pointed out in Chapter 1. A formal introduction of the mathematical distributions used in significance tests by R. A. Fisher was presented in *Econometrica* as early as 1935. The Neyman–Pearson approach to hypothesis-testing was introduced by Neyman to the 1936 Annual Meeting of the Econometric Society, not long after its development around 1930. (Interestingly, the part of Neyman's speech on hypothesis-testing was reported summarily in *Econometrica* by Frisch, who referred to the Neyman–Pearson approach as essentially a 'method of rejection' (Brown 1937).) The introduction induced a few modellers to have a try at the new theory of statistical tests. For instance, M. Friedman (1937) discussed the application of the analysis of covariance to test the significance of the differences among a group of regression equations as against a general regression of the whole group. The method was later applied by W. A. Wallis to testing the stability of US consumption patterns (1942). I. Hilfer (1938) developed 'a test of differential effect' based on the F distribution to test the existence and significance of different effects of regressors on the dependent variable. G. Tintner (1939) proposed a test, based upon Fisher's variance ratio z-test, for the approximate equality of the variance between two different-order difference series in the variate difference method, to judge the sufficiency of the number of differencing of a series. The criterion of sufficiency was that no systematic element could be found left in the series after that number of differencing (see Chapter 3).

Concurrently, the general concept of hypothesis-testing became popularized in the econometric circle, as more and more applied models were built in the area of business cycle analysis to test various theoretical hypotheses, since few well-established theories were available here. Accordingly, more emphasis was put on testing, and statistical results were given sway more often here, compared to demand analysis. A typical example was Tinbergen's 'Statistical Evidence on the Acceleration Principle' (1938a), where the acceleration principle was transformed and decomposed into the correlation and regression aspects, and much of its claimed power in explaining investment fluctuations was discredited by a number of simple correlation and regression results. Another example was the first macro-model of inter-industrial relations, the US model of 'patterns of resource use' (see Chapter 2). The modelling procedure here was described as one of setting up working hypotheses, testing them by means of correlation analysis, and improving the hypotheses in the light of the statistical results, even though probability theory was still considered as inapplicable (Means 1938).

Attempts at hypothesis-testing with econometric models reached its first climax with Tinbergen's ambitious macroeconometric model of the US economy (1939). Tinbergen's work explicitly defined statistical verification of economic theory as the chief objective, first by the title *Statistical Testing of Business-Cycle Theories* itself, followed by an explanation at the very beginning of the first volume: 'The purpose of this series of studies is to submit to statistical test some of the theories which have been put forward regarding the character and causes of cyclical fluctuation in business activity', or in short, 'to identify and to test' those 'direct causal relations' proposed by economic theory (pp. 11–12). Although by that time Tinbergen had been convinced of the structural approach advocated by Frisch (see Chapter 2), the conversion did not alter the course of testing economic theories that he had been pursuing. This could be seen from his following reiteration: 'the principles underlying the procedure are that economic theory has to suggest the factors to be considered, while the statistical testing process shows the maximum degree of accordance obtainable and the relative strength of each factor required to obtain that degree of accordance' (p. 34). Moreover, Tinbergen clarified the realm of testing, which, interestingly, expressed the similar idea implied in the Neyman and Pearson testing theory. He stated:

No statistical test can prove a theory to be correct. It can, indeed, prove that theory to be incorrect, or at least incomplete, by showing that it does not cover a particular set of facts: but, even if one theory appears to be in accordance with the facts, it is still possible that there is another theory, also in accordance with the facts, which is the 'true' one, as may be shown by new facts or further theoretical investigation. (Tinbergen 1939: 12)

Yet, the statistical tests that Tinbergen talked about had a broader and more general connotation than those in the Neyman–Pearson theory. Tinbergen took the idea as the guiding principle of his research, rather than as an object to be realized through invention of new statistical theory and methods. As for statistical methods, he simply adopted the suggestion by Koopmans (1937) to use a combination of Fisher's method with Frisch's method of bunch maps. In fact, the method of bunch maps served as a major tool of test in Tinbergen's experiments. He used it extensively for variable selection to see, by adding more variables to the basic relations, 'whether the correlation coefficients increase', 'whether the regression keeps stable', and 'whether the variate is significant' (Tinbergen 1939: 50). In conjunction, he frequently reported the conventional statistics of correlation coefficients and standard deviations as support for his estimates. Another idea that he adopted from Koopmans (1937) was to use sub-sample estimates as a test of the stability of the estimated relations over time, i.e. to divide the whole period of observation into two, performing estimation for the sub-periods and comparing the results. He inferred intuitively that 'similar results with coefficients of the same order of magnitude should be found: otherwise the significance must be doubted' (p. 42). The method was applied to testing the estimated relations of investment fluctuation in the USA, the UK, and Germany respectively from the 1870s to the 1910s (the dividing year being 1895). Tinbergen also used forecasting results as an additional test for the stability of the estimated relationships. However, he had no exact test statistics nor critical values. He just relied upon eye judgement.

Tinbergen's bold empirical undertaking of hypothesis-testing immediately encountered criticisms from the economic circle, noticeably by Keynes (1939), as well as the econometric circle, and by Frisch (1938), as described previously. Further formalization of econometrics became imperative. The theoretical enquiries by Koopmans (1937, 1941) were among the first of these attempts. It was pointed out in Chapter 1 that Koopmans (1937) introduced into econometrics the concept of 'sample' versus 'hypothetical population'. More interestingly in that book, he classified as the '*inductive* part' of the sampling theory, statistical inference from samples to population by means of tests (*t*-test mainly), and more widely empirical statistical studies of some hypothetical theories, in contrast to the other '*deductive* part' where specification, estimation, and distribution were designated. He extended his idea of statistical testing in his 1941 paper.

In that paper, Koopmans regarded economic theories as working hypotheses in general, and as components of various premisses defined in model specification in particular. He anatomized statistical testing of the theories into two layers. First, 'statistical censorship' of the adopted premisses through inspection of (*a*) the 'unexplained residuals' of regression analyses (e.g. large residuals or their cyclical patterns might indicate contradictions between specified premisses and data), and (*b*) the signs of estimated coefficients (i.e. whether they coincided with what had been expected from the premisses); and secondly, 'conditional conclusions' in 'the form of the calculation of certain "best estimates" of the coefficients and lags not specified in advance' (i.e. those not given by economic theory) 'according to certain technical criteria', given the data and the specified model. The two were discussed respectively in two sections of the paper. Discernibly, the first had a close link with the process of model specification ('the choice of the premisses') and embraced the basic idea of misspecification-testing; whereas the second was based upon model estimation and related closely to the classical theme of the significance test. Interestingly, Koopmans regarded the first part to be 'less technical' and the second 'more refined', apparently with respect to the degree of statistical formalization attained. Furthermore, Koopmans defined the test of a model as test of an entire list of premisses, and transformed the concept of 'sufficiency' or 'insufficiency' of all the premisses into that of 'relevance' of dubious premisses considered one at a time. He then introduced and emphasized the idea of statistical testing with specified alternatives to the dubious premisses, developed by Neyman and Pearson.

Koopmans's ideas of test were hardly pursued at all by the Cowles Commission, even though Koopmans himself was a leading figure there in their project of formalization of econo-

metrics. They were overwhelmed by the commitment to measurement and the structural modelling approach.

5.2 ADOPTION OF THE HYPOTHESIS-TESTING FRAMEWORK AND INVENTION OF ECONOMETRIC TESTS

As mentioned repeatedly in previous chapters, the main theoretical framework of econometrics was drafted by Haavelmo in his
The Probability Approach in Econometrics (1944). In this seminal
work, Haavelmo argued for a total adoption of the Neyman–
Pearson hypothesis-testing approach on the basis of probability
theory, and sketched a general representation of the issue of
testing economic relations in the form of the Neyman–Pearson
approach. By doing so, he was able to link up the problems of
identification, estimation, and model specification, with this
hypothesis-testing scheme built upon the general probability
foundation. His clarification thus put the idea and desire for
theory verification into a more precise and operational theme
of statistical inference.

Haavelmo praised the Neyman–Pearson approach as 'among
the very greatest achievements of scientific thought' (1944: 64),
for it 'opened up the way for a whole stream of high-quality
work, which gradually is lifting statistical theory to a real scientific level'.[1] He reported their work as providing a few 'very
general' and 'very simple' principles which 'specify clearly the
class of problems that fall within the field of statistical theory
and statistical inference' (p. 60). In his outline of the Neyman–
Pearson theory, Haavelmo emphasized two key points in the
statistical testing of hypotheses: (*a*) the formulation of 'a set of
a priori admissible hypotheses' upon which a test of a certain
hypothesis was actually conducted, and (*b*) the choice of 'best
critical regions', which formed the essence of the test technique.
The former stressed the interrelationship and interaction between
testing and specification of hypotheses. Tests, developed on the
basis of a given set of admissible hypotheses were powerful, only

---

[1] In a talk with D. F. Hendry in the summer of 1987, Haavelmo described
how he was converted from Frisch's thinking to Neyman's under the direct
influence of discussions with Neyman around 1940. He again recalled this
experience with Neyman in his Nobel Prize speech (1989).

relative to the chosen set of admissible hypotheses. These tests required explicit and precise specification of 'what we assume known beyond doubt, and what we desire to test' (p. 66) within the set of a priori admissible hypotheses. As for the latter, the common precaution against errors in induction from the particular to the general found expression in the definition of two types of errors in terms of critical regions, and the intuition to minimize these errors was conveyed in the quest for the 'best critical regions'. The concept of these regions provided not only an explicit representation of the function and the limitation of statistical inference, but also the link between testing and estimation, which could now 'be considered as a particular form of testing hypotheses' (p. 66).

Using principles of Neyman–Pearson theory, Haavelmo then gave 'a general, axiomatic, formulation of the problem of testing economic relations' (p. 69), with emphasis on the fundamentals of 'a *statistical formulation of hypotheses constructed in economic theory*' (p. 60). The formulation started from a 'fundamental assumption' assuming that economic data were samples of joint observations drawn from systems 'satisfying the requirements of a fundamental probability set' (p. 70). From this sample-population angle, economic theories to be tested were regarded as 'a system of restrictions' imposed upon the fundamental probability set. The imposition was carried out through model specification, namely, via (*a*) choosing the functional form; (*b*) assuming the properties of the joint probability of the error terms conditional upon the given values of all the independent variables; and (*c*) deducing from (*b*) the probability distribution of all the variables. Once economic theories were presented as hypothetical restrictions concerning the probability distributions of the observable variables, the principle of the Neyman–Pearson type of statistical tests became applicable.

Next, Haavelmo elaborated the issue as to the extent to which these tests could check for the 'correctness' of the formulated hypotheses. He dwelt on the following two points. First, these tests were efficacious only on the premiss that the correct hypothesis was within the set of admissible hypotheses specified in advance. Second, the 'goodness' of a relationship within an accepted hypothesis was judged by the properties of the error terms, especially their smallness and randomness. Further reflection on the issue brought Haavelmo to a more fundamental but confounding problem of what exact position econometricians should take between theory and data, or, in his words, what was 'the meaning of the phrase "to formulate theories by looking at the data". Acknowledging the problem as a common one of inductive science, Haavelmo admitted the limited role of statistical testing in verifying economic theory. He was aware of the fact that results of either acceptance or rejection did not contain the guarantee for the truth or falseness of the hypothesis tested, because it was never known whether the correct one had been included in the admissible set in the first place. Nevertheless, he argued that the usefulness of statistical tests lay in their provision of information concerning how to further restrict the class of hypotheses regarded a priori as admissible. Accordingly, the focus of testing should be placed on deciding the compatibility of a hypothetical relation with the data, rather than on its correctness.

It was clearly of crucial importance to choose the set of admissible hypotheses in the whole procedure of testing, because the set itself was assumed 'true' (in the sense of definitely including the correct hypothesis of interest), and exempt from the test. Haavelmo was not ignorant of this point. But he hardly specified any do's for the choice, except for the seemingly reluctant recognition that it was still 'a matter of general knowledge and intuition' (Haavelmo 1944: 81). In contrast, he was more specific about the don'ts, and warned, in particular, against making the set data-dependent (i.e. be a function of the sample) in order to maintain invariance of the method of testing across changing samples. He concluded by observing that the essential thing was '*not* the way in which we choose the hypothesis to be tested', but 'what we *know or believe* to be the class of *a priori* admissible hypotheses, and what power our test has of rejecting the hypothesis tested, if a "really different" one among the alternatives be true' (p. 83).

Compared with Koopmans's argument, there is a subtle shift of weight from a posteriori observations towards a priori theory in modelling in Haavelmo's exposition. Since judgement of statistical tests was limited to the compatibility of data with the theory concerned rather than its definite verification, since the power of a test presupposed the verity of a particular set of a priori admissible hypotheses, since no methods nor tests were considered which had the capacity to detect the situation when the set of hypotheses happened to exclude the correct theory, and since no explicit rules, except for common knowledge and intuition, were available in setting up the set of admissible hypotheses, it was natural to rely upon existing economic theory, perhaps the best summary of common knowledge, as the ground for the hypothesis set and therefore the background for tests. This helped reinforce the structural approach to modelling and relegate econometric tests to a perfunctory role. On a closer look, however, the structural approach did not seem compatible with the Neyman–Pearson hypothesis-testing approach, in that the former put the bulk of economic theory into the basic structural model allowing only for some auxiliary assumptions (e.g. identification assumptions) to be tested, whereas the latter meant to treat the theory proper as hypothetical restrictions. Apparently, Haavelmo did not notice this incompatibility. The idea that he tried to draw from the Neyman–Pearson approach should lead to specification tests, whose function was dubious under the structural modelling procedure. On the other hand, the faith in structural models posed a barrier to the notion of misspecification (diagnostic) tests, which were actually the most needed in the framework. Nevertheless, the incompatibility might explain why Haavelmo failed to work out exactly how to carry out econometric estimation under the general principle of hypothesis-testing. Compared with what he did in probability modelling, joint distribution specification, maximum-likelihood estimation, and identification, Haavelmo actually made little substantive progress in testing, despite all of his efforts in introducing the Neyman–Pearson approach.

Subsequently in the Cowles Commission Monograph 10 (Koopmans 1950), the issue of hypothesis-testing, which was classified within the problem of model choice, was hardly addressed. The choice of leaving open 'the choice of model' (Koopmans 1950: 44–5) was legitimate in so far as the domain of the analysis was limited to the 'deductive part' defined earlier by Koopmans (1937), and as the structural model contained the really correct structure. Indeed the Cowles research complied with the two conditions. This is obvious with the first. As with the second, this is embodied in the use of a very abstract form for the structural model, as presented in equation (2.7) in Chapter 2.

Consequently, description of classical tests, e.g. t-tests, was given minor weight in Monograph 10, since their function as specification tests was somewhat redundant in such a circumstance. The only substantive development that the Cowles group contributed to testing was the design of overidentification tests, the first strictly econometric test device.

Chapter 4 described how conditions for model identification were defined in Monograph 10 as a priori restrictions on structural relations, and how it was recognized that identifiability could be sufficiently guaranteed only by certain conditions of the actual data observations. Chapter 3 told the story of how LIML was invented for estimating individual equations in a simultaneous-equations system. It was in conjunction with these developments that T. W. Anderson and H. Rubin (1949, 1950) came to the idea of composing statistical tests for the validity of the identifying restrictions on single structural relations.

Anderson and Rubin made use of the properties of the reduced-form coefficient matrix, i.e. the properties that the elements of the matrix were actually the parameters of the joint distribution of the observations and, at the same time, the rank of the matrix contained information about the model identifying requirements transformed from the structural relations upon which those restrictions had been directly imposed. Hence by inspecting the rank conditions of the matrix of the reduced-form coefficients, one could cross-check the a priori rank requirement on the structural form against data. They constructed a likelihood ratio test for overidentifying restrictions following this intuition. The null and alternative hypotheses were defined by the different status of the rank of the matrix of the reduced-form coefficients. The smallest characteristic root of a matrix was used as the indicator of its closeness to singularity (i.e. its rank condition). The test statistic was developed as the ratio, in terms of the smallest root, of the restricted ML function to the unrestricted ML function. Anderson also proposed an alternative test of the rank condition based on small-sample theory (Koopmans 1950: 320–1). These identification tests implied a real need for specification testing to help build the structural model, originally thought to be set up completely a priori. But the Cowles people were very cautious in their claim to the specification aspect of the tests. They reiterated that 'any statistical inference regarding identifiable parameters of economic behaviour is conditional upon the validity of the model' (Hood and Koopmans 1953: 44–5). The validity depended upon making correct choice of model, which, they believed, required methods capable of testing 'the whole set of such models simultaneously' (Koopmans 1950: 45). Up to this point, they felt powerless because they could not find any satisfactory statistical theory from their stand. Therefore, they retained the position in Monographs 10 and 14 that 'no attempt' was made to approach the choice of models problem.

However, there are two other short articles on specification testing in Monograph 10. One was by H. B. Mann, which was an abstract of a paper published in 1945, in which he proposed two non-parametric tests for randomness against trends by means of ranks. The other was by R. L. Anderson, who illustrated the use of the analysis of variance in testing the hypothesis of no seasonal fluctuations in the context of time-series analysis. But a really interesting point about the two articles lay in the general attitude of the Cowles group towards them, reflected in Marschak's introduction, which stated clearly that these two articles were 'given by guests of the Cowles Commission, Mann and R. L. Anderson', who placed 'less reliance . . . on knowledge from economic theory' and 'correspondingly' made 'no attempts . . . to estimate economic structure' (Koopmans 1950: 47). Their topics were excluded from the subsequent explanatory volume of Monograph 14. Evidently, the Cowles people chose to assume the general theoretical relations as 'known beyond doubt' to circumvent the knotty step of model selection, which would involve heavy use of hypothesis-testing theory, because they considered the theory still immature for the task.

Contemporary with the Cowles contribution, fragmentary development of testing methods in the errors-in-variables context could be found mainly in Tintner's work. Tintner proposed a test for multicollinearity (1945), and then extended it to a test for the existence of linear relations between the weighted regression coefficients (1950b). The test statistics were obtained through the use of Lagrange multipliers and based on the latent roots of the variance–covariance matrix of the errors in variables. In the latter paper, he applied his test to the hypothesis of constant returns to scale in the US economy as assumed in the Cobb–Douglas production function, and rejected the hypothesis. However, Tintner's tests were left aside together with errors-in-variables models not long after by the mainstream econometric errors-in-equations formulation. So were most of the statistical tests in connection with the errors-in-variables form and periodogram analysis, which were painstakingly compiled in Tintner's textbook (1952), the only one of the time which devoted considerable space to discussing statistical tests in comparison with the space for describing estimation techniques.

5.3 HYPOTHESIS-TESTING VIA MODEL EVALUATION IN APPLIED ECONOMETRICS

As seen above, theory verification by means of statistical tests had remained more or less at the stage of introducing principles rather than seriously adapting techniques by the mid-1940s. The backwardness of testing theory in comparison with estimation theory and identification theory became discernible when the Cowles workers stepped out of the 'deductive' phase to try to demonstrate their newly invented tools in empirical modelling, with the high hope of exhibiting the power of these tools in policy analysis and forecasting. The contrast between their impressive theoretical success and the few tenuous empirical models that they attempted was so marked that serious scepticism was common about the value of refinements of the statistical aspect in econometrics (e.g. see Epstein 1987). However, at the time, the test part of modelling was not regarded as a main weak point. Instead, central problems were accredited to inadequacies in data collection, analysis, and utilization, and the absence of well-formulated operational economic theories, especially for utilizing a wider range of economic information (e.g. cross-section data, quarterly data). A strong view held then was that the adaptation of statistical tools for econometrics had much outpaced the data quality, the mathematization of economic theories, and the practice of empirical model building, as well as the computing capacity.[2] So revision of economic

---

[2] For instance, serious criticisms of overrefinement of methods to the Cowles Commission can be found in a number of unpublished referees' comments on

theories by the route of mathematical economics and development of various microeconometric models formed the two main
research directions, which absorbed much of the 'long-term'
interest of the Cowles group and its followers. Meanwhile, the
contrivance of different estimators and calculation procedures
to circumvent inadequate computing capacity absorbed much of
the enthusiasm of econometric theorists. Only minor attention
was given to the problem of how to select and settle on an
estimated model from the framework of a given structural
model. The problem was addressed under the name of 'multiple'
or 'additional' hypotheses, i.e. there were more hypotheses than
the number verifiable from the particular data available (see
Cowles Commission 1947). It was regarded virtually the same
as making choices among 'a set of overidentifying hypotheses'
in the circumstances (Koopmans 1947a). Hence it was thought
to be solvable, in principle, by the same approach as the tests
for overidentification restrictions proposed by Anderson and
Rubin, only requiring a better statistical device allowing for tests
of more than two alternatives simultaneously (Koopmans 1949b).
But since it was reckoned that such statistical theory was not
yet available, further discussion along this direction gradually
receded. Reliance on the structural modelling procedure was
strengthened. The statistical inference procedure of hypothesis-
testing sat on the bench of theoretical econometrics for most of
the time, while the door to the 'kitchen' where applied econometric models were produced remained shut.

But behind the door, crude statistical results, mainly the sizes
and signs of estimated parameters as well as of the residuals,
correlation coefficients, t-statistics, and standard errors, were
commonly used as working criteria to assist model processing.
On the other hand, empirical models and results, however
produced, when they were finally brought into the open, were
bound to meet with queries concerning not only the sustain-
ability of the underlying economic theories, but also the reliability
of these models themselves.

One of the earliest applied post-model tests was carried out
by G. C. Means and his colleagues at the beginning of the 1940s
(Means 1941), on their model of 'Patterns of Resource Use' built

the Cowles work, reported to the Rockefeller Foundation around 1950 (deposited
at the Rockefeller Archive Center).

in the late 1930s.[3] The test was to find out whether there existed the 'continuing relationships underlying economic activity', proposed and estimated in the original model (Means 1941: 1). The test contained 138 separate analyses ('formulae') of the eighty-one segments into which the US economy had been divided, based on data from the early 1920s to 1935. Four ways of testing these formulae were suggested: (a) comparison of the formulae with actual data; (b) tests of their reasonableness against common sense; (c) extensions of the time-period covered; and (d) future facts. The fourth was thought to be 'the most rigorous test' of models (Means 1938: 14–16). Around one-third of the formulae were considered as acceptable according to the first three types of tests when the model was being built. They were put to the fourth type of test subsequently against post-sample data of 1936–8 (Means 1941). Means admitted the crudeness of this test of his, for the test aimed to find out not the closeness of the analyses to the corresponding 'true' relationships, but rather the 'likelihood' of constancy of the analyses in 'the immediate future' (p. 5). The techniques used were also crude: either the ratios of forecasting errors to the original standard deviations or the percentages of forecasting errors in the calculated values, with arbitrarily set values of the ratios (e.g. 1.5) or the percentages (e.g. 7 per cent) as testing criteria. Although the numbers of close-fitting relations dropped considerably as they were projected further beyond the original period of estimation, Means still took the results optimistically as a confirmation of its being possible 'to discover relationships which can be usefully projected into the future' by the method (p. 14).

It was almost a decade later that the similar kind of post-model tests occurred. The tests were conducted on Klein's model III this time by A. W. Marshall, and then Carl Christ, and the results exerted considerable influence on the development of macroeconometric modelling. Marshall constructed a goodness-of-fit test for single structural equations on the basis of the tolerance interval technique, i.e. inferring whether a series of events was occurring continuously from an unchanging distribution by inspecting whether a large proportion of them fell into

[3] The test was almost totally ignored in the econometric circle. The only reference that I have found to Means's work is in Friedman's comments on C. Christ's testing of Klein's model, which is described below.

a certain probabilistic region. He applied the data of the post-sample period of 1946–7 to the Klein model, and calculated the residuals. He used these residuals to perform (*a*) an *ex post* test under the hypothesis that Klein's model should describe 1946 and 1947 equally as well as it did the sample period (1921–41); and (*b*) a comparative test of the prediction power of Klein's model against that of simple extrapolation models. The results rejected several of Klein's equations and put a few others on probation (Marshall 1950; also cf. Christ 1951). Following Marshall's work, Christ revised Klein's model, estimated it with the data for 1921–47, and tested the results (Christ 1951). Christ classified all available model tests into two groups: 'tests of internal consistency' and 'tests of success in extrapolation and prediction'. The first group included three tests. First, naïve visual judgement of the approximate magnitudes and the algebraic signs to be expected of the estimates and the sizes of the corresponding standard statistics (e.g. standard errors). Second, Anderson and Rubin's test of overidentification restrictions as 'a sort of overall test of the totality of restrictions and assumptions applied in estimating an equation'. Third, a serial correlation test using the von Neumann ratio. The second group consisted mainly of tests by Marshall's methods against data for 1948, with an additional comparative test of the goodness-of-fit of different estimation methods on the grounds of their predictive abilities. Christ's work was acknowledged as the first published piece of research focused entirely and explicitly on testing the validity of empirical econometric models after their construction,[4] though it contained some defects in data-handling and model revision.[5]

At a very broad level, these trial tests corresponded with Tinbergen's appeal to reformulate economic theories 'as refutable hypotheses' (Tinbergen 1949). However, the test results seemed to aggravate, at least not to alleviate, mistrust in structural macroeconometric modelling. As a sharp critic of the Cowles approach, M. Friedman interpreted the rejection of many of Klein's equations in Christ's tests as evidence of the

[4] Marshall's paper has not been published except for the short abstract quoted.
[5] Klein raised a number of objections to Christ's revised version of Klein's model III in his comment on Christ's paper (see the Comment following Christ's paper).

prematurity of macro-modelling of a whole economy, before dynamic models of parts of an economy were well developed (Christ 1951, Comment). The opinion apparently became increasingly shared in the applied circle. Many applied modellers shifted their interest in macro-modelling away from a whole economy to parts of economic activities where economic theories were relatively well developed. The principle of hypothesis-testing was enhanced significantly with this shift.

In fact, results from empirical studies had been exerting a significant impact, with their explicit verification purpose, on economists' thinking about how to formulate economic theory with respect to data evidence. The extent of the impact could be seen easily from Friedman's methodological discussion concerning the nature of positive economics (1953). In this methodological classic, Friedman attached great importance to testing and considered empirical evidence as the ultimate testimony for the validity of hypotheses. He argued that 'the only relevant test of the *validity* of a hypothesis is comparison of its predictions with experience' and that internal tests for 'logical completeness and consistency are relevant but play a subsidiary role'. He attributed the enormous difficulty in obtaining really convincing testing of economic hypotheses to the difficulty of interpreting the available test results, due to the impossibility of conducting controlled 'crucial' experiments. He also pointed out that the kind of indirect tests of the assumptions imposed to specify the circumstances in which a particular hypothesis should work only had limited power. This implied the restricted adequacy of inferring from model tests to theory verification. Friedman also pointed out that factual tests of hypotheses could turn out to form 'the raw material' for constructing new hypotheses or revising old ones at the same time. This led him to a rather pragmatic and instrumentalistic standpoint concerning the formation and uses of theory. Indeed, Friedman's 'permanent income hypothesis' was such an outcome from many (including his own) empirical studies of consumer behaviour with respect to the available consumption theories (Friedman 1957).

Similar theoretical advances driven by empirical evidence from econometric studies could be seen increasingly in different branches of applied economics after 1950. Consumption analysis took the lead. Two of the most prominent results were Stone's formulation of a testable 'linear expenditure system' and Modigliani's 'life-cycle hypothesis'. Stone's (1954*a*) linear expenditure system was produced out of vast empirical testing in general, and careful statistical testing in particular. Modigliani's 'life-cycle hypothesis' and its tests came from his attempt to circumvent the failure of previous consumption models in explaining and predicting data. The research led him to a separate treatment of the short-run and long-run consumers' behaviour in one theoretical model (e.g. Modigliani and Brumberg 1954; Modigliani and Ando 1957). The turn of 1960 also saw the generalization of the Cobb–Douglas function into a constant-elasticity-of-substitution (CES) function in production theory (e.g. Arrow *et al.* 1961), and the rise of the rational expectations hypothesis in price theory (e.g. Muth 1961). As applied econometric modelling flourished, economists were forced to construct, on the basis of older received theory, new hypotheses which were 'capable of accounting for, and integrating, all the macro and micro evidence' and 'which could, in turn, lead to new, testable implications' (Modigliani 1975). However, all these events were happening away from what became recognized as the technical process of hypothesis-testing in econometrics.

Around the time when Marshall started testing Klein's model III, Guy Orcutt was checking Tinbergen's model with a different method and from a relatively different angle, as mentioned in Chapter 3. His central interest was to find means of data experiments to verify whether applied econometric models had truly captured the generating mechanism of time-series data. This interest stemmed from his doctoral research, which involved a lot of sampling (Monte Carlo) experiments, using computers, on non-related series generated by separate processes with autocorrelated properties, to examine their effects on tests of significance. After joining the DAE project on the 'Analysis of Time Series' at Cambridge University, Orcutt extended his experiments to real economic data in an attempt 'to figure out what was the proper model' for economic time-series (Qin 1988*b*). Orcutt took the Tinbergen model as his first guinea-pig. He tested the fifty-two series used in that model against the hypothesis that these series were drawn 'from a single population of linear stochastic series having the same underlying autoregressive structure', and obtained a positive result with the help of correlograms together with *t*- and *F*-tests. Orcutt deduced that since Tinbergen's structural model was made up of a system of linear stochastic difference equations, the economic time-series entered in the system should behave 'very nearly as though they were drawings from some population of linear stochastic autoregressive series' (Orcutt 1948). Subsequently, he applied the same method to Stone's (1945) demand model, Girshick and Haavelmo's (1947) model, and Klein's (1950) models I–III, with the assistance of Cochrane. The findings reinforced the conviction that 'the error terms involved in most current formulations of economic relations are highly positively autocorrelated' and hence, an improved formulation for estimation would be to make first-order difference transformation of the original relations (Cochrane and Orcutt 1949; see also Orcutt and Cochrane 1949). Noticeably, Orcutt and Cochrane utilized the von Neumann ratio and its distribution to test for serial correlation of the residuals.

Orcutt and Cochrane's diagnosis had an immediate impact on the DAE project, headed by Stone, of empirical studies into British consumers' expenditure and behaviour (see Chapter 6; also, for a detailed description of Stone's econometric contribution, see Gilbert 1988). Their work also prompted the awareness among many applied econometricians of the importance of guarding against misspecification problems, especially by keeping an eye on the residual distributions from model estimation. This in turn motivated econometric theorists to search for better tests to help reduce rigorously what had been taken as 'beyond doubt' into what they should 'desire to test'.

5.4 DIAGNOSTIC TESTS FOR MODEL EVALUATION IN THEORETICAL ECONOMETRICS

As mentioned earlier, a great deal of technical effort had been concentrated on developing tools for estimation, identification, and computation in theoretical econometrics since the Cowles contribution. Of the minor effort spent on statistical tests, the target was turned to problems of structural models, quite apart from the ambition of direct verification of economic theories. The tests designed during that time concerned either of the following two issues: (*a*) checking the internal consistency of specified models, though often discussed in closer connection with estimation bias than with specification; and (*b*) assessing the external endurance of estimated models. Both required econometrics to integrate further with the theory of statistical inference, where, however, ready-made tools happened to be running short.

The initial path-breaking development came as a cross-product of econometrics and statistics in the domain of testing for specification bias caused by serial correlations (see Gilbert 1988, sect. 2.4). The earliest available statistical test was the von Neumann ratio, which came out during the beginning of the 1940s. But it was designed for testing serial correlation in a time-series of a variable, not in the residual series of a regression equation. The issue was touched on slightly in a short piece of work by R. L. Anderson in Cowles Monograph 10. There, Anderson stressed the need to deal with the problem of how to test from the residuals for 'independence of successive observations inherent in' the much advocated model form of stochastic difference equations systems. The issue was passed over to his collaborator in the serial correlation research, T. W. Anderson, who recognized it 'to be an important topic in time-series analysis and the application of statistics to economic time-series' from his participation in the econometrics research project at the Cowles Commission (Phillips 1986). The two Andersons constructed an exact test (called 'uniformly most powerful' (UMP) test in statistical terms) of residual autocorrelation for a special type of equation form (R. L. Anderson and T. W. Anderson 1950). The preparation of that joint paper led T. W. Anderson to a deeper perception of the problem. He immediately incorporated the available methods for testing serial correlation into the general framework of the Neyman–Pearson hypothesis-testing theory, established a general form of test statistic and demonstrated the non-existence of UMP tests in general cases (T. W. Anderson 1948). In fact, his 1948 results were among the first showing substantial progress along the lines of the Neyman–Pearson approach in econometrics since Haavelmo's theoretical justification. But this aspect of theoretical significance was overlooked by econometricians, probably because the generalization was presented entirely in terms of mathematical statistics concealing almost all its econometric motivation.

Anderson's work was carried on by James Durbin and Geoffrey Watson at the DAE, Cambridge, when they were working with Orcutt and Cochrane on the same project the 'Analysis of Time Series' in the late 1940s. They saw, from what Orcutt and Cochrane were doing, that there was an urgent need to have a statistical test for the [specification] bias caused by residual autocorrelation. They also saw the limited applicability of the Andersons' test and the impossibility of obtaining UMP tests in most cases. So they thought up the use of upper and lower bounds to the significance limits of the test statistic as a promising approach to bypass the difficulty in constructing more general tests for serial correlation. They chose a statistic in terms of the residuals u from a regression equation: $d = \sum(\Delta u_t)^2/\sum u_{t-1}^2$ (Δu_t being the backward difference of the residuals) on the basis of the general form suggested by Anderson (1948), and established the bounds to its distribution in the context of a general regression model (Durbin and Watson 1950). Subsequently, they tabulated the bounds of their test statistic d and illustrated how to use the test to detect residual autocorrelation with some econometric examples (1951). The test, known as the 'D–W test', together with the table of test statistics, was soon widely used in econometrics as a formal diagnostic device against first-order residual autocorrelation.

Shortly after the work on the residual autocorrelation test, Durbin turned to the problem of errors in variables and proposed the use of the IV method in that context (Durbin 1954a) (see Chapter 3). In that paper, Durbin suggested a test for the [specification] bias in the OLS estimate b of the parameter β: $y = \beta'x + \varepsilon$, when the expectation of the error ε conditional upon the observed values of x was not zero, i.e. $E(\varepsilon/x) \neq 0$, due to errors in the observations of x. The test was designed in effect to detect, in the errors-in-variables case, whether bias existed in taking the actual regressors to be independent of the error term, by examining the difference between the expectations of the OLS estimate b and the IV estimate b^* which had taken care of the errors-in-variables specification. Durbin reported these results at the 1953 European Meeting of the Econometric Society, and explained, in response to his discussant Wold, that 'the distinction between errors-in-variables and errors-in-equations models' did 'not seem to be of great significance' 'for his approach'

(Durbin 1954b). In spite of all these, this test was given a cold shoulder, contrasting sharply with what happened to the Durbin–Watson test, and was to be uncovered about twenty-five years later by Hausman (1978).

As described in Chapter 3, Sargan (1958) endeavoured to develop the IV estimation method for an extended simultaneous-equations model with the Cochrane–Orcutt type of residual auto-regressive specification. In transforming the model into its reduced form, Sargan noticed that the residual autoregressive specifica-tion could also be expressed in terms of structural constraints on the reduced-form coefficients, just as with overidentification constraints. He developed an asymptotic theory for IV estim-ators and suggested, on that basis, the route to 'a significance [specification] test for the existence of a relationship of the proposed [Cochrane–Orcutt] type' (Sargan 1959), following the same principle as the likelihood-ratio tests for overidentification developed by Anderson and Rubin (Phillips 1985). Since Sargan was preoccupied with the generalization of the IV estimator at the time, he did not elaborate the actual test and its applications till around the mid-1960s (Sargan 1964) (see Section 6.3).

While Durbin, Watson, and Sargan were tackling the prob-lems concerning residual autocorrelation, H. Theil grew worried about possible misspecification caused by 'omitted variables' (see Chapter 6). He became aware of this problem in handling the aggregation process from micro- to macro-data (Theil 1954). He established a theorem showing that, under the condition of non-stochastic regressor variables, the criterion of minimum residual variance (or equivalently maximum multiple correla-tion) could be used to discriminate incorrect specifications from the correct one, since the residual sum of squares of incorrect specifications should be 'on the average larger than the sum of squares of the residuals implied by the use of the correct specification' (Theil 1957). Theil's method was not yet a statist-ical test in a strict sense, but it pointed out a way to indicate possible omission of significant regressors by statistical measures based on information from regression residuals. It preceded Zellner's proposal (1962)[6] of a formal test for aggregation bias by means of a Wald test (Wald 1943).

[6] Zellner acknowledged that he did the research at the Netherlands School of Economics and had direct discussions with Theil there (Zellner 1962).

Concerns for model endurance had always been on the minds of early econometricians, and were particularly reflected in the discussion on the 'autonomy' of structural models, as previously described. But the issue was not formalized during the initial formative period of the 1940s. Developments of formal testing-tools for the constancy of structural models over time lagged a bit behind the above developments of tests concerning the internal logic of model misspecification. As described in the previous section, Marshall devised a method of prediction test using 'tolerance intervals'. However, a major problem with the tolerance interval technique was the absence of the standard hypothesis-testing procedure to back it up. Normally, the standard test by means of the analysis of covariance, as proposed by Friedman earlier (see Section 5.2), could be applied when the number of new data observations was sufficiently large to allow for a separate regression, which, however, was rarely so in reality.

T. E. Davis observed the shortcoming of Friedman's test, and proposed a modification of the available standard 'prediction limit statistic' for only one further observation outside of the original sample (which was essentially to form an F-statistic from the ratio between the squared prediction error and its estimated variance) (Davis 1952). Davis's proposal was to make a sequence of predictions, when there was more than one further observation but still insufficient for a separate regression, and base the F-test statistic on the two averages of all the prediction errors and their variances. He applied his method to the forecasting abilities of various types of existing consumption functions, e.g. static equations with one or two explanatory variables, static equations with a separate trend term, some kind of growth-rate equations, some kind of distributed lag equations with one lag. All the equations were rejected by the test as unacceptable for forecasting, though the latter two appeared to produce better results than the others.

A full solution to testing the constancy of linear regression coefficients over different time-spans (or sample sizes) was due to G. C. Chow. In an empirical study of the demand for automobiles in the USA, Chow found himself confronted with the problem of how to decide whether an economic relationship represented by a linear regression equation remained 'stable in two periods of time', or held 'for two different groups of

economic units'. The problem set him to construct a test of the
equality between sets of linear regression coefficients from the
general approach of linear hypothesis-testing (Chow 1960). He
pointed out that a major weakness of Davis's method was that
the prediction errors might cancel out in the averaging summation to give falsely small averages. Following the same route of
the test based on the prediction interval for one new observation, Chow chose to extend that F-test by using the ratio of the
difference between the residual sum of squares of the overall
regression and that of the original subset regression to the
residual sum of squares of the original subset regression, all
adjusted for the corresponding degrees of freedom. The Chow
test, as it has been commonly called since then, suited the
situation when the number of additional observations was more
than one but less than required for a separate regression, because
it was only built on the original observations and all the
observations as a whole. Chow further demonstrated how his
test was related to the previous ones on the basis of the
prediction interval, and the analysis of covariance within the
general framework of the theory of linear hypothesis-testing.

The invention of the above statistical tests, most noticeably
the D–W test and Chow test, greatly facilitated applied modelling activities. Applied modellers picked up these tests immediately to detect the possible deficiencies of a priori formulated
structural models, caused supposedly by the data complexities.
Their wide application encouraged theoretical econometricians
to work out more tests of the same kind for various kinds of
data complexities. Testing thus became generally regarded as a
technical phase of model evaluation within the established structural modelling procedure, a much narrower and more spe-
cialized scope than that implied in its original notion. Meanwhile
in economics, the general principle of hypothesis-testing against
data information spread in theory formulation, as applied
econometric results accumulated. However, problems gradually
accrued between the practice of such 'data-instigated' (this term
comes from Leamer 1978) theory formulation induced by testing
and the theorists' abidance by the structural approach, where
econometric modelling was to start from structural models given
a priori with complete certainty. Many of the problems were
reflected in the discussions and controversies over the applica-

tion of newly developed econometric tools to applied modelling, immediately after econometrics was formalized. They turned out to relate closely to the function of those techniques and the interpretation of their results with respect to model construction. A report on them forms the topic of the next chapter.

6

Model Construction Revisited

In the late 1940s, trial applications appeared of the newly developed tools of estimation and identification. Klein's famous first three macroeconomic models, known as Klein models I–III (Klein 1950) served as a paradigm. The models were expected to demonstrate that the structural approach 'would revolutionize economics', as anticipated by the Cowles group (Phillips 1986). However, the outcome looked somewhat disappointing. Serious weaknesses in the model construction phase of the structural approach were revealed in these preliminary applied modelling attempts. As some of the Cowles people put it, before their newly invented tools were applicable, 'we must know the form of all the equations that connect the several variables of the system; we must know which variables are endogenous and which are exogenous' (Klein 1950: 12). They also noted however 'that economic theory was not always specific enough; nor did the data always fit what theory suggested', as recalled by Anderson (1990). By the end of the 1940s, the Cowles group had recognized the urgency of 'the formulation of precise economic theories of practical relevance and the submission of these to statistical tests' (Cowles Commission 1949). Feeling restricted by computing technology and data availability as well as statistical theory, the group soon turned its research focus upon mathematical economics from the 1950s onwards. Meanwhile, developments in econometrics grew more diversified and contentious as the elegance and rigour of the structural modelling procedure became eroded by the substantial amount of equation search involved in applied modelling. The structural modelling procedure only explained how to estimate and identify a priori given structural models, while many of the empirical studies actually involved groping for the appropriate structural models given the data. Mismatch of the two sides gave rise to many problems and disputes, as the procedure and the associated techniques spread and formed the core of orthodox econometrics. At the time, problems and disputes appeared mostly in connection with the roles and ways that modellers attributed to individual tools of testing, identification, and estimation in the integrated process of empirical model construction.

This chapter therefore revisits the issue of model construction with particular respect to the roles of testing, identification, and estimation. It depicts how controversies arose as econometricians were swayed back to more data-based positions, away from the emphasis on a priori considerations, back to statistical results, away from reliance on economic theory, and back to dynamics, away from concerns over contemporaneous interdependency.[1]

Section 6.1 looks at modelling issues associated with hypothesis-testing. This appears to be the most backward area with hindsight, but the least disputed at the time. Problems about model formulation with respect to identification are examined in Section 6.2. Section 6.3 turns to the 'estimation' aspect of modelling. In contrast to Section 6.1, the most acute disputes occurred in this area despite the fact that estimation methods were then the most developed. A central discord arose of whether it was redundant or still essential for applied purposes to further the formalization efforts, as exemplified by those of the Cowles group. Section 6.4 leads the discord to the focal issue of the probability approach underlying established econometrics. By illustrating that most of the problems could be viewed as due to the incompleteness of the probability approach, as suggested in Chapter 1, this final section leaves the story with an open end.

6.1 TESTING AND MODEL CONSTRUCTION

As shown in the previous chapter, the practice of testing in the literature gradually polarised in two directions. The general idea of theory verification by means of econometric models was

---

[1] This chapter moves slightly away from the style used in the previous chapters. Instead of making an extensive survey of the historical events, it focuses on the most representative and controversial events in order to provide readers with a full perspective over the whole period of history examined. The literature covered here is therefore not exhaustive.

popularized in the contiguous area of applied econometrics and economics. In the contiguous area of theoretical econometrics and mathematical statistics, testing became a much narrower concept defining a technical process in model building within the established structural framework. This narrowing encouraged the mutual practice, in both applied and theoretical econometrics alike, of using econometric tests as diagnostic tools for uncovering many of the problems of inconsistency in matching data with theoretical models built by the structural approach. Such uncovered problems led to discernible differences in the ways in which the test results were explained and exploited in connection with model construction.

As mentioned above, Klein models I–III exemplified the Cowles new inventions. But they also exemplified a pragmatic modelling route, which retained quite a lot of Tinbergen's modelling style, i.e. modifying equations with respect to data features which emerged in estimation. Klein argued that 'academic economic theory is only one among alternative sources for the development of hypotheses. . . . We shall by no means be so narrow as to insist that econometric work be built on this particular foundation' (Klein 1953: 3). He pointed out that the final choice of a model depended largely on 'pragmatic considerations'. This pragmatic position of accommodating empirical flexibility to the structural approach was strengthened through Marshall's and Christ's tests, others' opinions on Klein model III, the forecasting results of the model, and experience of other modellers. It was further consolidated by the combined efforts of Klein and Goldberger to build better models than the Klein model III (Klein and Goldberger 1955).

The construction of the Klein–Goldberger model followed roughly the same approach as the Klein models I–III, except that the scale was enlarged with many more new variables and lagged terms. Although theoretical justifications for including these new elements were given prior to statistical analyses in the book, actual decisions on their inclusion were often made in inverse order. For example, many of the structural relations were finalized in forms through a great deal of statistical testing among various alternative schemes, and then wrapped up with theoretical considerations, because 'details of a priori analysis' were 'rarely' found to 'stand up against the facts of real life'

(Klein and Goldberger 1955: 56). In particular, whenever no statistically satisfactory theoretical relations could be found, 'empirical time-series expression' (i.e. autoregression) was adopted (p. 28). These data-instigated modelling activities were however somewhat obscured by the scant reports of the tried, but discarded, alternatives.[2] Nevertheless, statistical tests here were clearly used for diagnostic purposes, and the results were used effectively for formulating working theoretical relations. This way of making use of testing in model construction was implied in an earlier statement by Klein that 'a great deal of empirical work will be of the utmost importance in the formulation of hypotheses' (Klein 1953: 14–17).

Such a pragmatic modelling approach was developed into a more stepwise and more explicit procedure by H. Theil, called 'specification analysis' (now referred to as 'misspecification analysis') in the late 1950s. He first noticed the problem of misspecification while he was looking for the sufficient conditions to aggregate economic relations (Theil 1954). He then discovered its wide existence in his extensive survey of the previous macroeconometric forecasting records, which revealed that the phenomenon of 'underestimation of changes . . . with respect to a well-defined variable' prevailed (Theil 1961: 543–4). In tracing its causes, Theil soon became convinced that it was unfeasible in practice to follow rigidly the structural modelling procedure, namely, relying upon economic theory to provide correct postulates in the form of a well-defined structural model, or a 'maintained hypothesis' (i.e. the set of admissible hypotheses), and then obtain structural estimates by significance tests of individual parameters. The reason for this judgement was that such an approach 'greatly overestimates the economic theorist's knowledge and intellectual power'. He observed that the common practice in applied model revision often rejected and changed part of the original 'maintained' hypothesis, instead of rejecting the null hypothesis, when the original model had produced 'unsatisfactory results'. So Theil set out to systematize

---

[2] C. Christ gave an account of all the places in Klein and Goldberger (1955) where statistical selections among different equation forms were suggested, and commented that 'their work would be even more useful to others had they presented all the equations with which they experimented and the estimates obtained for each' (Christ 1956).

the applied modelling procedure of a trial-and-error type into explicit 'specification analysis' by 'an experimental approach' (pp. 206–7).

Noticeably, the problem how to set up the maintained hypothesis had been addressed by Haavelmo (see Chapter 5), but not as acutely as Theil put it. That was mainly because the two men had different types of economic theories on their minds when they discussed the problem. For Haavelmo, the economic theory underlying his maintained hypotheses was the most general type, since he remained at the purely theoretical level. Whereas for Theil from his applied stand, available economic theories were far from general, and therefore his maintained hypotheses were indeed far more fragile.

As for testing models, Theil agreed with the opinion that ' "the" criterion' for testing the goodness of an econometric model is that 'it predicts well'. But he argued that since 'it is neither always conclusive nor always feasible', two additional criteria of 'rather subjective' nature could be applied: 'plausibility' and 'simplicity' (Theil 1961: 205). These criteria supported his 'experimental' appeal towards model building, and especially his disapproval of 'the statistical theory which forbids the rejection of a "maintained" hypothesis'. It is worth while to quote his argument on this point:

What is incorrect, however, is to act as if the final hypothesis presented is the first one, whereas in fact it is the result of much experimentation. Since every econometric analysis is an essay in persuasion—just as is true for any other branch of science—the line of thought leading to the finally accepted result must be expounded. It is not true that analyses which are in the end not accepted are useless. The mere fact that a certain 'maintained' hypothesis can be excluded raises the plausibility of its rivals. This can be compared to a large extent with the function of standard errors of parameter estimates. Just as the standard errors contribute to an appraisal of numerical outcomes within a certain 'maintained' hypothesis, in just the same way alternative analyses of separate 'maintained' hypotheses contribute to an appraisal of the hypothesis which is finally preferred. (Theil 1961: 207)

To illustrate his point, Theil criticized the conventional practice of judging parameter estimates by 'correct' signs or plausible order of magnitudes. He pointed out that these simple methods implied erroneous construction of the maintained hypothesis, since the maintained hypothesis either was incomplete in so far as it excluded a priori known information about those signs and orders of magnitudes, or violated the rules of construction in so far as some of the information included was actually uncertain (Theil 1961: 233). He argued therefore that a more explicit model construction strategy should be adopted and accompanied by a schematic 'analysis of specification errors' by means of statistical inference.

Like his contemporaries, Theil started his 'specification analysis' from particularly specified, simple structural models, using the standard regression conditions as the criteria. The analysis began with the problem of diagnosing wrong choices of explanatory variables. He dealt with it in two consecutive steps. First, he set up a measure for the consequences of erroneous choices of explanatory variables by transforming the estimated coefficients of the erroneous equation into a weighted sum of all the coefficients of the true equation, so as to express the degree of misspecification in terms of the difference between the two, denoted 'the specification bias' (Theil 1957; see also Griliches 1957). This measure of specification bias was applied to illustrate the consequences of omitted variables, incorrect equation forms, and errors in the variables (Theil 1957, 1961). Secondly, he established 'the criterion of minimum residual variance' as a primitive test criterion for selection among several alternative equations (hypotheses) when the true one was not known. This meant that selection among competing equations was made by comparison of their residual variances provided the regressors were non-stochastic or otherwise independent of the error term (Theil 1957). The next problem that Theil tried to tackle was multicollinearity. The problem was recognized by considerable sampling variances of the parameter estimates. Theil did not provide a general solution to the problem. But he opposed the thoughtless practice of dropping some explanatory variables in case of high multicollinearity. He suggested 'that we can rearrange our problem in such a way that the multicollinearity difficulty is avoided' (Theil 1961: 217). He used, as an example, Koyck's transformation of a model with geometric distributed lags into a partial adjustment model (Koyck 1954) (see also Section 6.3). Theil then turned to the problem of residual autocorrelation. He adopted the diagnosis and the prescription by the DAE people at Cambridge, i.e. to detect the autocorrelation by D–W tests and to cure it by using growth-rate models (see below). As for the problem of simultaneity, its well-known symptom was Haavelmo bias. Theil recommended his own device of the 2SLS method as the prescription. Finally, he proposed a method of 'mixed estimation' (together with Goldberger, cf. Theil and Goldberger 1961) for the problem of omitted a priori information in the specified model. The method was to specify the extra information not already included in the model, e.g. the expected signs and orders of magnitude of parameters, explicitly in the form of constraints on the parameters concerned, so as to utilize them 'in the same way as observational information' (Theil 1961: 233) (see also Section 6.4).

It is discernible that Theil's specification analysis was designed to reach a working structural model from a simple a priori theoretical model, which was consistent with various statistical tests of the data. The revisions of the original theoretical model due to statistical tests were regarded also as part of the theoretical model, and were given economic interpretations. By openly allowing successive extensions of the maintained hypothesis, Theil reinforced the pragmatic approach that statistical tests were used mainly for constructing part of the theory not yet formulated a priori rather than for verifying the original model.

But the revised parts of an a priori model were not always taken as parts of the theory by all the applied modellers. For those who were more concerned with theory verification, model revisions through diagnostic tests could be interpreted somewhat differently. For instance, the issue of how to test theories by applied econometric models using the structural modelling procedure was on the research agenda of the Department of Applied Economics at Cambridge headed by R. Stone at the end of 1950. Noticeably, the DAE group paid close attention to the connection and the relationship between empirical findings and established economic theories. This was especially reflected in Stone's writings of the period. In a monograph *The Role of Measurement in Economics*, Stone ranked 'facts and empirical constructs' as 'the first-class' questions in empirical analyses (1951: 7), and thought of them as forming the basis for testing economic theories, 'deductively formulated' from certain postulates (pp. 12–15). Elsewhere, he maintained that 'the role of theory is to reduce the number of possibilities to be examined at any one stage and to permit the investigator to interpret the results of his analysis. It is a simple device for economizing and should be used for that reason wherever possible' (Stone 1954*b*: p. xxx). Stone reckoned that the purpose of testing theory lay in 'satisfying ourselves that for practical purposes the actual world behaves as if the postulates of the theory held true in it' (1951: 15). These statements implied a more strict view on theory formulation than the one held by Klein and Theil for example, though the emphasis on empirical knowledge and the faith in the structural modelling procedure were shared. For Stone and his group, theory should be 'deductively formulated' and then verified through empirical work, whereas in the pragmatic approach described earlier, theory formulation was finalized during the empirical modelling exercise. This subtle difference was revealed in the way in which the DAE people interpreted the model revisions resulting from specification analysis. A good illustration of this was their response to the problem of detected residual autocorrelations, originally by von Neumann ratio tests and later by D–W tests. Their prescription, due to Orcutt and Cochrane as described in Chapters 3 and 5, was to append an error autoregressive equation to the relevant structural equation. The simplest case would be:

$$y_t = \beta x_t + u_t \tag{6.1}$$

$$u_t = \rho u_{t-1} + \varepsilon_t \qquad |\rho| < 1; \ \varepsilon_t \sim IN(0, \sigma_\varepsilon^2). \tag{6.2}$$

(6.1) and (6.2) laid the basic form for the later appeared 'common factor' (or COMFAC) analysis (see e.g. Sargan 1980). The two equations implied a quasi-difference expression:

$$y_t - \rho y_{t-1} = \beta(x_t - \rho x_{t-1}) + \varepsilon_t. \tag{6.3}$$

(See Orcutt and Cochrane 1949.) When $\rho \to 1$, (6.3) would reduce to a first-difference model:

$$\Delta y_t = \beta \Delta x_t + \varepsilon_t. \tag{6.4}$$

Model (6.4) was widely used in the DAE empirical consumption studies (Stone 1948, 1954*b*). Their justification for using it was: 'analyses made with the original data showed, in general, a significant amount of positive serial correlation in the observed residuals', and 'this correlation could, in general, be effectively removed by working with first differences' (Stone 1954b: 308). However, they ignored a loophole in so far as the consequence of substituting variables in levels in the original theoretical analyses by variables in differences implied an alteration of the theoretical meaning underlying the model. Equation (6.1) embodied a long-term relationship whereas (6.4) could only depict a short-term relationship as it was, by nature, a growth-rate model.

What shielded the loophole was just the way in which model revisions in light of the diagnostic tests were interpreted. With strong belief in the theory (6.1), the addition of (6.2) resulting from residual correlation tests was not thought of as carrying any economic implications. It was merely a statistical adjustment to take care of the 'inexactness' involved in moving from pure theory to rather complicated data observations, so as to secure 'the appropriate estimation procedure' for identifying and obtaining estimates of those a priori formulated structural parameters (Stone 1954b: 239). In this way, the originally deductively formulated structural model was seemingly kept intact for measurement and verification, but at the expense of having some auxiliary specifications added between it and the data. Changes induced by these specifications in the economic implications of the model were likely to be overlooked, as long as they were regarded as covering up certain 'estimation problems', such as residual autocorrelation, multicollinearity, measurement errors etc. (see Stone 1954b, ch. 19). But it was almost impossible to maintain this position in all the applied studies. The applied studies by the DAE people also showed instances of data-instigated model formulation, e.g. Stone's 1945 work on market demand and his 1954 work on the linear expenditure systems, as cited in the previous chapters.

Up to the end of the 1950s, test developments and applications in econometrics were aimed at diagnosing the places where the a priori specified models were incompatible with data. The efforts of applied modellers to deal with such incompatibilities led to the trial-and-error practice of specification searches for better models with respect to 'all-over performance testing of the models in question' (Koopmans 1957). Stop-gap remedies were commonly used to patch up the incompatibility bit by bit. Modellers viewed the remedies differently, however. For those who considered the additionally respecified part of the model as devoid of any economic meaning, theory measurement and therefore model estimation absorbed their central attention. Although they were concerned with theory verification, the estimated results actually had very low power for that purpose with the respecified part added between the original theory and the data. For many who employed tests in search of data-instigated structural models, test results served actually for hypothesis-formulation rather than hypothesis-testing. Furthermore, since this kind of specification search involved constant changes of the model framework (i.e. the maintained hypothesis), the test results seldom offered much guidance, having detected faults, to the definite directions along which the tested model should be rebuilt. Therefore, such tests were later labelled as 'non-constructive tests' (see Goldfeld and Quandt 1972). Model reconstruction was thus often based upon arbitrary and *non sequitur* decisions in practice. Few people however recognized and worried about these decisions at the time, for there were more obviously arbitrary decisions in model construction to occupy the worries of econometricians. One of the particular topics of concern was model identification.

6.2 IDENTIFICATION AND MODEL CONSTRUCTION

As described in Chapter 4, the necessary condition for model identifiability (i.e. the order condition) was found to be closely connected with the specification of exogenous variables in setting up 'complete' models 'for statistical purposes' (Koopmans 1950). In applied circumstances, the identification requirement frequently resulted in the imposition of additional exogenous variables to the original structural models, since the particular economic theories underlying the structural models often turned out to be short of the requirement of 'complete'. The formalized identification theory disregarded the issue of whence the imposition should come, and left the job to model construction, specification, and testing. However, these steps could never stay apart in the applied world. With little theoretical guidance at hand, applied modellers were induced to make too much use of identification restrictions in model specification merely for the sake of identification. This situation gave rise to the frequent occurrence of the arbitrary imposition of identifying restrictions in applied model construction. The need for checking the validity of these restrictions grew prominent and imminent, when it came to applying the estimated model results to real economic problems.

Indeed it was the practical motives of forecasts and policy making that induced Orcutt (1952) to ponder over the common practice of specifying a priori endogenous and exogenous variables in model building. From the policy-makers' standpoint, he held that 'more emphasis needs to be placed on building and testing models or components of models which include as exogenous variables those variables that we know how to control, and that we contemplate using for control purposes'. He observed that in econometric modelling 'the specification of which variables are to be considered exogenous is either done on the basis of theoretical convenience from the standpoint of limiting the field of interest or is done on the basis of some *a priori* knowledge of unspecified source. In any case, *the specification is not subject to any test whatsoever*. . . . Little or no attention has been given to evidence or lack of evidence of relationship between movements of those variables selected as exogenous.' To spell out his points, Orcutt criticized further the situation where 'frequently the literature is far from explicit about the difference between endogenous and exogenous variables. And sometimes the distinction is merely used for the purpose of arbitrarily setting the limits of the problem under consideration', and where 'the interest of econometricians has been too much preoccupied with estimating interrelationships in the economic system to the almost complete neglect of testing hypotheses about which variables are wholly or partially exogenous to the economic system.' He then stressed the fact that 'the interpretation of the obtained econometric models depends critically' on the 'choice of exogenous variables', so as to reinforce his appeal for a 'partial redirection of econometrics' toward testing and 'discovery of exogenous variables and of as complete a specification as possible of their impact'. In particular, Orcutt called for more studies on 'the continuity properties of economic time-series' in association with 'the impact of instruments of control or policy actions'. This precautionary statement preceded the 'Lucas critique' (1976) by over twenty years.

Orcutt's appeals met a sympathetic response from Koopmans (1952). Koopmans interpreted Orcutt's observations largely as concerns about 'the problem of specification: the choice of the model, and the nature of the evidence that can be adduced in support of that choice'. Deeply involved in the structural approach, Koopmans explained dishearteningly the near impossibility of performing statistical tests on specifications of most exogenous variables due to the constraint of identifiability, upon which the estimability of test statistics was conditioned. He wrote that 'assurance that a given variable is exogenous can only be obtained by qualitative knowledge of the variables causally involved in *its* generation. If the model can be extended by additional equations describing the generation of the presumably exogenous variables, the needed information is of the same type as that required for identifiability.' Koopmans further accredited the difficulty to the specification of 'sufficiently strong' maintained hypotheses, which were prerequisite to and exempt from any statistical tests, in order to ensure the identifiability of the parameters to be tested. Since the maintained hypotheses included inevitably '*a priori* specification as to which variables are exogenous' so as to enable certain parameters to be identified, 'this specification then escapes all possibility of a test'. Koopmans therefore concluded that 'the evidence on which the choice of exogenous variables rests must be sought primarily in qualitative knowledge about the place of the variables in question in the causal hierarchy, with slight chances of corroboration from statistical tests utilizing time series', although he held no objection that 'it would be very important to have a test of exogeneity' (Koopmans 1952).

This viewpoint of Koopmans's was seconded by Tinbergen, who maintained that 'in principle' 'the specification of the variables chosen as exogenous . . . should be based, in my opinion, on *a priori* rather than on statistical considerations' (Tinbergen 1952). All these encouraged econometricians to lean, in model construction and specification, upon a priori theory and knowledge, which was 'not subject to conclusive test' (Koopmans 1952).

Noticeably, Koopmans referred heavily to Simon's 1953 paper concerning the concepts and relationship between causality, exogeneity specification, and identifiability, instead of to the paper by Reiersøl and himself (1950), in his comments on Orcutt's paper. This put much emphasis upon the a priori side of the identification issue. As described already in Chapter 4, Section 4, Simon's exposition strongly helped to insulate model construction and specification from statistical testing with his 'inverse' interpretation of identifiability. In addition, Simon seemed to have included all the predetermined variables in his classification of exogenous variables, as he derived it from the imaginary process of reducing 'self-contained subsets' from the original full structure (Simon 1953). His definition significantly strengthened the outlook of a simultaneous and deterministic economic mechanism at the expense of dynamics and the probability approach. But the insulation of model specification from statistical testing by identification was obscured by the purely theoretical level at which Simon proceeded with his discussion, since concerns about true correspondence with respect to reality here were of little relevance. The discussion over causality and identifiability aroused by Simon was soon converted into the dispute over simultaneity versus causal chain-modelling strategies between H. Wold and defenders of the Cowles methodology. The dispute appeared more difficult to settle, being at a purely theoretical level where no common testing criteria could be resorted to (see the next section).

Back in the applied world, overidentified models prevailed gradually, with the popularization of the structural modelling procedure. As already pointed out, identifiability even became one of the model building criteria in the 1950s. The first person who stood out to challenge this 'habit' was T.-C. Liu. During the construction of a forecasting model for the US economy in the early 1950s, Liu noticed that overidentifying restrictions would create differences between estimates obtained by the 'reduced-form solutions' via the restricted maximum-likelihood route set by the Cowles group, and those obtained directly from regression equations by least-squares (Liu 1955). This placed weight on the soundness of the overidentifying restrictions. He noticed from his empirical modelling experience that actually 'all structural relationships are likely to be "underidentified"' 'in economic reality' (Liu 1955), and there was a great deal of arbitrariness in formulating overidentifying restrictions. This brought him around to resist the orthodox structural route in his modelling practice, and eventually motivated him to launch his famous critique of the Cowles structural approach (he referred to it as 'the reduced-form solutions approach') (Liu 1960, 1963, written in 1957).

Liu built his argument from the specification of 'the joint distribution of the current values of the endogenous variables, given the predetermined variables'. He noted that 'the reduced-form function' was in fact a representation of this distribution function, and that identification conditions under the Cowles methodology amounted to 'compromising' the maximum-likelihood principle 'in the reduced-form solutions approach' with respect to 'the so-called *a priori* restrictions' (Liu 1955). He then contested that these so-called a priori restrictions were 'really mostly oversimplifications of economic reality' rather than 're-quired by "economic theory" concerned', as 'often expressed in the Cowles Commission literature' (Liu 1963). Thus he reasoned that since the situation of whether the structural model was over- or under-identified, did 'not constitute any constraint' on the unrestricted ML function, i.e. the reduced form, estimation should be based directly upon and start from the reduced form instead of going through the Cowles route of reduced-form solutions (1955, 1963). It is worth noting that Liu's argument implied the generality of the reduced form over the structural model. But this point was obscured by his emphasis on demonstrating the superiority of the least-squares reduced-form estimation over the Cowles structural approach in forecasting. It was not until two decades later that his point was readdressed in C. Sims's (1980) paper for the method of vector autoregression (VAR). At the time, attention soon focused on the more superficial question of the competing merits of the LS and ML principles in estimation (see the next section).

Liu's argument was in effect underpinned by acute considerations about the correspondence of the estimated relationships with the 'true' ones with respect to economic reality. In the absence of a testing scheme, Liu skirted round the issue of how to detect misspecifications in the a priori identifying restrictions to seek more fundamental solutions through reconstruction of applied models. His applied experience taught him that models with more dynamic factors, i.e. with 'more finely divided time-periods' (e.g. quarterly or monthly) or further disaggregated sectors, could get around the underidentification problem, because the chance of identification would go up by increasing the number of lagged (predetermined) variables (1960). Here he turned his sharp eye upon the error autoregressive model form, initiated by Orcutt and Cochrane, and questioned its validity in handling residual serial correlation. His argument was simple but forceful:

To consider an autoregressive scheme for an error term as a part of structural estimation is clearly unsatisfactory. For the use of such a scheme amounts to a confession that an economic explanation for a systematic (nonrandom) part of the movement in the variable to be explained has not been found. . . . The omission of relevant variables is an important, if not the main, reason for the existence of serial correlation in the estimated residuals (Liu 1960).

From this standpoint, he advocated the strategy of introducing more lagged variables into theoretical models, recommending particularly two models in this context (1960). One was Klein and Barger's recursive quarterly US model (Klein and Barger 1954), which was regarded by Liu as 'a fundamental reversal of the position underlying the simultaneous-equation approach'. The other was the experimental analysis of adaptive expectations by M. Nerlove.

Nerlove's model resulted from his doctoral research in estimating farmers' responses to prices (1958; written in 1954–6). The applied problem led him to study the issue of correspondence between data information and theory. Nerlove observed that 'insufficient attention has been devoted to the problem of identifying the price variable to which farmers react', and one of his major objectives was to 'identify' the appropriate price variable connected to farmers' response with one or several observable variables (pp. 24–5). The connotation associated with his use of the term 'identify' differed significantly from that in the Cowles identification theory. It contained a certain reversion towards the original identification problem. It anticipated the development of a different notion of identification in the later literature of economic time-series analysis, e.g. in Box and Jenkins (1970). Nerlove resorted to dynamic models for solutions to his identification problem. He believed that dynamic models could mimic reality better than static models (1956, 1958). In particular, he chose the hypothesis of adaptive expectations to account for farmers' adjustment to price response and derived a theoretical relationship, later known as the 'partial adjustment model'. Its simple form is:

$$y_t = \alpha x_t + \beta y_{t-1} + v_t. \tag{6.5}$$

Actually, the relationship that Nerlove developed at the time and used mainly was the type which is now labelled 'dead-start':

$$y_t = \alpha x_{t-1} + \beta y_{t-1} + v_t. \tag{6.6}$$

Nerlove found that his model produced better-estimated results than those produced by static models and reduced the symptoms associated with residual autocorrelation at the same time. Since this apparently satisfied his main object of estimation, Nerlove did not explore further the implications of his model specification, but just demonstrated that his adjustment model implied 'certain forms of *distributed lags*' (Nerlove 1958) (see the next section).

It is interesting to observe that there was a certain degree of similarity in people's attitudes to testing and identification with respect to model construction. Here, for those who looked at the identification problem more from the angle of data information, the part of a model instigated by identification considerations was interpreted as an inherent part of the theoretical model. Identification served hypothesis formulation. As for those who approached the problem more from the theoretical angle, the imposed identification conditions were treated largely as additional to the structural model. Identification then helped tuck the original model further away from statistical tests against data. Neither way of interpreting the identification conditions in model construction brought the issue closer to hypothesis-testing. In fact, model estimation attracted the central interest of econometricians from both sides.

6.3 ESTIMATION AND MODEL CONSTRUCTION

The most heated controversies over model construction from the late 1940s till the early 1960s involved methods of estimation, mainly between the ML camp and the LS camp. As mentioned in Chapter 3, least-squares estimators held on to their popularity with applied modellers, in spite of the advantages of the maximum-likelihood technique demonstrated by the Cowles group. Super-ficially, the popularity had much to do with the obvious computing advantages of the LS estimators. But a deep and crucial reason for the unceasing controversies lay in the very fact that the choice of estimators depended upon the type of structural models specified. Thus the validity of the choice depended vitally upon the validity of the specified model. This was clearly at the heart of the debate between H. Wold and proponents of the SEM.

As described in earlier chapters, Wold started his econometric career as a purely statistical time-series analyst. He was espe-cially won over by the method of regression analysis taught by H. Cramér and the disequilibrium approach of the Swedish macroeconomic school by means of 'sequence' analysis, when he began his econometric practice by building applied models for demand analysis (1943–4).[3] From his knowledge and experi-ence, Wold developed an approach called 'recursive' or 'causal-chain' modelling to challenge the simultaneous-equations modelling approach (see Epstein 1987; Morgan 1991).

Wold's interest in the causal implications of models was provoked primarily by the early debate over the choice of regression directions in connection with demand analysis (Wold 1965). Looking from a dynamic viewpoint, Wold maintained that the problem of 'regression direction' should be solved by formulating applied models, such as demand models, in terms of non-simultaneous systems according to the subject-matter of research. Furthermore, he established a device called 'condi-tional regression analysis' based upon the implicit causal links provided by the subject-matter to solve the problem of high interdependency (or collinearity) among explanatory variables. It was designed to condition certain explanatory variables on some other available information, e.g. to estimate the price elasticity of demand conditioned upon the estimated income elasticity obtained from cross-section data, so as to avoid the collinearity between price and income. Least-squares could therefore always be valid estimators (Wold 1943–4). From the same viewpoint, Wold interpreted Tinbergen's macroeconometric model as a recursive model, and Tinbergen's approach as a

---

[3] Actually Wold had a part of his demand studies published in Swedish as early as 1940, see the reference in Wold (1943).

significant approval of his own. (Tinbergen (1939: i.13) explicitly referred to the 'sequence analysis' of Swedish economists in formulating dynamic economic theory.)

The discovery of Haavelmo bias and the consequent development of the simultaneous-equations model by the Cowles group greatly upset Wold, because it seemed to invalidate all the results that he had worked out on the basis of the LS method. So Wold, together with R. Bentzel, investigated the degree of OLS bias in the context of a dynamic system (i.e. a recursive model) underlying all his previous applied studies (Bentzel and Wold 1946). Their original model was:

$$x_t^{(i)} = F_i(x_t^{(1)}, x_{t-1}^{(1)}, \ldots, x_t^{(i-1)}, x_{t-1}^{(i-1)}, \ldots; x_{t-1}^{(i)}, x_{t-2}^{(i)}, \ldots,$$
$$x_{t-1}^{(n)}, x_{t-2}^{(n)}, \ldots) + \xi_t^{(i)}$$
$$(i = 1, \ldots, n; t = 1, \ldots, T). \tag{6.7}$$

A simpler representation of the model was in linear matrix form:

$$y_t = Ay_t + Bz_t + v_t \text{ with } E(y_t/\hat{y}_t, z_t) = Ay_t + Bz_t, \tag{6.8}$$

where $\{y_t z_t\} = x_t$ (see Wold 1965).

Wold and Bentzel regarded the system (6.7) to be adequately general to represent the gist of sequence analysis, for it described an economic structure in a clearly defined causal chain in a recursive manner, 'i.e. $x_t^{(i)}$ can for every i be calculated from the development of $x^{(1)}, \ldots, x^{(n)}$ up to the time point $t - 1$' (Bentzel and Wold 1946). They found with relief that the LS method could, under fairly general assumptions, still apply to their type of dynamic system. This discovery drew their attention from defending the LS method to defending their model system. Thus the focus of dispute was shifted from different estimation techniques to different strategies in formulating theoretical models, when Wold and Bentzel's 1946 paper came out (see Wold 1965).

The findings with Bentzel strengthened Wold's belief in the recursive system as the most basic structural model representing a 'discrete process' of 'a joint probability distribution which specifies . . . an infinite sequence of variables' (Wold and Juréen 1953).[4] In order to maintain this position, Wold undertook a

[4] Notice that Wold only considered 'stationary' processes in his statistical discussions.

series of studies exploring the 'attractive features' of his recursive model (1965). He showed that the recursive model guaranteed a straightforward causal interpretation (1949, 1954), and that any given set of time-series could be represented formally as a causal chain system satisfying the basic regression requirements (1948, 1951). Meanwhile, Wold and his colleagues cast serious doubt on Haavelmo and the Cowles simultaneous-equations formulation, which he referred to as an interdependent (ID) system. He criticized it for failing to specify clear-cut causal relations and their dynamic motion (Bentzel and Wold 1946; Wold and Juréen 1953; Wold 1954, 1956; Bentzel and Hansen 1955). This immediately got entangled with Simon's (1953) causality and identifiability observation described above in Section 6.2 (Wold 1954, 1955; Simon 1955). The debate over causality instigated Wold to find a 'precise causal interpretation . . . to the coefficients of ID systems' using his causal chain systems (1965). The outcome of his investigation was that if an interdependent system was causally interpretable, it was then 'either an approximation to the recursive system or a description of its equilibrium state' (Strotz 1960; also Strotz and Wold 1960). This outcome seems to suggest that any identifiable interdependent system could be 'encompassed' by a recursive system using the present terminology.

Using causal chains as the main criterion, Wold further criticized the simultaneous-equations approach by warning that 'specification errors' would occur when causal relations were ill-defined or important variables were omitted (1954, 1956). He explained that these errors were different from sampling errors and tended to be of much larger order of magnitude than sampling errors in the case of large samples. Worse still, he wrote, 'the presence of a specification error is not signalled by the standard error of a regression coefficient, for this accounts only for the sampling error. . . . No routine methods are available for guarding ourselves against a specification error' (Wold 1954; see also Strotz 1960). Thus Wold saw the need to further clarify the rationale of non-experimental modelling with respect to causal interpretation. This led him to the idea that 'the general procedures of operation with relations' in model building should be best 'specified in terms of conditional expectations', which he termed 'eo ipso predictors' (1965; see also Wold 1961, 1963).

Despite his opposition to the simultaneous-equations model formulation, Wold's overall view on modelling procedures was very much the same as that of the simultaneous-equations camp, especially in view of his strong claim on the priority of theory in formulating a good causal model. He relied upon economic theory for arbitration among multiple hypotheses, and believed that '*ad hoc* tests' should be used only on the basis of 'theoretical or empirical evidence' to detect possible specification errors. In case the error did exist, correction could be made by adding 'further factors as explanatory variables' to the model (Wold 1954). His unanimity with the Cowles group on the structural modelling procedure can best be seen in his conviction that a system of statistical relations, i.e. the reduced-form type, was 'less general' than structural models, and that structural models in the form of the causal chain system were less general than those in the form of the simultaneous-equations system. Therefore, he adhered to the structural modelling procedure, even when he derived the same reduced form from alternative or even rival structural systems (Wold 1956). In his 1965 paper, Wold outlined that there were three types of structural models: (A) the vector regression system:

$$y_t = Rz_t + \epsilon_t \text{ with } E(y_t/z_t) = Rz_t; \qquad (6.9)$$

(B) the causal-chain system (6.8) and (C) the interdependent system:

$$y_t = C'y_t + Dz_t + \omega_t \text{ with } E(y_t/\hat{y}_t, z_t) \neq Ay_t + Bz_t. \qquad (6.10)$$

Wold showed that all three had the same reduced form. But he did not stop to ponder over the implication of this, probably for the reason of its label of '*reduced form*'. It was the original structural models that he was interested in. He asserted, from the standpoint of economic theory, that 'models A–C represent three levels of increasing generalization', and that the only trouble with (C) was that its 'cause–effect specification' and 'chainwise forecasting' broke down (Wold 1965). Therefore the causal-chain system appeared to be the most appropriate type. The remedy that he suggested for (C) was to respecify it into an 'expectational interdependent system' using the rationale of Theil's 2SLS method. Up to this point, Wold seemed to feel relieved for having finally justified the validity of the LS estimation method.

Apparently, Wold came quite near to unveil the myth of generality of an SEM, and the discrepancy in modellers' concepts of economic theory, from the angle of recursive analysis. But the structural approach had deeply indoctrinated him with the generality of any structural models over their statistical counterparts (reduced forms). So his argument was somewhat confused on the issues of model generalization and causality versus testability.

Wold was far from a lone defender in that respect. As described earlier, Theil based his procedure of constructing and specifying forecasting models mainly upon LS estimators; Liu advocated the reduced-form LS approach also for forecasting purposes. Moreover, Fox (1956) re-estimated the Klein–Goldberger model by LS and found that the degree of Haavelmo bias was smaller than expected. A number of Monte Carlo studies demonstrated fairly good performance of the LS estimators as compared with the ML estimators in finite samples (cf. Christ 1960; Hildreth 1960).[5] As the position of the LS methods was consolidated increasingly by empirical findings, modellers gradually shifted their attention from structural estimates more and more to estimates of statistical relations and hence to reduced-form equations. In particular, this was reflected in Klein's (1960) remark that 'in practically all the situations, the reduced-form equations are the important ones to consider even though they are derived from the more basic structural equations. . . . This is true whether we are considering a fixed or changing structure'. Underlying this shift of attention was actually the old concern over the 'true' correspondence of model results with reality, and the fact that this correspondence problem had not yet been adequately tackled in the formalization of the structural modelling procedure. Without definite confirmation of the true correspondence, the status of structural models in applied circumstances was inevitably weakened.

It was in this context that Waugh (1961) presented an open opposition to the route of 'structural analysis'. Waugh pointed out that Haavelmo bias was widely misunderstood by the profession, for the nature of the bias did not lie in the statistical

---

[5] These two papers together with Liu (1960) were components of a 'symposium on simultaneous-equation estimation' originating from a panel discussion on the topic at the 1958 meeting of the Econometric Society in Chicago.

sense but in the imposition of a simultaneous-equations model as the structural model. He demonstrated that the bias arose from the fact that the parameter of *de facto* conditional expectation of one variable upon another estimated by least-squares was not the same parameter of interest formulated a priori in an SEM, or in his words, 'the basic structural true equations give biased estimates of the expected value of the dependent variable'. Waugh observed from his own empirical experience that the parameters of interest in most practical circumstances belonged to the type of conditional expectations, and therefore the LS methods were adequate for applied purposes. Since the construction of an SEM was carried practically through in the attribution of endogeneity/exogeneity to the variables in question, Waugh criticized strongly the 'metaphysical rituals about endogenous and exogenous variables' in the 'routine' practice of structural modelling for impeding empirical economists from appreciating 'the exact meaning of the available statistical data' (Waugh 1961).

The debates around LS versus ML and causal chain versus simultaneity made it clear that 'the choice between different estimation techniques must be decided upon from case to case with regard to the theoretical model that underlies the application at issue' (Wold 1965). But on the other hand a working theoretical model could rarely be deduced with certainty from a priori economic theory. In most of the applied circumstances, its formulation involved frequent adjustments in respect to the various results of trial estimations. Such uses of estimations deranged the role of estimation in the structural approach formalized not long before, i.e. measuring merely the magnitudes of the coefficients of given structural models as accurately as possible. Similar to the cases with testing and identification, estimation in practice also transgressed its formal scope, and overlapped with testing and identification in exerting an indispensable 'feedback' effect on applied model construction. The transgression is perceivable in the debates described above. Some accounts of the feedback effect are now described.

As mentioned previously, the purely theoretical models of the interdependent type were found to be conveniently transformable into the SEM framework in econometrics, whereas the dynamic part (i.e. the lagged terms) of an SEM could rarely find a transformable counterpart in economic theory. Consequently, dynamic specification was the place where estimation was found in practice to serve hypothesis formulation the most significantly. Innovative research of this sort during the 1950s was best represented by the works of T. M. Brown, L. M. Koyck, M. Nerlove, and J. D. Sargan. The pragmatic and inventive style of these works bore a close resemblance to that of the early applied works of the 1920s and 1930s. Their studies resulted in the formulation of the model types of 'distributed lags', 'partial adjustment' (as seen in Section 6.2 above), and 'error correction'.

T. M. Brown (1952) started his study by estimating the aggregate Canadian consumption function. In trying to find the best fit with the data, he experimented with three types of relations: (a) a simple static equation embodying the conventional economic theory; (b) an equation with the lagged explanatory variable (i.e. a distributed lag relation):

$$C = a_0 + a_1 Y + a_2 Y_{-1} + u \qquad (6.11)$$

and (c) an equation with the lagged explained variable (i.e. a partial adjustment relation):

$$C = a_0 + a_1 Y + a_2 C_{-1} + u. \qquad (6.12)$$

Brown found that (b) produced a better statistical fit than (a), especially with respect to residual serial correlation, and that the statistical fit in (c) was 'quite good'. He thus observed that 'lagged values of some variables involved exert an important influence on current consumer behaviour', and justified (b) and (c) as representing consumers' 'habit persistence' or 'inertia' behaviour in adjusting to income changes. Both types, and the explanation of inertia reaction, were soon adopted in modelling other areas by the profession, e.g. in the Klein–Goldberger model (Klein and Goldberger 1955).

About the same time, L. M. Koyck (1954) studied 'distributed lags' in its general form in relation to investment analysis:

$$y_t = \sum_{i=0} \alpha_i x_{t-i} + u_t. \qquad (6.13)$$

His explanation for (6.13) was that it represented a certain 'time-shape of an economic reaction' (p. 3). To circumvent the difficulty in estimating the α's in the case of high multicollinearity (i.e. high interdependency between one variable and its lags), Koyck restricted the α's to be geometrically decreasing coefficients:

$$y_t = \alpha \sum_{i=0} \lambda_i x_{t-i} + u_t \qquad (0 \leqslant \lambda < 1). \qquad (6.14)$$

This enabled him to transform the distributed lags into the following relation with only the concurrent exogenous variables plus the one-lagged dependent variables:

$$y_t = \alpha x_t + \lambda y_{t-1} + u_t - \lambda u_{t-1}. \qquad (6.15)$$

Klein immediately saw the similarity of Koyck's result to the Brown hypothesis (6.12) that he had used. Klein made his preference of (6.12) to (6.15) as a basic structural form, for the reason that (6.12) did not induce additional residual autocorrelation if there was no residual autocorrelation to start with, and that it was difficult to find an acceptable theoretical rationale for the imposition of both geometric lags and the autocorrelated disturbances in (6.15) (Klein 1958). Concurrently, the scheme (6.12) was further linked to the theory of adaptive expectations by Nerlove, and developed formally into the partial adjustment rationale, as shown in Section 6.2.

Unlike Brown, Koyck, and Nerlove, whose researches concerned directly applied issues, Sargan made his contribution through developing estimators for a generalized simultaneous-equations model incorporated with the error autoregressive expression (see Chapter 5). During the derivation of an ML estimator for the model, Sargan noticed that the additional autoregressive expression amounted to imposing only an extra set of restrictions upon the 'restricted' ML estimation of the structural form, while the ML estimation of the reduced form remained 'unrestricted' (1961). Subsequently, Sargan elaborated and applied his above findings in a paper called 'Wages and Prices in the United Kingdom: A Study in Econometric Methodology' (1964).

In that paper, Sargan showed explicitly that the error autoregressive equation was equivalent to 'a set of non-linear restrictions' imposed upon a general equation with autoregressive and distributed lags (ADL), 'transformed' by combining a simultaneous-equation model with an error autoregressive scheme. Roughly, Sargan's formulation runs as follows (in matrix form):

The simultaneous-equation system: $AX'_t = u_t$.
A first-order error autoregression: $u_t - ku_{t-1} = e_t$.
The combination of the two: $AX'_t - kAX'_{t-1} = e_t$.

This implied a 'transformed equation' with autoregressive and distributed lags:

$$B\xi'_t = e_t, \ B = (A, \ -kA), \ \xi_t = (X_t, \ X_{t-1}).$$

He proposed a likelihood ratio (LR) test based upon the unrestricted ML estimates of the general 'transformed equation' versus the restricted ML estimates of the structural equations to check 'if the autoregressive assumption is correct'. He deduced from the unrestricted ADL equation that if the autoregressive assumption was rejected, 'a more complicated structure of lags, or a longer lag is required in the structural equation on at least one of the variables'. Then he observed, first, that the coefficients of the general 'transformed equation' could 'indicate' the direction of 'modification' (i.e. respecification) of the lags if the results of the test results so required, and, secondly, that the modification often ended up with the autoregressive coefficient ceasing to be significant (i.e. its value approaching zero). These findings led him to the conclusion 'that its [the autoregressive coefficient] significance in the original form of the structural equation was due to the variables in the equation having the wrong lags' (Sargan 1964). His conclusion formally verified Liu's intuitive criticism of the error autoregressive scheme, as described in Section 6.2.

Sargan applied his method to modelling wages and prices in the UK. He believed from his theoretical deduction that 'the only criterion' regarding 'the most appropriate form of equation' was having non-autocorrelated errors. He therefore turned down the growth-rate model, recommended formerly by the Cambridge group, and modified it by adding a 'correction' factor made of the difference between the lagged wages and prices. The resulting wage-determination equation in essence looks like:

$$\Delta w_t = \alpha_0 + \alpha_1 \Delta p_t + \alpha_2(w_{t-1} - p_{t-1}) + e_t. \qquad (6.16)$$

Sargan explained the economic interpretation of (6.16) as allowing potentially for separate expressions of the 'equilibrium' wage level $E(w_t)$ and the wage 'dynamic adjustment' process

Δw_t. An alternative explanation, that he pointed out, was the rationale of dynamic 'correction' behaviours, given by A. W. Phillips in a theoretical study of the relationship between unemployment and wage rates (1958).[6] The factor $(w_{t-1} - p_{t-1})$ in (6.16) could also be seen as embodying such a 'correction' mechanism. Thereafter, the equation form:

$$\Delta y_t = \alpha_0 + \alpha_1 \Delta x_t + \alpha_2 (y_{t-1} - kx_{t-1}) + e_t \qquad (6.17)$$

similar to (6.16) got its name 'error correction'.

It is discernible that Sargan's 1964 paper carried, within itself and reflected in its subtitle 'A Study in Econometric Methodology', the seeds to construct models using a different approach from the stereotypical structural route. His demonstration of the generality and importance of the 'transformed equation' not only provided a formal approval of Liu's argument in favour of the reduced-form approach, but also suggested a constructive way to implement the hypothesis-testing principle for choosing among alternative hypotheses. However, the seeds were overshadowed by Sargan's dominant interest in methods of estimation. He stated this explicitly in commencing his 1964 paper: 'the primary intention of this study was to develop methods of estimation, and to compare different methods of estimation when estimating structural relationships from economic time-series when the errors in the relationships are autocorrelated.'

The applied studies described above implied that 'an acceptable rationale' with respect to economic theory and 'a feasible estimation procedure applicable to a wide range of problem' were essential for applied model construction (Griliches 1967). This soon became extensively accepted as the general criteria for a good econometric model design, through the common practice of constructing empirical models with heavy reference to estimation results in the 1960s and 1970s.

[6] Actually, Phillips (1954) first came up with the theory in an effort to formulate stabilization policy in a dynamic context. In the paper, Phillips made the hypothesis that whenever there occurred an error, i.e. the difference between the actual level and the desired level of a variable, a certain stabilizing factor 'will be changing in a direction which tends to eliminate the difference and at a rate proportional to the difference', and suggested the use of a 'derivative correction' mechanism, opposite to the acceleration mechanism, to depict such an adjustment movement towards the desired level.

6.4 MODEL CONSTRUCTION AND THE PROBABILITY APPROACH

It has been stated in Section 1.5 that Haavelmo's probability revolution was not complete, and that what got through was merely the adoption of probability theory as the pillar of those statistical methods found applicable in the structural modelling framework. This has been illustrated through Chapters 2 to 5, where we saw that the part backed up by the success of the revolution showed faster and smoother developments (e.g. methods of estimation and identification) than the part without the backing (e.g. methods of model building and testing). The problem of the incomplete revolution is more evident in the arguments and debates described in the first three sections of this chapter. There we saw that even the relatively well-formulated part (identification and estimation) was in question, because it could not stand independent of the fragile part of model construction and testing in any applied circumstances. In particular the fact, described in Section 4.3, that the LS methods remained the most used in practice despite the theoretical beauty of the ML principle, made it clear that it was quite immaterial for the majority of applied modellers to remember constantly to start off their modelling by thinking of all the variables as jointly distributed in probability terms, which had been such a crucial point in the partial victory of the probability approach.

In Section 1.5, the incomplete revolution has been attributed to the 'deterministic' attitude towards economic theory in the structural modelling procedure. We saw, especially from the early part of this chapter, that econometricians actually began to realize that there was a significant discrepancy between the very abstract and seemingly incontestable theory of the general equilibrium model—the cornerstone of the structural approach—and the rather restrictive and uncertain economic theories available as a basis for any applied studies. Therefore, to mend the weak state of economic theory was the immediate response of many econometric theorists. For instance, the end of 1950 saw the Cowles Commission taking a 'shift toward theoretical work to obtain better models preparatory to another phase of empirical work' (Christ 1953: 47). Its subsequent theoretical work bearing the closest link with its SEM formulation in econometrics was on issues concerning the general equilibrium, and particularly the dynamic path of the equilibrium of an economic system. Here, a number of momentous contributions were produced from the late 1940s to the mid-1950s, associated with the names of Koopmans, Hurwicz, K. Arrow, G. Debreu, and E. Malinvaud (cf. Arrow and Intriligator 1982; Weintraub 1985; Debreu 1986).[7] However, it was hard to discern, from their models, any serious concern with the issue of theory testability against data information, or the need of having 'in mind some actual experiment, or some design of an experiment' (Haavelmo 1944: 6). The demarcation of econometrics and mathematical economics apparently made theorists feel justified in dissociating their research from economic data altogether.

Since in the circumstances the discrepancy between actual theories and the ideal theory was neither eliminated, nor in any hope of being eliminated, by newly developed theoretical models in economics, applied modellers often found themselves compelled to violate the structural modelling procedure, trying and appending various *ad hoc* alterations and assumptions to the original structural model in order to make it data-permissible. The original 'maintained hypothesis' was either too uncertain to maintain, or too simple to allow for making economically meaningful choice between the null and the alternative hypotheses, or both. However, once the maintained hypothesis was free to alter, as suggested by Theil (1961), the 'deterministic' view of treating the structural model as 'maintained' seemed no longer maintainable. The issue of (structural) model choice had to be faced and given explicit treatment. The debate on causality between Wold and the Cowles people, for instance, posed serious doubt about the maintainability of the SEM in the dynamic context. Interestingly, H. Wold (1965) later regarded the debate as a reflection of 'the transition from deterministic to stochastic models', and R. L. Basmann (1963) thought of it as one over specifications of the 'jointly determined variables'. Their opinions brought the problems of model construction back to the

[7] Their main contributions include (Debreu 1951; Koopmans 1951; Hurwicz and Arrow 1952; Malinvaud 1953; Arrow and Debreu 1954). Notice that Malinvaud did his work during his visit at the Cowles Commission as a guest for one year during 1950–1.

probability approach, and indicated that the approach had not yet been carried through.

Actually, the problems of how to view the probability approach with respect to the establishment of the structural modelling procedure were taken up by R. Vining in the well-known Cowles versus the (US) National Bureau of Economic Research (NBER) debate in the late 1940s. The debate started from Koopmans's review of Burns and Mitchell's 1946 book *Measuring Business Cycles*. Since this work represented the strongly data-orientated research methodology of the (US) National Bureau of Economic Research, Koopmans's review led to a methodological debate between the Cowles approach versus the NBER's approach (see also Epstein 1987).

Koopmans criticized the NBER's approach to business cycle analysis as one of thorough empiricists' 'measurement without theory' (Koopmans 1947*b*). Vining produced a sharp review of the work of the Cowles group in response. He observed:

Some of his [Koopmans] discussion suggests that we have already at hand a theoretical model. . . . Koopmans doesn't give his hypotheses specific economic content. He discusses the mathematical form that the model should (or must) take; and suggests the kind of content it should have in very general terms. . . . But apparently all he has to insist upon at present is the mathematical form, and from his discussion it appears not unfair to regard the formal economic theory underlying his approach as being in the main available from works not later than those of Walras. (Vining 1949)

Vining thus concluded that the 'entire line of development' of the Cowles group was to solve 'the problem of statistical estimation that would be presented by the empirical counterpart of the Walrasian conception'. But he pointed out that 'the adequacy of this model' still awaited evidence, and expressed the view that 'the Walrasian conception' was 'in fact a pretty skinny fellow of untested capacity'. With regard to the uncertainty of actual economic theory, Vining argued that 'statistical economics is too narrow in scope if it includes just the estimation of postulated relations'. He related this further to the probability approach and wrote:

Probability theory is fundamental as a guide to an understanding of the nature of the phenomena to be studied and not merely as a basis for a theory of the sampling behaviour of estimates of population parameters the characteristics of which have been postulated. In seeking for interesting hypotheses for our quantitative studies we might want to wander beyond the classic Walrasian fields and to poke around the equally classic fields once cultivated by such men as Lexis, Bortkievicz, Markov, and Kapteyn. (Vining 1949)

From this standpoint, he praised the studies of Burns and Mitchell as representing 'an accumulation of knowledge', for they aimed at 'discovery and hypothesis-seeking' (Vining 1949).

In reply, Koopmans agreed with Vining's probability argument:

Probability, randomness, variability, enter not only into estimation and hypothesis-testing concerning economic behaviour parameters. These concepts are an essential element in dynamic economic theory, in the model we form of the conditioning (rather than determination) of future economic quantities by past economic developments. (Koopmans 1949*a*)

However, Koopmans's real intention was to defend the Cowles position of strong reliance on economic theory. He observed pessimistically that hypothesis-seeking touched on some 'unsolved problems at the very foundations of statistical theory'. Although 'a formal view' purported that 'hypothesis-seeking and hypothesis-testing differ only in how wide a set of alternatives is taken into consideration', 'there remains scope for doubt whether all hypothesis-seeking activity can be described and formalized as a choice from a preassigned range of alternatives' (Koopmans 1949*a*).

Plainly, the Koopmans–Vining debate brought up the issue of how to construct models with tentative and indefinite hypothetical theories. Both sides recognized that the structural modelling procedure in the Cowles formalization was incapable of handling the strong uncertainty of theories, for the uncertainty overruled the basic assumption that the theory underlying the structural model should be known as true and general. Noticeably, both sides also admitted that the probability approach should not be narrowly confined to the specification of distribution functions of variables for estimation. But neither was able to suggest constructive, systematic methods for the uncertainty in model construction by the probability approach.

During the 1950s, more and more people came to the view that theoretical uncertainty was creating a bottleneck for econometric model construction. The issue was chosen as the central theme of the presidential address at the 1957 conference of the Econometric Society (Haavelmo 1958). Haavelmo acknowledged the phenomenon that 'the concrete results of our efforts at quantitative measurements often seem to get worse the more refinement of tools and logical stringency we call into play'. His explanation was that the previous econometric work was essentially 'repair work' on the basis of an economic model being 'in fact "correct" or "true"', whereas in reality 'the "laws" of economics are not very accurate in the sense of a close fit'. Hence he appealed to econometricians to overcome their 'passive attitude' to economic axioms and cut down the amount of 'repair work' so as 'to bring the requirements of an econometric "shape" of the models to bear upon the formulation of fundamental economic hypotheses from the very beginning'. He further emphasized:

We have a very important task of formulating and analysing alternative, feasible economic structures, in order to give people the best possible basis for choice of the kind of economy they want to live in. By formulating alternatives in the language of econometrics we may also be in a position to judge the amount of quantitative information concerning these alternatives that could conceivably be extracted from data of past and current facts of our economy. . . .

I believe the econometricians have a mission in fostering a somewhat bolder attitude in the choice of working hypotheses concerning economic goals and economic behaviour in a modern society. (Haavelmo 1958)

But, like Koopmans, Haavelmo could not offer a concrete way out of the 'model choice' problem. Indeed, with the strengthening of the newly established structural approach, it was almost impossible for Koopmans, Haavelmo, and their associates to turn and challenge squarely the very foothold upon which they had just set up the whole structural enterprise. However, as long as economic theory kept its general and 'maintained' position in the form of structural models, the principle of hypothesis-testing remained powerless in discriminating between models, and data information had no explicit channel to feed its effect on new model construction. Therefore, the probability revolution was incomplete.

Around the turn of 1960, Haavelmo's advocacy for the probability approach was effectively submerged in mainstream econometrics. Meanwhile, the approach revived partially in the emergence of a heterodox school of econometrics—the Bayesian school. The early 1960s saw the first introduction of Bayes's principle of inference into econometrics, e.g. through the pioneer works of W. D. Fisher (1962), J. Drèze (1962), and T. J. Rothenberg (1963). The pioneers reckoned that Bayes's principle offered a convenient way to handle the uncertainty in a priori formulated theories, because these theories could be expressed in the form of prior distribution densities in model specification in the Bayesian framework. The Bayesian method thus put forth a formal way to represent the uncertainty of theory in model construction in line with the probability approach. However, the early Bayesian econometricians did not pursue this route much farther. Instead of challenging the structural modelling procedure, they based themselves upon it, with the belief that their approach provided a better set of instruments for it, particularly with respect to the aspect of modelling various policy scenarios. Hence they devoted almost all their efforts in devising Bayesian tools of estimation and identification, equivalent to those of the standard econometrics within the same structural modelling paradigm (see Qin 1991). Nevertheless, their continuation of the probability approach was hardly noticed at the time, since the Bayesian method was strongly rejected from the outset by orthodox econometricians for its subjective image.

Econometricians would still have to try all the paths in the labyrinth of structural modelling for years before they would stumble upon some way out. To achieve that, they would have to recoordinate the steps of model estimation, identification, testing, specification, and construction in a systematic way, in addition to making refinements on each, such that these together would embody a progressive searching process for better econometric models. More fundamentally, they would have to push along the probability revolution. This required them to move away from 'repair work' and take a 'bolder attitude' to challenge 'fundamental economic hypotheses' (Haavelmo 1958), to overcome the narrow outlook of regarding probability theory 'merely as a basis for a theory of the sampling behaviour of estimates of population parameters the characteristics of which have been

postulated' (Vining 1949), to change 'deductively formulated
theories' or postulates (Stone 1951) from the position of maintained hypotheses to that of any testable hypotheses, and to in-
stil their stochastic, non-experimental viewpoint into the largely
deterministic, metaphysical camp of economics. Before then
many problems awaited solution. Yet many more would still
arise thereafter.

The History Revisited

The controversies over he probability approach, estimation, identification, and testing in relation to model construction, as reported in the previous chapter, appeared to have caused only limited and transient repercussions in the profession. When the standard form of textbook econometrics emerged in the early 1960s, there were few traces of these controversial issues in most of the textbooks. Compiled largely with reference to the works of the Cowles group, these textbooks have since fosteed the spread of a stereotyped structural modelling procedure, and exerted considerable influence on the scope and direction of research of both applied and theoretical econometricians. Mainstream econometric research in the 1960s and the 1970s comprised primarily technical refinements and extensions of the structural procedure.

Therefore, I mark an end-point around 1960 in the historical study of the formation of econometrics. In retrospe't, we would naturally pose the following question: What should we and can we learn from this period of history with respect to present and future econometric research? One might then naturally turn to the philosophy of science, and not find it difficult to apply the popular notions of either Lakatos's 'scientific research programme' (SRP) (Lakatos 1978), or Kuhn's 'paradigm' (Kuhn 1970), to account for the history. The events around Haavelmo's probability treatise and Cowles Commission Monograph 10 can be viewed as the formation of either the 'hard core' of an SRP, or the 'shared symbolic generalizations', 'models', 'values', and 'metaphysical principles' of a paradigm, and hence can be called a scientific revolution. The subsequent events can be viewed accordingly either as further developments of 'the negative heuristic' and 'the positive heuristic' of the hard core, or as 'a period of normal science'. Either of the two explanatimhs can be adopted to depict one perspective of the evolution of econometrics over the long run. But neither seems to answer the above question specifically enough to the satisfaction of most econometricians and economists.[1] They are quite practical in their concerns, with far less interest in the long-run suppositions than in the short-run explanations of econometric developments.

It has gradually dawned on me during the historical investigation that the key points of historic significance are the junctures at which economic thinking and mathematical statistics merged at the practical request of matching economics with data information. In the following, I try to draw some more concrete lessons from these junctures. I hope that the discussion may provide some useful points, particularly with respect to issues pertinent to present econometric developments.

My prime impression of the history is that most important econometric advances have resulted from ingenious interfusion of statistical ideas with economic thinking, in regard to applied problems of interest. The single most significant event of this sort is, perhaps, the acceptance of probability theory. The acceptance turns crucially upon Haavelmo's argument that the notion of probability is not only perfectly interpretable, but also constructive in handling the issue of matching economics with data. Haavelmo's approach offered a new perspective from which economic theories could be formulated in the logic and manner of mathematical statistics, ready in principle for correspondence with data. Another event of significance is the formalization of identification theory. It is rather interesting to see how econometricians' understanding of the identification problem converged, shifted, and deepened, as the presentation of the problem evolved from a deterministic simultaneous-equations system to the probability distribution function related to the system. It is particularly thought-provoking to see how the different presentations led econometricians to different views and interpretations of the problem from either the standpoint of a priori given economic theory, or the standpoint of available data.

However, we noticed that not only the effects of such an interfusion of ideas often died out very quickly, but also the original economic thinking was easily submerged in the adoption of statistical methods. For instance, we saw in Chapter 3 how

---

[1] The disappointment of economists in purely methodological discussions in the manner of the philosophy of science is reflected recently in Hausman (1989) and Weintraub (1989).

the desire to obtain the best parameter estimates with respect to their economic meaningfulness was left behind in the adoption of standard statistical estimation methods; and we hardly found any suspicions thereafter that the statistical optimality underlying these methods did not equate with the desired 'best' in its original and full sense. We saw in Chapter 4 how the desire to relate the estimated relations to reality was left behind in the establishment of identification conditions concerning the existence of unique solutions of given structural models; and we found most modellers applying the conditions without realizing that they did not guarantee true correspondence after all those efforts of formalization. We saw in Chapter 5 how the desire to verify economic theory against data was left behind in the derivation of test statistics for the purpose of evaluating econometric models; and we found almost no econometricians who ever remarked on the conceptual reduction of testing with respect to economic theory, when they devised tests or applied them to econometric models. More importantly, we saw, throughout the book and particularly in Chapters 1 and 6, how the message that economic theory should be formulated in such a stochastic form as to enable its verification in Haavelmo's general theme of the probability revolution was left behind in the formalization of the structural approach; and we found most econometricians viewing the probability approach as equivalent to the systematic application of statistical techniques. On the whole, we found that econometricians tended to devote most of their efforts to deriving econometric methods patterned after mathematical statistics, once they felt the issues of concern more or less translatable into statistical terms, and that very few of them became aware of the possibility that the issues might not have been accurately mapped into the mathematical statistical ideas underlying the utilized statistical tools in the first place, even when they were confronting problems which emerged in applying their methods.

It is a well-recognized fact that any theory, as an abstraction of empirical information, entails disregard of certain aspects of the information (cf. Cartwright 1989). Being a bridge between economic theory and data, econometrics is no exception. The real issues here are: whether the abstraction is fully recognized, and whether the disregarded aspects are truly irrelevant to the subject in question. The instances mentioned above suggest negative answers to both questions. They thus raise a puzzling paradox—the use of mathematical statistics seems to have, to some extent, confused, instead of clarified, the abstraction process in econometrics.[2]

My historical investigation has led me to the following explanation. In general, what happened is due to the commonly held opinion that mathematical statistics can be treated only as a passive and formal tool without substantial ideas in the formation of econometrics; in other words, mathematical statistics provides merely a formal vehicle of linking up data and theory for its operational accuracy and convenience. In particular, it is due to the use of mathematical statistics to fulfil two tasks at the same time—converting non-mathematical economic ideas into a mathematical form, and building a bridge between theory and data. Notice that the two tasks impose different demands on mathematical statistics. Mathematical statistics should serve as a form of perfect substitution in the former, and a means of abstraction in the latter. Substitution allows no loss of information, whereas abstraction is bound to discard the part of information considered as irrelevant to the subject-matter. From the 'passive-tool' standpoint, econometricians naturally took the substitution as perfect, at least in principle. They showed much more awareness of the process of substitution than that of abstraction, and they might well regard the latter process also as one of substituting the intrinsic abstraction process in the formulation of economic theory. Hence little room has been left for doubt that the possibility of the substitution might be imperfect, because the abstraction process of mathematical statistics might not match exactly that of economic theory.

In the above light, we are now able to see that most of the problematic places in the formation of econometrics were those where the ideas of mathematical statistics underlying the particular techniques being adopted were at variance with the existing economic thinking. We are also better able to under-

<hr />

[2] A popular view about the essential problem of structural econometrics puts the blame generally on the unavailability of mathematically precise models for scientific discovery. It leads therefore to the conclusion that 'there will never be an objective econometric algorithm that generates empirically creative models' (Heckman 1992). But I find the view too sweeping in respect to the history, and non-constructive in respect to the present.

stand the many confusions, controversies, and slow recognitions of useful results in the history. In particular, we are able to explain why Wold still maintained the generality of a structural model over the reduced form, even when he derived the same reduced form of his causal-chain model from his opponents' model of the simultaneous type; why the error autoregressive scheme could be accepted as a useful addition to the simultaneous-equations system already generalized by the Cowles Commission; why Koopmans and Reiersøl's approach to identification was not pursued till much later, e.g. by Rothenberg (1971); why Durbin's test for independence between regressors and the error term remained ignored for over twenty years; and, more generally, why developments in testing lagged behind developments in estimation and identification; and why Haavelmo's general probability theme was not carried through.

What then caused econometricians to hold such a passive view of mathematical statistics? The primary reason seems to be associated with the urgent need of econometrics, in its infant stage, to gain recognition by economists. The urgency was mainly boosted by a deep anxiety about the methodological validity of econometric practice in its heavy involvement in inductive inference. The anxiety found refuge in the structural modelling approach. The rise of the approach helped econometrics win recognition by establishing its subordinate status to economics. The status was further strengthened by the demarcation of mathematical economics from econometrics, because the job of formalizing and developing the 'thinking' part of economics was seen as one which could be and was delegated to theoretical economists. On the other hand, the initial formalization of econometrics opened up a whole new frontier to explore, and set up a paradigm to emulate. Many followers were absorbed by the new tool-making profession, so that the course adopted gradually moved apart from the applied world, as well as from theoretical economics.[3] Econometrics lost much of its creativity at its maturity in the 1960s, marked by the appearance of its standardized textbook form.

---

[3] Morgan (1990: 264) has concluded from her history study that 'by the 1950s the founding ideal of econometrics, the union of mathematical and statistical economics into a truly synthetic economics, had collapsed'.

I wrote at the beginning of this discussion that most controversies reported in Chapter 6 were transient. However, that is not a totally correct statement. In fact, the current major schools in econometrics—the Bayesian school, the VAR (Vector AutoRegression) school, and the dynamic specification school, have grown out of distinct perspectives on the older controversies. The direct bearing of Liu's critique on Sims's championing of VAR is a ready illustration. The importance of Sargan's 1964 paper to the dynamic specification approach is another. It is remarkable to see that the observation still holds in these analyses currently revived, namely, key results have come from careful comparisons and ingenious recombination of economic and statistical ideas with respect to the practical request of matching economics with data information.

The historical investigation has straightforward implications. Econometric progress in principle entails the intermingling of economic thinking with mathematical statistics, inspired and monitored by applied requirements. Narrow tool-making practice is necessary, but not sufficient, for progress. A consistent combination of economic thinking with mathematical statistical ideas is essential; yet fruitful combinations have come from real interest in, and good understanding of, the applied world.

Bibliography

Aitken, A. C. (1934–5), 'On Least Squares and Linear Combinations of Observations', *Proceedings of Royal Society*, 55: 42–8.

Aldrich, J. (1989), 'Autonomy', *Oxford Economic Papers*, 41: 15–34.

—— (1992), 'Haavelmo's Identification Theory', Discussion Paper 18, University of Southampton.

Allen, R. G. D. (1938), 'Review of Koopmans: "Linear Regression Analysis of Economic Time Series"', *Economica*, 5: 105–6.

—— (1939), 'The Assumptions of Linear Regression', *Economica*, 6: 191–204.

—— (1946), 'Review of Haavelmo: "The Probability Approach"', *American Economic Review*, 36: 161–3.

Alt, F. L. (1942), 'Distributed Lags', *Econometrica*, 10: 113–28.

Anderson, R. L. (1942), 'Distribution of the Serial Correlation Coefficient', *Annals of Mathematical Statistics*, 13: 1–13.

—— (1945), 'Review of T. Haavelmo: "The Probability Approach in Econometrics"', *Journal of American Statistical Association*, 40: 393–4.

—— and Anderson, T. W. (1950), 'Distribution of the Circular Serial Correlation Coefficient for Residuals from a Fitted Fourier Series', *Annals of Mathematical Statistics*, 21: 59–81.

Anderson, T. W. (1948), 'On the Theory of Testing Serial Correlation', *Skandinavisk Aktuarietidskrift*, 31: 88–116.

—— (1990), 'Trygve Haavelmo and Simultaneous Equation Models', *Technical Report*, 39 (Econometric Workshop, Stanford University).

—— and Rubin, H. (1949), 'Estimation of the Parameters of a Single Equation in a Complete System of Stochastic Equations', *Annals of Mathematical Statistics*, 20: 46–63.

—— —— (1950) 'The Asymptotic Properties of Estimates of the Parameters of a Single Equation in a Complete System of Stochastic Equations', *Annals of Mathematical Statistics*, 21: 570–82.

Archibald, G. C. (1959), 'The State of Economic Science', *British Journal for the Philosophy of Science*, 10: 58–69.

Arrow, K. J. (1951), *Social Choice and Individual Values*, Cowles Commission Monograph 12 (New York).

—— and Debreu, G. (1954), 'Existence of an Equilibrium for a Competitive Economy', *Econometrica*, 22: 265–90.

—— Chenery, H. B., Minhas, B. S., and Solow, R. M. (1961), 'Capital-Labour Substitution and Economic Efficiency', *Review of Economics and Statistics*, 43: 225–50.

Arrow, K. J. and Intriligator, M. D. (1982) (eds.), *Handbook of Mathematical Economics* (Amsterdam).

Basmann, R. L. (1957), 'A Generalized Classical Method of Linear Estimation of Coefficients in a Structural Equation', *Econometrica*, 25: 77–83.

—— (1963), 'The Causal Interpretation of Non-Triangular Systems of Economic Relations' and 'On the Causal Interpretation of Non-Triangular Systems of Economic Relations: A Rejoinder', *Econometrica*, 31: 439–48; 451–3.

Bentzel, R., and Hansen, B. (1955), 'On Recursiveness and Interdependency in Economic Models', *Review of Economic Studies*, 22: 153–68.

—— and Wold, H. (1946), 'On Statistical Demand Analysis from the Viewpoint of Simultaneous Equations', *Skandinavisk Aktuarietidskrift*, 29: 95–114.

Bodkin, R. G., Klein, L. R., and Marwah, K. (1991), *A History of Macroeconometric Model-Building* (Aldershot).

Boland, L. A. (1991), *The Methodology of Economic Model Building* (London).

Box, G. E. P., and Jenkins, G. M. (1970), *Time Series Analysis: Forecasting and Control* (San Francisco).

Brown, E. H. P. (1937), 'Report of the Oxford Meeting, September 25–9, 1936', *Econometrica*, 5: 361–83.

Brown, T. M. (1952), 'Habit Persistence and Lags in Consumer Behaviour', *Econometrica*, 20: 355–71.

Burns, A. F., and Mitchell, W. C. (1946), *Measuring Business Cycles* (New York).

Cartwright, N. (1989), *Nature's Capacities and their Measurement* (Oxford).

Champernowne, D. G. (1948), 'Sampling Theory Applied to Autoregressive Sequences', *Journal of the Royal Statistical Society, Series B*, 10: 204–31.

—— (1969), *Uncertainty and Estimation in Economics* (Edinburgh).

Chow, G. C. (1960), 'Tests of Equality between Sets of Coefficients in Two Linear Regressions', *Econometrica*, 28: 591–605.

Christ, C. F. (1951), 'A Test of an Econometric Model for the United States, 1921–1947', in *Conference on Business Cycles* (with comments by M. Friedman, L. R. Klein, G. H. Moore, and J. Tinbergen) (New York), 35–106.

—— (1952), 'History of the Cowles Commission, 1932–1952', in *Economic Theory and Measurement* (Chicago).

—— (1956), 'Aggregate Econometric Models', *American Economic Review*, 46: 385–408.

—— (1960), 'Simultaneous Equations Estimation: Any Verdict Yet?' *Econometrica*, 28: 835–45.

—— (1985), 'Early Progress in Estimating Quantitative Economic Relationships in America', *American Economic Review*, 75: 39–52.

Cochrane, D., and Orcutt, G. (1949), 'Application of Least Squares Regression to Relationships Containing Autocorrelated Error Terms', *Journal of American Statistical Association*, 44: 32–61.

Cobb, C. W., and Douglas, P. H. (1928), 'The Theory of Production', *American Economic Review* (Suppl.), 18: 159–66.

Cowles Commission (1936), *Abstracts of Papers Presented at the Research Conference on Economics and Statistics* (Colorado).

—— (1937), *Report of Third Annual Research Conference on Economics and Statistics* (Colorado).

—— (1938), *Report of Fourth Annual Research Conference on Economics and Statistics* (Colorado).

—— (1939), *Report of Fifth Annual Research Conference on Economics and Statistics* (University of Chicago).

—— (1947), *Five-Year Report 1942–46* (University of Chicago).

—— (1952), *Economic Theory and Measurement* (Chicago).

Davis, H. T. (1941a), *The Analysis of Economic Time Series* (Bloomington, Ind.).

—— (1941b), *Theory of Econometrics* (Bloomington, Ind.).

Davis, T. E. (1952), 'The Consumption Function as a Tool for Prediction', *Review of Economics and Statistics*, 34: 270–7.

Debreu, G. (1951), 'The Coefficient of Resource Utilization', *Econometrica*, 19: 273–92.

—— (1986), 'Theoretic Models: Mathematical Form and Economic Content', *Econometrica*, 54: 1259–70.

Department of Applied Economics (1951), *Second Report: Activities in the Years 1948–51* (Cambridge).

De Finetti, B. (1968), 'Probability: Interpretations', in *International Encyclopedia of the Social Sciences* (New York).

De Marchi, N. (1988), 'Popper and the LSE Economists', in de Marchi (ed.), *The Popperian Legacy in Economics* (Cambridge).

—— and Gilbert, C. (1989), 'Introduction (to the Special Issue: History and Methodology of Econometrics)', *Oxford Economic Papers*, 41: 1–11.

Douglas, P. H. (1934), *The Theory of Wages* (Chicago).

Drèze, J. (1962), 'The Bayesian Approach to Simultaneous Equations Estimation', *ONR Research Memorandum*, 67 (Northwestern University, Evanston, Ill.).

Durbin, J. (1953), 'A Note on Regression when there is Extraneous Information about One of the Coefficients', *Journal of American Statistical Association*, 48: 799–808.

—— (1954a), 'Errors in Variables', *Review of the International Statistical Institute*, 22: 23–32.

Durbin, J. (1954*b*), 'Regression Techniques in Econometrics: Errors in Variables', *Econometrica*, 22: 102–3.

—— (1960*a*), 'The Fitting of Time-Series Models', *Review of the International Statistical Institute*, 28: 233–43.

—— (1960*b*), 'Estimation of Parameters in Time-Series Regression Models', *Journal of the Royal Statistical Society*, series B, 22: 139–53.

—— and Watson, G. S. (1950), 'Testing for Serial Correlation in Least Squares Regression. I', *Biometrica*, 37: 409–28.

—— —— (1951), 'Testing for Serial Correlation in Least Squares Regression. II', *Biometrica*, 38: 159–78.

Engle, R. F., Hendry, D. F., and Richard, J.-F. (1983), 'Exogeneity', *Econometrica*, 51: 277–304.

Epstein, R. J. (1987), *A History of Econometrics* (Amsterdam).

—— (1989), 'The Fall of OLS in Structural Estimation', *Oxford Economic Papers*, 41: 94–107.

Ezekiel, M. (1933), 'Some Considerations on the Analysis of the Prices of Competing or Substitute Commodities', *Econometrica*, 1: 172–180.

Fisher, F. M. (1959), 'Generalization of the Rank and Order Conditions for Identifiability', *Econometrica*, 27: 431–47.

—— (1962), 'The Place of Least Squares in Econometrics: Comment', *Econometrica*, 30: 565–7.

—— (1965), 'Near-Identifiability and the Variance of the Disturbance Terms', *Econometrica*, 33: 409–19.

—— (1966), *The Identification Problem in Econometrics* (New York).

Fisher, M. R. (1956), 'Exploration in Savings Behaviour', *Bulletin of the Oxford University Institute of Statistics*, 18: 201–77.

—— (1957), 'A Reply to the Critics', *Bulletin of the Oxford University Institute of Statistics*, 18: 179–99.

Fisher, W. D. (1962), 'Estimation in the Linear Decision Model', *International Economic Review*, 3: 1–29.

Foote, R. J., and Waugh, F. V. (1957), 'Results of an Experiment to Test the Forecasting Merits of Least Squares and Limited Information Equations', in *Agricultural Marketing Service* (US Department of Agriculture, Washington DC).

Fox, K. A. (1956), 'Econometric Models of the United States', *Journal of Political Economy*, 64: 128–42.

—— (1989), 'Some Contributions of US Agricultural Economists and Their Close Associates to Statistics and Econometrics, 1917–33', *Oxford Economic Papers*, 41: 53–70.

Freeman, H. A. (1938), 'Review of Koopmans: Linear Regression Analysis of Economic Time Series', *American Economic Review*, 28: 608–9.

Friedman, M. (1937), 'Testing Significance of the Differences among a Group of Regression Equations', *Econometrica*, 5: 194–5.

—— (1953), 'The Methodology of Positive Economics', in id., *Essays in Positive Economics* (Chicago), 3–43.

—— (1957), *A Theory of the Consumption Function* (Princeton NJ).

Frisch, R. (1929), 'Correlation and Scatter in Statistical Variables', *Nordic Statistical Journal*, 1: 36–102.

—— (1933a), 'Editorial', *Econometrica*, 1: 1–4.

—— (1933b), *Pitfalls in the Statistical Construction of Demand and Supply Curves*, New Series 5 (Leipzig).

—— (1933c), 'Propagation Problems and Impulse Problems in Dynamic Economics', in *Economic Essays in Honour of Gustav Cassel* (London), 171–205.

—— (1934), *Statistical Confluence Analysis by means of Complete Regression Systems* (Oslo).

—— (1936), 'Time Series and Business Cycle Analysis: Economic Macro Dynamics' in Part 2 of *Report of the Work Done under the Direction of Professor I. Wedervang, at the University Institute of Economics, Oslo, January 1932–June 1936* (Rockefeller Archive Centre).

—— (1937), 'An Ideal Programme for Macrodynamic Studies', *Econometrica*, 5: 365–6.

—— (1938), 'Statistical versus Theoretical Relations in Economic Macrodynamics', reproduced by University of Oslo in 1948 with Tinbergen's comments, *Memorandum* (Oslo); also in D. F. Hendry and M. S. Morgan (eds.), *The Foundations of Econometric Analysis* (Cambridge, forthcoming).

—— and Waugh, F. V. (1933), 'Partial Time Regression as Compared with Individual Trends', *Econometrica*, 1: 387–401.

Geary, R. C. (1942), 'Inherent Relations between Random Variables', *Proceedings of Royal Irish Academy*, 47: 63–76.

—— (1943), 'Relations between Statistics: The General and the Sampling Problem', *Proceedings of Royal Irish Academy*, 49: 177–96.

—— (1948), 'Studies in Relations between Economic Time Series', *Journal of the Royal Statistical Society*, series B, 10: 140–58.

—— (1949), 'Determination of Linear Relations between the Systematic Parts of Variables with Errors of Observations the Variances of which are Unknown', *Econometrica*, 17: 30–58.

Gigerenzer, G., Swijtink, Z., Porter, T., Daston, L., Beatty, J., and Krüger, L. (1989), *The Empire of Chance* (Cambridge).

Gilbert, C. L. (1988), 'The Development of Econometrics in Britain Since 1945', Ph.D. thesis (Oxford).

Gilboy, E. W. (1930), 'Demand Curves in Theory and in Practice', *Quarterly Journal of Economics*, 44: 601–20.

Girshick, M. A. (1936), 'Principal Components', *Journal of American Statistical Association*, 31: 519–28.

—— and Haavelmo, T. (1947), 'Statistical Analysis of the Demand for Food: Examples of Simultaneous Equations Estimation', *Econometrica*, 15: 79–110.

Goldfeld, S. M., and Quandt, R. E. (1972), *Nonlinear Methods in Econometrics* (Amsterdam).

Greenstein, B. (1935), 'Periodogram Analysis with Special Application to Business Failures', *Econometrica*, 3: 170–98.

Griliches, Z. (1957), 'Specification Bias in Estimates of Production Functions', *Journal of Farm Economics*, 39: 8–20.

—— (1967), 'Distributed Lags: A Survey', *Econometrica*, 35: 16–49.

—— (1974), 'Errors in Variables and Other Unobservables', *Econometrica*, 42: 971–8.

—— and Intriligator, M. D. (1983) (eds.), *Handbook of Econometrics* (Amsterdam).

Haavelmo, T. (1938), 'The Method of Supplementary Confluent Relations, Illustrated by a Study of Stock Prices', *Econometrica*, 6: 203–18.

—— (1939), 'Statistical Testing of Dynamic Systems if the Series Observed are Shock Cumulants', in *Report of Fifth Annual Research Conference on Economics and Statistics* (Cowles Commission).

—— (1940a), 'The Inadequacy of Testing Dynamic Theory by Comparing the Theoretical Solutions and Observed Cycles', *Econometrica*, 8: 312–21.

—— (1940b), 'The Problem of Testing Economic Theories by means of Passive Observations', in *Report of Sixth Annual Research Conference on Economics and Statistics* (Cowles Commission).

—— (1941), 'A Note on the Variate Difference Method', *Econometrica*, 9: 74–9.

—— (1943a), 'Statistical Testing of Business Cycle Theories', *Review of Economics and Statistics*, 25: 13–18.

—— (1943b), 'The Statistical Implications of a System of Simultaneous Equations', *Econometrica*, 11: 1–12.

—— (1944), *The Probability Approach in Econometrics*, *Econometrica* (Suppl.), 12; mimeo 1941.

—— (1947), 'Methods of Measuring the Marginal Propensity to Consume', *Journal of American Statistical Association*, 42: 105–22 (repr. in Hood and Koopmans, 1953).

—— (1957), 'Econometric Analysis of the Savings Survey Data', *Bulletin of the Oxford University Institute of Statistics*, 19: 145–9.

—— (1958), 'The Role of Econometrician in the Advancement of Economic Theory', *Econometrica*, 26: 351–7.

—— (1989), 'Econometrics and the Welfare State', Nobel Prize Lecture, *Sosialøkonomen*, 11: 2–5.

Hagstroem, K.-G. (1938), 'Pure Economics as a Stochastical Theory', *Econometrica*, 6: 40–7.

Hamouda, O., and Rowley, J. C. R. (1988), *Expectation, Equilibrium and Dynamics* (Hemel Hempstead).

Hausman, D. M. (1989), 'Economic Methodology in a Nutshell', *Journal of Economic Perspectives*, 3: 115–27.

Hausman, J. A. (1978), 'Specification Tests in Econometrics', *Econometrica*, 46: 1251–70.

Heckman, J. (1992), 'Haavelmo and the Birth of Modern Econometrics: A Review of *The History of Econometric Ideas* by Mary Morgan', *Journal of Economic Literature*, 30: 876–86.

Hendry, D. F. (1980), 'Econometrics: Alchemy or Science?', *Economica*, 47: 387–406.

—— and Morgan, M. S. (1989), 'A Re-analysis of Confluence Analysis', *Oxford Economic Papers*, 41: 35–52.

—— and Richard, J.-F. (1982), 'On the Formulation of Empirical Models in Dynamic Econometrics', *Journal of Econometrics*, 20: 3–33.

Hildreth, C. (1960), 'Simultaneous Equations: Any Verdict Yet?', *Econometrica*, 28: 846–54.

—— (1986), *The Cowles Commission in Chicago 1939–1955* (New York).

Hilfer, I. (1938), 'Differential Effect in the Butter Market', *Econometrica*, 6: 270–84.

Hood, W., and Koopmans, T. (eds.) (1953), *Studies in Econometric Method*, Cowles Commission Monograph 14 (New York).

Hooper, J. W. (1959), 'Simultaneous Equations and Canonical Correlation Theory', *Econometrica*, 27: 245–56.

Hotelling, H. (1933), 'Analysis of a Complex of Statistical Variables into Principal Components', *Journal of Educational Psychology*, 24: 417–41, 498–520.

—— (1936), 'Relations Between Two Sets of Variables', *Biometrica*, 28: 321–77.

Hurwicz, L. (1950), 'Generalization of the Concept of Identification', in Koopmans, 1950: 245–57.

—— and Arrow, K. J. (1952), 'Dynamic Aspects of Achieving Optimal Allocation of Resources' (abstract), *Econometrica*, 20: 489–90.

Johnson, S. R., Reimer, S. C., and Rothrock, T. P. (1973), 'Principal Components and the Problem of Multicollinearity', *Metroeconomica*, 25: 306–17.

Kalecki, M. (1935), 'A Macrodynamic Theory of the Business Cycle', *Econometrica*, 3: 327–44.

Kendall, M. G. (1961), 'A Theorem in Trend Analysis', *Biometrica*, 48: 224.
—— (1968), 'The History of Statistical Method', in *International Encyclopedia of the Social Sciences* (New York).
Keynes, J. M., and Tinbergen, J. (1939), 'Professor Tinbergen's Method, review of J. Tinbergen: League of Nations, I, 1939', *Economic Journal*, 49: 558–68; 'A Reply' by Tinbergen and 'Comment' by Keynes, *Economic Journal*, 50 (1940), 141–56.
Klappholz, K., and Agassi, J. (1959), 'Methodological Prescriptions in Economics', *Economica*, 26: 60–74.
Klein, L. R. (1950), *Economic Fluctuations in the United States 1921–1941*, Cowles Commission Monograph No. 11 (New York).
—— (1953), *A Textbook of Econometrics* (New York).
—— (1955), 'On the Interpretation of Theil's Method of Estimation of Economic Relations', *Metroeconomica*, 7: 147–53.
—— (1958), 'The Estimation of Distributed Lags', *Econometrica*, 26: 553–61.
—— (1960), 'Single Equation vs. Equation System Methods of Estimation in Econometrics', *Econometrica*, 28: 865–71.
—— and Barger, H. (1954), 'A Quarterly Model for the US Economy', *Journal of American Statistical Association*, 49: 415–37.
—— and Goldberger, A. S. (1955), *An Econometric Model of the United States 1929–1952* (Amsterdam).
Koopmans, T. C. (1937), *Linear Regression Analysis of Economic Time Series*, Netherlands Economic Institute (Haarlem).
—— (1941), 'The Logic of Econometric Business-Cycle Research', *Journal of Political Economy*, 49: 157–81.
—— (1942), 'Serial Correlation as Quadratic Forms in Normal Variables', *Annals of Mathematical Statistics*, 13: 14–33.
—— (1945), 'Statistical Estimation of Simultaneous Economic Relations', *Journal of American Statistical Association*, 40: 448–66.
—— (1947*a*), 'Statistical Problems of Importance to the Cowles Commission Program' (Cowles Foundation Archive).
—— (1947*b*), 'Measurement without Theory', *Review of Economics and Statistics*, 29: 161–72.
—— (1949*a*), 'Reply to Rutledge Vining', *Review of Economics and Statistics*, 31: 86–91.
—— (1949*b*), 'Identification Problems in Economic Model Construction', *Econometrica*, 17: 125–44.
—— (1950) (ed.), *Statistical Inference in Dynamic Economic Models*, Cowles Commission Monograph 10 (New York).
—— (1951) (ed.), *Activity Analysis of Production and Allocation*, Cowles Commission Monograph 13 (New York).

—— (1952), 'Comments to "Toward Partial Redirection of Econometrics"', *Review of Economics and Statistics*, 34: 200–5.

—— (1957), *Three Essays on the State of Economic Science* (New York).

—— and Reiersøl, O. (1950), 'The Identification of Structural Characteristics', *Annals of Mathematical Statistics*, 21: 165–81.

Koyck, L. M. (1954), *Distributed Lags and Investment Analysis* (Amsterdam).

Krüger, L., Gigerenzer, G., and Morgan, M. (1987) (eds.), *The Probabilistic Revolution* (Cambridge).

Kuhn, T. S. (1970), *The Structure of Scientific Revolutions*, 2nd edn. (Chicago).

Lakatos, I. (1978), *The Methodology of Scientific Research Programmes*, in J. Worrall and G. Currie (eds.) (Cambridge).

Leamer, E. E. (1978), *Specification Searches: Ad Hoc Inference with Non-Experimental Data* (New York).

Leavens, D. H. (1937), 'Chicago, December 28–30, 1936, Report', *Econometrica*, 5: 184–97.

Leontief, W. W. (1948), 'Econometrics', in H. S. Ellis (ed.), *A Survey of Contemporary Economics* (Illinois).

Liu, T.-C. (1955), 'A Simple Forecasting Model for the US Economy', *International Monetary Fund Staff Papers*, 4: 434–66.

—— (1960), 'Underidentification, Structural Estimation and Forecasting', *Econometrica*, 28: 855–65.

—— (1963), 'Structural Estimation and Forecasting: A Critique of the Cowles Commission Method', *Tsing-Hua Journal of Chinese Studies*, 3–4: 152–71.

Lucas, R. E. (1976), 'Econometric Policy Evaluation: A Critique', in K. Brunner and A. H. Meltzer (eds.), *The Phillips Curve and Labour Markets* (Amsterdam), 19–46.

Malinvaud, E. (1953), 'Capital Accumulation and the Efficient Allocation of Resources', *Econometrica*, 21: 233–68.

—— (1988), 'Econometric Methodology at the Cowles Commission: Rise and Maturity', *Econometric Theory*, 4: 187–209.

Magnus, J. R., and Morgan, M. S. (1987), 'The Et Interview: Professor J. Tinbergen', *Econometric Theory*, 3: 117–42.

Mann, H. B. (1945), 'Nonparametric Tests against Trend', *Econometrica*, 11: 173–220.

—— and Wald, A. (1943), 'On the Statistical Treatment of Linear Stochastic Difference Equations', *Econometrica*, 11: 173–220.

Marschak, J. (1937), 'Utility and Probabilities in Human Choice', in *Report of Third Annual Research Conference on Economics and Statistics* (Cowles Commission).

Marschak, J. (1938), 'Review of Koopmans: Linear Regression Analysis of Economic Time Series', *Economic Journal*, 48: 104–6.

—— (1942), 'Economic Interdependence and Statistical Analysis', in O. Lange, F. McIntyre, and T. O. Yntema (eds.), *Studies in Mathematical Economics and Econometrics—In Memory of Henry Schultz* (Chicago).

—— (1946), 'Quantitative Studies in Economic Behaviour (Foundations of Rational Economic Policy)', Report to the Rockefeller Foundation (Rockefeller Archive Centre).

—— (1954), 'Probability in the Social Sciences', *Cowles Commission Paper*, New Series, 82 (Cowles Commission).

Marshall, A. W. (1950), 'A Test of Klein's Model III for Changes of Structure' (abstract), *Econometrica*, 18: 291.

Means, G. C. (1938), *Patterns of Resource Use* (US National Resources Planning Board, 1938).

—— (1941) 'Supplement to *Patterns of Resource Use*', *Technical Paper*, No. 1 (US National Resources Planning Board).

Ménard, C. (1987), 'Why was there no Probabilistic Revolution in Economic Thought?', in L. Krüger and M. S. Morgan (eds.), *The Probabilistic Revolution*, 2: 139–46.

Metzler, L. (1940), 'The Assumptions Implied in Least Squares Demand Technique', *Review of Economics and Statistics*, 22: 138–49.

Mirowski, P. (1989a), *More Heat than Light: Economics as Social Physics: Physics as Nature's Economics* (Cambridge).

—— (1989b), 'The Probabilistic Counter-Revolution, or How Stochastic Concepts Came to Neoclassical Economic Theory', *Oxford Economic Papers*, 41: 217–35.

Modigliani, F. (1975), 'The Life Cycle Hypothesis of Saving Twenty Years later', in M. Parkin (ed.), *Contemporary Issues in Economics* (Manchester), 2–36.

—— and Ando, A. K. (1957), 'Tests of the Life Cycle Hypothesis of Savings', *Bulletin of the Oxford University Institute of Statistics*, 19: 99–124.

—— and Brumberg, F. (1954), 'Utility Analysis and the Consumption Function: An Interpretation of Cross-section Data', in K. Kurihara (ed.), *Post-Keynesian Economics* (New Brunswick, NJ).

Moore, H. L. (1914), *Economic Cycles: Their Law and Cause* (New York).

—— (1923), *Generating Economic Cycles* (New York).

Morgan, M. S. (1987), 'Statistics without Probability and Haavelmo's Revolution in Econometrics', in L. Krüger and M. S. Morgan (eds.), *The Probabilistic Revolution*, 2: 171–97.

—— (1989), *The History of Econometric Ideas* (Cambridge).

—— (1991), 'The Stamping Out of Process Analysis in Econometrics', in N. de Marchi and M. Blaug (eds.), *Appraising Economic Theories: Studies in the Methodology of Research Programmes* (Aldershot), 237–72.

Muth, J. F. (1961), 'Rational Expectations and the Theory of Price Movements', *Econometrica*, 29: 315–35.

Nerlove, M. (1956), 'Estimates of the Elasticities of Supply of Selected Agricultural Commodities', *Journal of Farm Economics*, 38: 496–509.

—— (1958), *The Dynamics of Supply: Estimation of Farmers' Response to Price* (Baltimore).

—— (1966), 'A Tabular Survey of Macro-Econometric Models', *International Economic Review*, 7: 127–75.

—— (1990), 'Trygve Haavelmo: A Critical Appreciation', *Scandinavian Journal of Economics*, 92: 17–24.

Neumann, J. von, and Morgenstern, O. (1947), *Theory of Games and Economic Behavior* (Princeton, NJ).

Neyman, J. (1937a), 'Survey of Recent Work on Correlation and Covariation' (abstract), *Econometrica*, 5: 367–8.

—— (1937b), *Outline of a Theory of Statistical Estimation Based on the Classical Theory of Probability* (London).

Orcutt, G. (1948), 'A Study of the Autoregressive Nature of the Time Series used for Tinbergen's Model of the Economic System of the United States 1919–1932', *Journal of the Royal Statistical Society*, Series B, 10: 1–45.

—— (1952), 'Toward Partial Redirection of Econometrics', *Review of Economics and Statistics*, 34: 195–200.

—— and Cochrane, D. (1949), 'A Sampling Study of the Merits of Autoregressive and Reduced Form Transformations in Regression Analysis', *Journal of American Statistical Association*, 44: 356–72.

Patinkin, D. (1976), 'Keynes and Econometrics: On the Interaction between the Macroeconomic Revolutions of the Interwar Period', *Econometrica*, 44: 1091–1123.

Persons, W. M. (1916), 'Construction of a Business Barometer', *American Economic Review*, 6: 739–69.

—— (1922–3), 'Correlation of Time Series', *Journal of American Statistical Association*, 18: 713–26.

—— (1925), 'Statistics and Economic Theory', *Review of Economics and Statistics*, 6: 179–97.

Phillips, P. C. B. (1985), 'The Et Interview: Professor J. D. Sargan', *Econometric Theory*, 1: 119–39.

—— (1986), 'The Et Interview: Professor T. W. Anderson', *Econometric Theory*, 2: 249–88.

Phillips, P. C. B. (1988), 'The Et Interview: Professor James Durbin', *Econometric Theory*, 4: 125–57.

—— (1989), 'Reflection on Econometric Methodology', *Cowles Foundation Papers*, 727 (Cowles Foundation).

Phillips, W. M. (1954), 'Stabilisation Policy in a Closed Economy', *Economic Journal*, 64: 290–323.

—— (1958), 'The Relation between Unemployment and the Rate of Change of Money Wage Rates in the United Kingdom, 1861–1957', *Economica*, 25: 283–300.

Qin, D. (1988a), 'An Interview with Professor P. Samuelson' (Oxford).

—— (1988b), 'An Interview with Professor G. Orcutt' (Oxford).

—— (1989), 'Formalization of Identification Theory', *Oxford Economic Papers*, 41: 73–93.

—— (1991), 'Rise of Bayesian Approach in Econometrics' (Oxford).

Reiersøl, O. (1941), 'Confluence Analysis by means of Lag Moments and Other Methods of Confluence Analysis', *Econometrica*, 9: 1–24.

—— (1945), 'Confluence Analysis by means of Instrumental Sets of Variables', *Arkiv for Mathematic, Astronomi, och Fysik*, 32A: 1–119.

—— (1947), 'Confluence Analysis when the Model Contains both Shocks and Errors', *Cowles Commission Discussion Papers and Minutes (Statistics)*, 306 (Cowles Foundation Archive).

—— (1950), 'Identifiability of a Linear Relationship between Variables which are Subject to Error', *Econometrica*, 18: 375–89.

Roos, C. F. (1934), *Dynamic Economics*, Cowles Commission Monograph 1 (Bloomington, Ind.).

—— (1937), 'A General Invariant Criterion of Fit for Lines and Planes where all Variates are Subject to Error', *Metron*, 13: 3–20.

Rothenberg, T. J. (1963), 'A Bayesian Analysis of Simultaneous Equations Systems', *Econometric Institute Report*, 6315, Netherlands School of Economics (Rotterdam).

—— (1971), 'Identification in Parametric Models', *Econometrica*, 39: 577–91.

Rowley, J. C. R., and Hamouda, O. (1987), 'Troublesome Probability and Economics', *Journal of Post Keynesian Economics*, 10: 44–64.

Samuelson, P. A. (1947), *Foundations of Economic Analysis*, Harvard University Press.

—— (1987), 'Paradise Lost and Refound: The Harvard ABC Barometers', *Journal of Portfolio Management*, Spring, 4–9.

Sargan, J. D. (1957), 'The Danger of Over-Simplification', *Bulletin of the Oxford University Institute of Statistics*, 19: 171–8.

—— (1958), 'The Estimation of Economic Relationships using Instrumental Variables', *Econometrica*, 26: 393–415.

——— (1959), 'The Estimation of Relationships with Autocorrelated Residuals by the Use of Instrumental Variables', *Journal of the Royal Statistical Society*, series B, 21: 91–105.

——— (1961), 'The Maximum Likelihood Estimation of Economic Relationships with Autoregressive Residuals', *Econometrica*, 29: 414–26.

——— (1964), 'Wages and Prices in the United Kingdom: A Study in Econometric Methodology', in P. E. Hart, G. Mills, and J. K. Whitaker (eds.), *Econometric Analysis for National Economic Planning* (London), 25–63.

——— (1980), 'Some Tests of Dynamic Specification for a Single Equation', *Econometrica*, 48: 879–97.

Schoeffler, S. (1955), *The Failures of Economics: A Diagnostic Study*, Harvard University Press.

Schultz, H. (1925), 'The Statistical Laws of Demand', *Journal of Political Economy*, 33: 481–504, 577–637.

——— (1928), *Statistical Laws of Demand and Supply with Special Application to Sugar* (Chicago).

——— (1930), 'The Meaning of Statistical Demand Curves', *Veröffentlichungen der Frankfurter Gesellschaft für Konjunkturforschung* (Leipzig).

——— (1933), 'A Comparison of Elasticities of Demand obtained by Different Methods', *Econometrica*, 1: 274–302.

——— (1939), *The Theory and Measurement of Demand* (Chicago).

Schumpeter, J. (1939), *Business Cycles* (New York).

Shackle, G. L. S. (1938), *Expectations, Investment and Income* (Oxford).

Simon, H. A. (1953), 'Causal Ordering and Identifiability', in Hood and Koopmans, 1953, 49–74.

——— (1955), 'Causality and Econometrics: Comment', *Econometrica*, 23: 193–5.

Sims, C. A. (1980), 'Macroeconomics and Reality', *Econometrica*, 48: 1–48.

Slutsky, E. (1937), 'The Summation of Random Causes as the Source of Cyclic Processes', *Econometrica*, 5: 105–46 (originally published in Russian in 1927).

Spanos, A. (1989), 'On Rereading Haavelmo: A Retrospective View of Econometric Modelling', *Econometric Theory*, 5: 405–29.

Staehle, H. (1933), 'Lausanne, September 1931, Compte rendu', *Econometrica*, 1: 73–86.

Stigler, G. J. (1962), 'Henry L. Moore and Statistical Economics', *Econometrica*, 30: 1–21.

Stone, J. R. N. (1945), 'The Analysis of Market Demand', *Journal of the Royal Statistical Society*, 108: 286–382.

Stone, J. R. N. (1946), 'Review of T. Haavelmo: *The Probability Approach*', *Economic Journal*, 56: 265–9.

—— (1947), 'On the Interdependence of Blocks of Transactions', *Journal of the Royal Statistical Society*, 9 (suppl.): 1–45.

—— (1948), 'The Analysis of Market Demand: An Outline of Methods and Results', *Review of the International Statistical Institute*, 16: 23–35.

—— (1951), *The Role of Measurement in Economics*, Monograph 3 of the University of Cambridge Department of Applied Economics (Cambridge).

—— (1954a), 'Linear Expenditure Systems and Demand Analysis', *Economic Journal*, 64: 511–27.

—— (1954b), *The Measurement of Consumers' Expenditure and Behaviour in the United Kingdom 1920–1938* (Cambridge).

Strotz, R. H. (1960), 'Interdependence as a Specification Error', *Econometrica*, 28: 428–42.

—— and Wold, H. (1960), 'Recursive vs. Nonrecursive Systems: An Attempt at Synthesis', *Econometrica*, 28: 417–27.

—— —— (1963), 'The Causal Interpretability of Structural Parameters: A Reply', *Econometrica*, 31: 449–50.

Theil, H. (1953), *Estimation and Simultaneous Correlation in Complete Equation Systems* (The Hague).

—— (1954), *Linear Aggregation of Economic Relations* (Amsterdam).

—— (1957), 'Specification Errors and the Estimation of Economic Relationships', *Review of International Statistical Institute*, 25: 41–51.

—— (1961), *Economic Forecasts and Policy* (Amsterdam, 1st edn. published in 1958).

—— and Goldberger, A. S. (1961), 'On Pure and Mixed Statistical Estimation in Economics', *International Economic Review*, 2: 65–78.

Tinbergen, J. (1930), 'Bestimmung und Deutung von Angebotskurven: Ein Beispiel', *Zeitschrift für Nationalökonomie*, 1: 669–79 (English trans. by Koopmans).

—— (1935), 'Annual Survey: Suggestions on Quantitative Business Cycle Theory', *Econometrica*, 3: 241–308.

—— (1937), *Econometric Approach to Business Cycles Problems* (Paris).

—— (1938a), 'Statistical Evidence on the Acceleration Principle', *Economica*, 5: 164–76.

—— (1938b), 'On the Theory of Business-cycle Control', *Econometrica*, 6: 22–39.

—— (1939), *Statistical Testing of Business-Cycle Theories* (Geneva).

—— (1940), 'Econometric Business Cycle Research', *Review of Economic Studies*, 7: 73–90.

—— (1942), 'Critical Remarks on Some Business-Cycle Theories', *Econometrica*, 10: 129–46.

—— (1949), 'Reformulation of Current Business Cycle Theories as Refutable Hypotheses', in *Conference on Business Cycles*, US National Bureau of Economic Research Special Conference Series No. 2 (New York), 131–48.

—— (1952), 'Comments to "Toward Partial Redirection of Econometrics"', *Review of Economics and Statistics*, 34: 205–6.

—— and Polak, J. J. (1950), *The Dynamics of Business Cycles* (London).

Tintner, G. (1935), *Prices in the Trade Cycle* (Vienna).

—— (1938*a*) 'A Note on Economic Aspects of the Theory of Errors in Time Series', *Quarterly Journal of Economics*, 53: 141–9.

—— (1938*b*), 'The Maximization of Utility over Time', *Econometrica*, 6: 154–8.

—— (1939), 'On Tests of Significance in Time Series', *Annals of Mathematical Statistics*, 10: 139–44.

—— (1940*a*), 'The Analysis of Economic Time Series', *Journal of American Statistical Association*, 35: 93–100.

—— (1940*b*), *The Variate Difference Method*, Cowles Commission Monograph 5 (Bloomington, Ind.).

—— (1944), 'An Application of the Variate Difference Method to Multiple Regression', *Econometrica*, 12: 97–113.

—— (1945), 'A Note on Rank, Multicollinearity and Multiple Regression', *Annals of Mathematical Statistics*, 16: 304–8.

—— (1949), 'Foundations of Probability and Statistical Inference', *Journal of the Royal Statistical Society*, Series A, 112: 251–86.

—— (1950*a*), 'Some Formal Relations in Multivariate Analysis', *Journal of the Royal Statistical Society*, Series B, 12: 95–101.

—— (1950*b*), 'A Test for Linear Relations between Weighted Regression Coefficients', *Journal of the Royal Statistical Society*, Series B, 12: 273–7.

—— (1952), *Econometrics* (New York).

—— (1968), *Methodology of Mathematical Economics and Econometrics* (Chicago).

—— and Sengapta, J. K. (1972), *Stochastic Economics* (New York).

Van Uven, M. J. (1930), 'Adjustment of N Points to the Best Linear (N − 1)-Dimensional Space', *Proceedings of the Section of Science*, 23: 143.

Vining, R. (1949), 'Koopmans on the Choice of Variables to be Studied and of Methods of Measurement, A Rejoinder', *Review of Economics and Statistics*, 31: 77–86; 91–4.

Wagner, H. M. (1958), 'A Monte Carlo Study of Estimates of Simultaneous Linear Structural Equations', *Econometrica*, 26: 117–33.

Wald, A. (1940), 'The Fitting of Straight Lines if Both Variables are Subject to Error', *Annals of Mathematical Statistics*, 11: 284–300.

Wald, A. (1943), 'Tests of Statistical Hypotheses concerning Several Parameters when the Number of Observations is Large', *Transactions of the American Mathematical Society*, 54: 426–82.
—— (1950), 'Note on the Identification of Economic Relations', in Koopmans 1950: 238–44.
Walker, G. (1931), 'On Periodicity in Series of Related Terms', *Philosophical Transactions of the Royal Society*, Series A, 131: 519–32.
Wallis, W. A. (1942), 'The Temporal Stability of Consumption Pattern', *Review of Economics and Statistics*, 24: 177–83.
Waugh, F. V. (1942), 'Regression between Sets of Variables', *Econometrica*, 10: 290–310.
—— (1961), 'The Place of Least Squares in Econometrics', *Econometrica*, 29: 386–96.
—— (1962), 'Further Comment', *Econometrica*, 30: 568–9.
Weintraub, E. R. (1985), *General Equilibrium Analysis: Studies in Appraisal* (Cambridge).
—— (1989), 'Methodology Doesn't Matter, but the History of Thought Might', *Scandinavian Journal of Economics*, 91: 477–93.
Wilks, S. S. (1938), 'Review of Koopmans: Linear Regression Analysis of Economic Time Series', *Journal of the American Statistical Association*, 33: 273–5.
Wilson, E. B. (1934), 'The Periodogram of American Business Activity', *Quarterly Journal of Economics*, 48: 375–417.
—— (1946), 'Review of T. Haavelmo: *The Probability Approach in Econometrics*', *Review of Economics and Statistics*, 28: 173–4.
Wold, H. (1938), *A Study in the Analysis of Stationary Time Series* (Uppsala).
—— (1943–4), 'A Synthesis of Pure Demand Analysis, I–III', *Skandinavisk Aktuarietidskrift*, 26: 84–119, 220–63; 27: 69–120.
—— (1948), 'On Prediction in Stationary Time-Series', *Annals of Mathematical Statistics*, 19: 558–67.
—— (1949), 'Statistical Estimation of Economic Relationships', *Econometrica*, 17 (Suppl.): 1–22.
—— (1951), 'Dynamic Systems of the Recursive Type—Economic and Statistical Aspects', *Sankhyá*, 11: 205–16.
—— (1954), 'Causality and Econometrics', *Econometrica*, 22: 162–77.
—— (1955), 'Causality and Econometrics: Reply', *Econometrica*, 23: 196–7.
—— (1956), 'Causal Inference from Observational Data', *Journal of Royal Statistical Society*, Series A, 119: 28–61.
—— (1958), 'A Case Study of Interdependent Versus Causal Chain Systems', *Review of International Statistical Institute*, 26: 5–25.
—— (1960), 'A Generalization of Causal Chain Models', *Econometrica*, 28: 443–63.

—— (1961), 'Unbiased Predictors', in *Proceedings of the Fourth Berkeley Symposium on Mathematical Statistics and Probability*, 1: 719–61.

—— (1963), 'Forecasting by the Chain Principle', in M. Rosenblatt (ed.), *Time Series Analysis Symposium* (New York), 471–97.

—— (1965), 'A Letter to Professor P. C. Mahalanobis', in C. R. Rao (ed.), *Essays on Econometrics and Planning* (Oxford).

—— (1969a), 'Econometrics as Pioneering in Non-experimental Model Building', *Econometrica*, 37: 369–81.

—— (1969b), 'E. P. Mackeprang's Question Concerning the Choice of Regression—A Key Problem in the Evolution of Econometrics', in M. Beckmann *et al.* (eds.), *Economic Models, Estimation and Risk Programming: Essays in Honour of G. Tintner* (Berlin).

—— and Juréen, L. (1953), *Demand Analysis: A Study in Econometrics* (New York).

Working, H. (1925), 'The Statistical Determination of Demand Curves', *Quarterly Journal of Economics*, 39: 503–43.

Wright, P. (1928), *The Tariff on Animal and Vegetable Oils* (New York).

Yule, G. (1921), 'On the Time-Correlation Problems with Especial Reference to the Variate-Difference Correlation Method', *Journal of Royal Statistical Society*, 84: 497–526.

—— (1926), 'Why Do We sometimes get Nonsense-Correlations between Time Series?', *Journal of the Royal Statistical Society*, 89: 1–64.

—— (1927), 'On a Method of Investigating Periodicities in Disturbed Series, with Special Application to Wolfert's Sun Spot Numbers', *Philosophical Transactions of the Royal Society*, Series A, 226: 267–98.

Zellner, A. (1962), 'An Efficient Method of Estimating Seemingly Unrelated Regressions and Tests for Aggregation Bias', *Journal of American Statistical Association*, 57: 348–68.

—— (1984), *Basic Issues in Econometrics* (Chicago).

INDEX OF NAMES

INDEX OF SUBJECTS